Inside .Mac

Other Macintosh resources from O'Reilly

Related titles

Mac OS X: The Missing
Manual, Panther Edition

Mac OS X Panther in a
Nutshell

Mac OS X Panther Pocket
Guide

Mac OS X Unwired

**Macintosh Books
Resource Center**

mac.oreilly.com is a complete catalog of O'Reilly's books on the Apple Macintosh and related technologies, including sample chapters and code examples.

A popular watering hole for Macintosh developers and power users, the Mac DevCenter focuses on pure Mac OS X and its related technologies, including Cocoa, Java, AppleScript, and Apache, to name just a few. It's also keenly interested in all the spokes of the digital hub, with special attention paid to digital photography, digital video, MP3 music, and QuickTime.

Conferences

O'Reilly brings diverse innovators together to nurture the ideas that spark revolutionary industries. We specialize in documenting the latest tools and systems, translating the innovator's knowledge into useful skills for those in the trenches. Visit *conferences.oreilly.com* for our upcoming events.

Safari Bookshelf (*safari.oreilly.com*) is the premier online reference library for programmers and IT professionals. Conduct searches across more than 1,000 books. Subscribers can zero in on answers to time-critical questions in a matter of seconds. Read the books on your Bookshelf from cover to cover or simply flip to the page you need. Try it today with a free trial.

Inside .Mac

Chuck Toporek

O'REILLY®

Beijing · Cambridge · Farnham · Köln · Paris · Sebastopol · Taipei · Tokyo

Inside .Mac
by Chuck Toporek

Copyright © 2004 O'Reilly Media, Inc. All rights reserved.
Printed in the United States of America.

Published by O'Reilly Media, Inc., 1005 Gravenstein Highway North, Sebastopol, CA 95472.

O'Reilly books may be purchased for educational, business, or sales promotional use. Online editions are also available for most titles (*safari.oreilly.com*). For more information, contact our corporate/institutional sales department: (800) 998-9938 or *corporate@oreilly.com*.

Editor:	Chuck Toporek
Production Editor:	Mary Brady
Cover Designer:	Edie Freedman
Interior Designer:	David Futato

Printing History:

May 2004:	First Edition.

RepKover™ This book uses RepKover™, a durable and flexible lay-flat binding.

ISBN: 0-596-00501-6
[C]

To my parents, who brought me into this world and taught me that anything was possible if you put your mind to it.

To Jeff, who taught me many life-lessons without realizing it, and left the world far too early for all of us. We miss you, pal.

Table of Contents

Preface

If you're like me, your Mac is like the Sun at the center of the solar system. It's the hub of all your activity. You use your Mac for work and play, and more importantly, to keep in contact with the outside world. In today's connected, Internet world, your Mac plays a vital role in how you communicate and share information with others, whether they're friends or cohorts at work.

When Steve Jobs revealed Apple's Digital Hub strategy (see Figure P-1), the thought was that your Mac would be the center of everything you do digitally. Whether that meant creating and playing music, editing and producing digital video, or how you connected with the outside world, your Mac would be the center of it all.

To help make your Mac the center of the Digital Hub, Apple produced some truly innovative applications, including the iLife suite (consisting of iTunes, iPhoto, iMovie, iDVD, and now GarageBand), as well as a group of iApps for your Mac, including iCal, iSync, iChat, and others such as Address Book, Mail, and Safari.

With your Mac at the center of all you do, there was one missing connection: a way to extend your digital lifestyle. In July 2002, Apple took its iTools services to the next level, expanded its capabilities and integrated those services with the various iApps for Mac OS X Jaguar, and relaunched the service as .Mac (pronounced "dot-Mac"). By integrating .Mac services into each of the iApps, your Mac became a greater part of the Digital Hub, and Apple made it easier for you to share your digital life, as well as to make your Mac safer.

iApp Integration with .Mac

Everyone knows that Apple's iApps are great for things like managing photos and music, or for creating movies and burning them to DVDs. But few people realize how tightly integrated the iApps are with the .Mac services. For example:

- From iPhoto, you can create Photo Albums and then publish them directly to your .Mac HomePage. You can also create screensavers from images in your collection to use on your Mac or share with other Mac OS X users (as long as they're using Mac OS X v10.2 or higher).

Figure P-1. The Digital Hub.

- From iMovie, you can export the movies you create directly to your iDisk's *Movies* folder and build a .Mac HomePage from which it can be viewed.

- With iCal, you can opt to publish your calendars to your iDisk, making them viewable on the Web from any browser that supports current-day web standards.

- iSync can be used to place information you store in your Address Book, iCal, and even Safari's bookmarks on your iDisk, making them available to you online using a web browser. Your Address Book contacts can then be used with .Mac's web-based Mail service as well, so your contacts will always be available to you, even if you're on the road or on vacation without your trusty Mac.

- Mail can be configured to use IMAP to gather and manage your .Mac email.

- You can save the tracks you create with GarageBand to your iDisk's *Public* folder and share them with your friends or other GarageBand users.

By combining the iApps and your .Mac account, your Mac becomes that much more powerful, making it easier for you to extend your digital lifestyle with the world around you.

What You Get with .Mac

So now that you know what you can do with .Mac and how the iApps fit to enhance your .Mac experience, let's look at what you get with your .Mac membership:

- A Mac.com email account with 15 MB of storage space on Apple's .Mac servers. You can access your .Mac mail over the Web via IMAP or download messages directly to your Mac using POP.

- An iDisk with 100 MB of space for storing, backing up, and sharing files. Your iDisk is also used for serving up your .Mac HomePage, which can include Photo Album pages you create with iPhoto or the movies you create with iMovie.

- HomePage web-building tools (based on Apple's own WebObjects technology), which you can use to build your own web site and host it on the .Mac servers (*http://homepage.mac.com/membername*).

- Backup, a Cocoa-based backup and recovery application that lets you back up data from your Mac to your iDisk, CD, or DVD, or to an external or networked drive.

- Virex (from McAfee Securities), anti-virus software for Mac OS X. Virex can be used to scan email attachments and the files on your hard drive for viruses, in order to protect your Mac from viruses that plague other systems.

- Address Book, iCal, and Safari Bookmark syncing with the aid of iSync. Once your contacts, calendars, and bookmarks have been synced to your iDisk, you can gain access to your vital information using any web browser from any platform, including Windows and Linux machines. Once synchronized, your iCal calendars can be viewed over the Web, making it easy for your friends, family, and colleagues to keep track of what you're up to.

- iCards (send electronic postcards) that you can send to your friends and family, as well as create custom iCards from digital images on your computer.

- Easy access to .Mac's Customer Support team. You'll also be able to discuss problems with other .Mac users and get answers from Apple's customer service representatives.

- The .Mac Learning Center, which gives you quick access to online tutorials to help you learn more about Mac OS X, its applications and utilities, and .Mac itself. The Learning Center also provides access to relevant articles from Apple's Knowledge Base and TechNotes so you can stay on top of the latest happenings with Mac OS X and .Mac.

- Mac Slides Publisher, a standalone application that can be used for creating .Mac screensavers. Once you've created a .Mac slide show, that screensaver can be shared with anyone else who is using a Mac OS X system (Jaguar, Panther, or higher).

- FreePlay Music, thousands of free AAC-encoded audio tracks that you can use as background tracks for use with iMovie, iDVD, GarageBand, Final Cut Express, and Final Cut Pro.

 You're not restricted to using the FreePlay Music clips with Apple's applications; you can also use them with any image or sound-editing tool. The only real restriction is that the FreePlay Music clips are provided for personal use only; they are not intended for commercial use.

In addition to all this, .Mac members are given exclusive access to QuickTime-based training sessions to help them learn more about their Macs, discounts on select software, a free VersionTracker Plus membership, free games, exclusive sound effects from Skywalker Sound (in MP3 format), and more. When you think about it, there really is a lot more to Apple's .Mac service than meets the eye.

The Benefits of a .Mac Membership

To borrow a tagline from American Express, "Membership has its privileges"; the very same adage applies to your .Mac membership. If you look beyond the instant gratification of having a Mac.com email address that lets everyone know you're a Mac user, take the time and look at everything that's included with your annual .Mac membership. But first, let's look at the ISP issue.

ISPs, Email, and Your Web Site

In order to connect to the Internet from home, you have to pay a gross amount of money to someone for that connection. Nowadays, the chosen path is cable modems and DSL for home users who want high-speed Internet access. Since most broadband providers charge an average of $30–$40 per month (or more), you're already shelling out $360 or more per year just to send email and cruise the Web.

And with that ISP, you most likely get one main email account and possibly a few more email addresses that you can assign to family members in your household. And most ISPs offer web-hosting on their servers, typically with a limit of about 50 MB of storage.

But the one problem with ISPs these days is that they're being bought and sold constantly, and every time your ISP changes hands, you get a new email address and your web address changes. That means you have to send a message to all your friends to let them know about the change, and what's worse, you typically don't get the same email address name as you had before. For example, in the two years I lived in Boston, my cable company (and broadband Internet service) shifted hands more than counterfeit $20s; from MediaOne, to AT&T, and then to Comcast. Every time the ISP changed hands, we got a new email address.

If you've been through an ISP switch, think about how much of a headache it is to send email out to everyone in your Address Book, plus not to mention the time it takes you to reconfigure your mail settings and realign the planets so people can get to your web site.

Through it all, the one constant in our lives has been our .Mac accounts. We've grown to rely on the Mac.com address as our primary source of email communication. Our friends and family know that their mail will always find us, no matter how frequently we move across the country, or how many times our ISP gets bought and sold. And since we have .Mac accounts, we have our own web sites, which we don't have to move around either. Everything stays put, just like it should.

.Mac's Extras

Beyond having a Mac.com email address, there's a lot more to .Mac membership that makes it a great deal. For example, let's consider Virex and Backup just by themselves.

Virex is a virus protection application for your Mac that's included with your .Mac membership. All you need to do is download and install the latest version of Virex from the Mac.com web site (or from your iDisk), and you can start regularly scanning your Mac for viruses. Virex can be set up so that it scans your computer for viruses every time you start your Mac. It also has an eUpdate feature that checks your iDisk for updates to ensure that Virex is always up to date in tracking down viruses on your Mac. If you purchase virus-protection software separately (such as Norton AntiVirus), you could pay upwards of $50.

The one thing that every computer owner should do regularly is back up their computer. If you don't, and if something happens to your computer's hard drive, you're basically out of luck. Smart computer owners realize the value of having a backup and often invest $50–$100 on backup software alone.

If you were to purchase the anti-virus and backup software separately, you can expect to spend about $100 right there. Add on to that 100 MB of drive space you can use to host a web site or a place to back up your files to, you've equaled the annual cost of your .Mac membership.

Then consider the thousands of royalty-free audio tracks, which can be downloaded from your iDisk. Each track is available in varying lengths, which makes them easy to download and use in any iMovie or Final Cut Express project on which you might be working. These tracks are always at your disposal, yet they don't cost you a dime. Apple makes these freely available to anyone with a .Mac membership. If you were to go out and purchase CDs full of stock, royalty-free audio tracks, the cost would be about 10 times the cost of your annual .Mac membership.

And finally, let's go back to that web page of yours. Sure, your ISP gives you space on its server to place your web site, but what if you don't have the foggiest clue of how to build a web page? ISPs don't give you any tools to use, and you're pretty much left to figure it out for yourself, which probably means that you won't take the time to publish your own web site.

But with .Mac, you can build your web site using the HomePage tools to create your web page with very little effort. Of course, you're not limited to using the HomePage tools—you can always build your site using Dreamweaver, Contribute, GoLive, or BBEdit and upload the site to your iDisk's *Sites* folder—but they're there if you need them. And if you have a digital camera and use iPhoto for storing digital images on your Mac, you can select images and post them on your .Mac HomePage or create a screensaver with a few clicks and the push of a button.

So, is the annual cost of a .Mac membership worth it? You betcha, it is! You can't get this level of integration anywhere or on any other system. There's nothing like a .Mac membership to extend your digital lifestyle.

System Requirements

As with most software these days, there are some minimum requirements for running all of .Mac's services and applications on your Mac. These include:

- Mac OS X Jaguar (Version 10.2.8) or better; along with running Mac OS X, keep in mind its minimum system and RAM requirements as well.
- An Internet connection, either dial-up, broadband, or LAN access; the faster your connection, the better your experience will be.
- A web browser, such as Apple's Safari (*http://www.apple.com/safari*), that supports web standards like the latest versions of HTML and Cascading Style Sheets (CSS).

Now, this doesn't mean that you can't have a .Mac membership if you have only a Mac OS 9 machine—because you can. I have a legacy Mac at home that's still running Mac OS 9.1.1, and I use that machine to mount my iDisk and access my Mac.com email all the time. While I can't use applications such as Backup or iSync on my Mac OS 9 machine, I can still get to my iDisk on the older Mac with some assistance from an application called Goliath (see Chapter 3).

.Mac memberships can also be used by people who use Windows by day and Mac by night. If you find yourself having to use a Windows machine during the day while you're at work but have a Mac at home, this book will show you how you can access your Mac.com mail online using .Mac's web-based Mail service, and also how to mount your iDisk on your Windows PC. Apple recently released an iDisk Utility for Windows XP, and we'll cover how to install and use that in Appendix C.

So, while on the outside it looks like you need a Mac OS X system to have a .Mac membership, you really don't. You can use Mac OS 9 or a Windows machine as well, and the web-based Mail and HomePage tools can be used from any computer, including Linux or FreeBSD machines. However, to get the most from your .Mac membership, you'll need a Mac that's running Mac OS X (Version 10.2.8 or higher).

How This Book Is Organized

This book is organized into the following chapters:

Part I, *.Mac's Core Services*

This first part of the book provides you with an overview of the services at the core of every .Mac member's account. The chapters in this part include:

Chapter 1, *Setting Up Your .Mac Account*

This chapter will show you how to configure and administer your .Mac account, including information on changing your .Mac account's password and configuring iCal to periodically remind you to change your password.

Chapter 2, *Inside Mac.com*

This short chapter provides you with a quick overview of what you'll find on Apple's hub for .Mac members: the Mac.com web site.

Chapter 3, *Using Your iDisk*

At the center of every .Mac account is the iDisk, which with a base membership includes 100 MB of online storage space. This chapter provides an in-depth look at the iDisk, showing you how to mount and unmount one, and it's use with *Public* folders.

Chapter 4, *.Mac Maill*

With .Mac, you have two options for checking your mail: with Mail.app (or any other email client), or over the Web, using .Mac's web-based Mail. This chapter focuses on using your .Mac email account over the Web and provides you with tips for managing your Mail and dealing with spam.

Part II, *Protecting Your Mac*

Whether you use your Mac at work or home, the data stored on your hard drive is no doubt very important to you. Your .Mac membership includes two great utilities to help you protect that data by screening it for viruses and to help you back up and restore that data if necessary.

Chapter 5, *Using Virex*

With all the worms and Trojan horse viruses that get sent around these days, everyone needs some protection from viruses. This chapter shows you how to use Virex to ensure your Mac is always protected.

Chapter 6, *Using Backup*

Without a doubt, the most important thing you can do as a computer owner is back up your system. Thankfully, .Mac comes with a powerful application, Backup, for just that purpose. You'll not only learn how to use Backup to back up and restore your precious data, you'll also learn some tips for getting into the habit of routinely backing it up.

Part III, *.Mac and Your Digital Life*

> This part of the book shows you how your .Mac membership fits in as an integral cog in Apple's Digital Hub strategy.

Chapter 7, *Building a .Mac HomePage*

> With 7 different page styles and over 50 different page themes, building a .Mac HomePage can be really simple. This chapter shows you where to save files on your iDisk and provides you with tips on how to build and show off your .Mac HomePage.

Chapter 8, *Blogging with iBlog*

> This chapter shows you how to add a web log to your HomePage using Lifli Software's application, iBlog.

Chapter 9, *Using iSync with .Mac*

> This chapter introduces you to iSync, which can be used to synchronize your Address Book, iCal information, and Safari's bookmarks with your iDisk and portable devices, such as an iPod, PDA, and/or cellular phone.

Chapter 10, *Slide Shows and iCards*

> This chapter covers the use of the Mac Slides Publisher and iPhoto 2 for creating Public Slide Shows (screensavers) from your photos, and how to create and send iCards.

Part IV, *Appendixes*

> There are also three appendixes to this book:

Appendix A, *.Mac's Keyboard Shortcuts*

> This appendix lists all of the keyboard shortcuts you can use with the .Mac applications, including Backup, Virex, iSync, and more.

Appendix B, *Common iDisk Error Codes*

> On occasion, you might encounter some cryptic error code when trying to connect or upload a file to your iDisk. This appendix provides you with a listing of some of the more commonly seen iDisk error codes and provides you with some guidance on what they mean so you'll know what to do when you see them.

Appendix C, *Installing and Using the iDisk Utility for Windows XP*

> Believe it or not, there are some people out there who use Windows by day and a Mac at home by night. This appendix has been provided for those folks who might need to access their iDisk from Windows XP; it shows you how to install and use the iDisk Utility on that other platform.

Combined, the chapters in this book provide you with a complete overview of .Mac's services and software, showing you how to effectively integrate your Mac with Apple's web services.

Conventions Used in This Book

The following typographical conventions are used in this book:

Italic

> Used to indicate new terms, URLs, filenames, file extensions, directories, commands and options, program names, and to highlight comments in examples. For example, a path in the filesystem will appear as */Applications/Utilities*.

`Constant Width`

> Used to show the contents of files or the output from commands.

`Constant Width Bold`

> Used in examples and tables to show commands or other text that should be typed literally by the user.

`Constant Width Italic`

> Used in examples and tables to show text that should be replaced with user-supplied values.

Menus/Navigation

> Menus and their options are referred to in the text as File → Open, Edit → Copy, etc. Arrows will also be used to signify a navigation path when using window options; for example, System Preferences → Desktop & Screen Saver → Screen Saver means that you would launch System Preferences, click on the icon for the Desktop & Screen Saver preferences panel, and then select the Screen Saver pane within that panel.

Pathnames

> Pathnames are used to show the location of a file or application in the filesystem. Directories (or folders for Mac and Windows users) are separated by a forward slash. For example, if you see something like "...launch the Terminal application (*/Applications/Utilities*)" in the text, that means the Terminal application can be found in the *Utilities* subfolder of the *Applications* folder.

↵

> A carriage return (↵) at the end of a line of code is used to denote an unnatural line break; that is, you should not enter these as two lines of code, but as one continuous line. Multiple lines are used in these cases due to printing constraints.

$, #

> The dollar sign ($) is used in some examples to show the user prompt for the *bash* shell; the hash mark (#) is the prompt for the root user.

Menu Symbols

> When looking at the menus for any application, you will see some symbols associated with keyboard shortcuts for a particular command. For example, to open a document in Microsoft Word, you could go to the File menu and select Open (File → Open), or you could issue the keyboard shortcut, z-O.

> Figure P-2 shows the symbols used in the various menus to denote a shortcut.

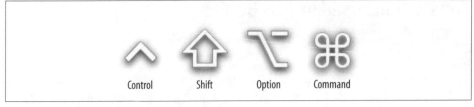

Figure P-2. Keyboard accelerators for issuing commands.

Rarely will you see the Control symbol used as a menu command option; it's more often used in association with mouse clicks or for working with the *tcsh* shell.

Indicates a tip, suggestion, or general note.

Indicates a warning or caution.

We'd Like to Hear From You

We have tested and verified all of the information in this book to the best of our ability, but you may find that features have changed (or even that we have made mistakes!). Please let us know about any errors you find, as well as your suggestions for future editions, by writing:

O'Reilly Media, Inc.
1005 Gravenstein Highway North
Sebastopol, CA 95472
800-998-9938 (in the U.S. and Canada)
707-829-0515 (international/local)
707-829-0104 (fax)

You can also send us messages electronically. To be put on the mailing list or to request a catalog, send email to:

info@oreilly.com

To ask technical questions or comment on the book, send email to:

bookquestions@oreilly.com

We have a web site for the book, where we list examples, errata, and any plans for future editions. You can access this page at:

http://www.oreilly.com/catalog/indotmac/

For more information about this book and others, see the O'Reilly web site:

http://www.oreilly.com/

Finally, you can also reach the author through his .Mac web page, located at:

http://homepage.mac.com/chuckdude/

Acknowledgments

If you've never written a book before—let alone edited one—it's hard to comprehend just how much time it takes to write a bunch of words and take a few screenshots. While working on this book, I spent many nights writing alone into the wee hours. Of course, this meant that I missed a lot time with my wife, our kitty Max, family, friends, and my bike; those who mean the most to me deserve a great deal of thanks. You're about to read more "Thank-You's" than what you'll hear on Oscar night, but trust me, these are well-placed and I won't get on my soapbox and preach politics at you.

First and foremost, I need to thank my wife, Kellie, for putting up with me taking on another solo book project, and for understanding that I'd rather be writing than editing most days. Kel puts up with a lot from me—writing, editing, ranting about writing and editing—and still manages to keep me around the house.

Thanks to my family for their support and encouragement with everything I do (especially through all those bike accidents). On my side of the fam, we have my folks, Greg and Carol, my brothers, Skip, Jerry, and Doug, their wives, children, pets, etc. On the in-law side, I'd like to thank Red (Bob) and Carole, Sheri and Jason and their munchkins, Mazzy and Aiden, and last but not least, Jeff.

Other friends I'd like to thank include (in alphabetical order this time so there's no fuss about who was listed first): Shirley Brooks, Kirk and Lisa Elrod (and the rest of the Elrod clan), James Duncan Davidson, Katie and Joe Johnson, Jamie Lavery, Susan Nimmo, Marsha Petty, Greg Tocco, and Bill Whytock and Rowan (the *Happy Dog*). Thanks for understanding that your dorky friend, Chuck, likes to write and play with computers, and sorry that I couldn't hang with you all those times when you wanted to go out and party. (But I do appreciate those of you who realized my Kryptonite was ice cream.)

Many thanks to the good folks at Apple, especially those of you on the .Mac team, for providing valuable feedback on early drafts of this book, and for welcoming me into your department for a week to make final tweaks to the manuscript. While I can't say who you are without causing ripples on the Loop, this book wouldn't have been as complete (or accurate) without your guidance and input. Thanks!

I know this one's odd, but I'd like to thank the cartoonists and comedians who have kept me laughing through the rough spots life has thrown my way. These kind folks

(I can only presume, right?) include Bill Amend (*FoxTrot*), Berke Breathed (*Bloom County* and *Outland*, Opus and Bill rule!), Dana Carvey, Bill Cosby, Michael Jantze (*The Norm*), Steve Martin, Bill Murray, Adam Sandler, Bill Waterson (*Calvin & Hobbes*), and Robin Williams (yes, reality is just a concept).

Finally, this book is dedicated to the memory of my brother-in-law, Jeff Robinson. A faithful Mac user, my fourth brother, and a crack-up in his own right. Jeff passed away from complications of surgery for Crohn's disease soon after I started writing this book. A portion of the proceeds from this book will be donated to the CHILD Foundation (Children with Intestinal and Liver Disorders) in Vancouver, British Columbia. Additional information about Crohn's disease can be found on CHILD's web site at *http://www.child.ca*. And while you're there, break out that wallet and make a donation, will ya?

.Mac's Core Services

This first part of the book provides you with an overview of the services at the core of every .Mac member's account.

This part of the book provides an overview of how to set up your .Mac account and introduces you to the basic services offered to every .Mac member. You'll also learn more than you probably ever wanted to know about your iDisk, including how to interpret some of the error codes you might run into when interacting with your iDisk.

Finally, you'll learn more about .Mac's web-based Mail service. This chapter introduces you to Mail's web-based interface, and includes information on how to send and view attachments in emails, and manage your Mail space, as well as how to bring your Mac's Address Book in-sync with .Mac's web-based Mail so you don't have to fish around for email addresses when you're on the road.

The chapters in this part include:

- Chapter 1, *Setting Up Your .Mac Account*
- Chapter 2, *Inside Mac.com*
- Chapter 3, *Using Your iDisk*
- Chapter 4, *.Mac Mail*

Setting Up Your .Mac Account

When you install Mac OS X or start up a new Mac for the first time, you are given an opportunity to enter the information for your .Mac account or to sign up for an account. If you don't have a .Mac account, or aren't sure of what your username and password are, you can always go back later and take care of these.

Apple offers four ways to sign up for a .Mac account:

- When you start up a new Mac for the first time while entering your user account information.
- When you install (or reinstall) Mac OS X.
- When you purchase a "boxed set" for a .Mac account from an Apple Store or Apple's web site.
- Online via the Mac.com (*http://www.mac.com*) web site.

Once you've signed up for your .Mac membership, you'll need to configure your Mac OS X system to use its services and software. This chapter shows you how to configure your Mac OS X system to work with the .Mac services.

The goal of this chapter is to help you get up and running with your .Mac account as soon as possible. Future chapters go into greater detail on using your iDisk, .Mac Mail, and the other applications and services that come as part of your .Mac membership.

Before You Sign Up

If you haven't already signed up for your .Mac account, there are some things you might want to take into consideration before doing so, including selecting a member (or user) name and choosing a password.

Try .Mac Before You Buy

If you don't already have a .Mac account, go to the Mac.com web site and click on the big red Free Trial button. This will take you to a page where you can sign up for a 60-day free trial .Mac membership. The trial .Mac membership includes the following:

- A Mac.com email address with 5 MB of email storage
- An iDisk with 20 MB of storage
- Software to back up to your iDisk
- Use of the HomePage web page builder

The trial .Mac membership should give you a taste of what's to come if you decide later that you want the full membership.

 If you have a trial .Mac membership, you should be aware that the Backup application (discussed in Chapter 6) only permits you to backup data to your iDisk. You won't be able to use Backup to make backups to CDs, DVDs, or to a networked or external drive.

Read the Fine Print

Before you sign up for your .Mac membership, there are a couple online documents that you should read. These include:

Privacy Policy
Apple's privacy policy (*http://www.apple.com/legal/privacy*) describes how the information you provide to Apple will be used and protected.

Terms & Conditions
The .Mac Terms & Conditions (*http://www.mac.com/1/membership_terms.html*) details the rules and usage terms by which all .Mac members must abide. Make sure you read this in its entirety, particularly the Acceptable Use Policy Guidelines section.

Selecting a Member Name

When selecting the username for your .Mac account, keep in mind that your member name will also be your Mac.com email address (e.g., *membername@mac.com*), as well as the lead-in for your Mac.com HomePage (*http://homepage.mac.com/membername*). So, you should select your username with care, being conscious that the username you select will be your permanent moniker.

You can opt for a plain-vanilla member name by combining your first and last names (e.g., *chucktoporek* or *chuck_toporek*), or something radically different to reflect your persona or personality (e.g., *chuckdude* or *chuckanut*). Member names can consist of letters or numbers, and may include hyphens (–) or underscores (_). The letters in your member name are case insensitive, meaning, if you enter an a member name by mixing upper- and lowercase letters, all of those letters will be interpreted as lowercase. For example, if I were to enter *chuckDUDE* as my member name, it would be interpreted as *chuckdude*.

Choosing a Password

The password you select will be used for all aspects of your .Mac account, such as logging in to check email, connecting to your iDisk, and accessing your account information on the Mac.com web site.

When selecting a password for your .Mac account, I *highly* suggest that you choose something other than the password you use when logging on to your Mac. Also, your password cannot be the same as your .Mac member name. As with any system, you should have different passwords for different systems and accounts. While this may make it more difficult for you to keep track of which username and password is used for which system, it also makes it harder for people to crack your account. If you use the same password for everything, all a cracker needs to do is guess one password correctly, and they'll have access to everything you do.

Your .Mac password needs to be 4–8 characters in length. The characters can either be lower- or uppercase letters, numbers, or a combination of the three. Try to pick something that's easy for you to remember, but not something so easy that someone else can guess it correctly. You should also stray away from using "dictionary" words (i.e., words commonly found in any English-language dictionary), since crackers tend to use those first when trying to break into an account. Another common practice is for people to use numbers in place of letters. For example, if you wanted your password to be "smile" you could use "5m1L3" instead, using 5 instead of an "s," a 1 instead of an "i," an uppercase "L," and a 3 instead of an "e."

Of course, it's all up to you as to what your password will be. The more difficult you make it, the harder it will be for someone to crack into your account, and the more often you change your password, the harder it will be for someone to catch on to what you're doing.

For a tip on how to remind yourself to change your .Mac account's password, see the section, "Changing Your .Mac Password," later in this chapter.

Your First Stop: System Preferences

Now that we've cleared the air about member names and passwords, it's time to configure your Mac OS X system to accept your .Mac account. For the purpose of this book, we'll assume that you didn't enter the settings for your .Mac account during the install or when you first started up a new Mac.

The .Mac Pane

To configure the settings for your .Mac account, you'll need to launch the System Preferences application by clicking on its icon in the Dock, and then clicking on the icon for .Mac in the Internet & Network section; the .Mac panel is shown in Figure 1-1.

Figure 1-1. The System Preferences .Mac preferences pane.

As you can see from Figure 1-1, the .Mac preference panel has two tabbed panes:

.Mac
> This pane has two fields for entering your .Mac Member Name and the Password you've chosen for your account. The information you enter in these fields will be used when you access your Mac.com email account or attempt to log on to your iDisk.

iDisk
> The iDisk pane, described more in the next section, contains information about the state of your iDisk.

If you don't already have a .Mac membership, click on the Sign Up button in the .Mac pane. This launches your default web browser and takes you to Apple's .Mac web site (*http://www.mac.com*), from which you can purchase a membership.

If you aren't comfortable with making a purchase and giving your credit card information over the Web, you can also purchase a boxed .Mac membership from any Apple Store. To find the Apple Store nearest you, go to *http://www.apple.com/retail* or call 1-800-MY-APPLE (or 1-800-692-7753).

The iDisk Pane

As mentioned in the previous section, the iDisk pane (System Preferences → .Mac → iDisk), shown in Figure 1-2, is mainly used to keep track of how much space you have on your iDisk. However, the iDisk pane also gives you a quick way to purchase additional storage space (by clicking on the By More button), and to control the access privileges to your iDisk's *Public* folder.

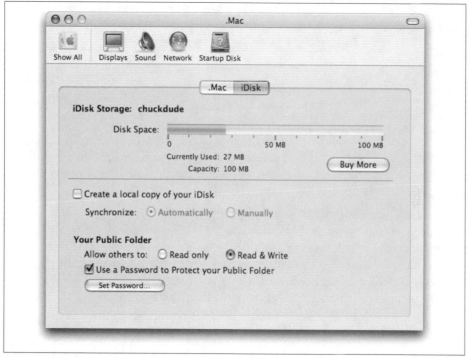

Figure 1-2. The iDisk pane.

When you click on the iDisk tab, your Mac quickly connects to your iDisk over the Internet to gather information about how much disk space you have used. If you are not connected to the Internet, an alert sheet slides out of the window's titlebar informing you that you cannot connect to your iDisk. When you dismiss the sheet by clicking on the OK button, you are returned to the .Mac pane.

Clicking on the iDisk pane does not mount your iDisk. Instead, it simply probes your iDisk over the Net to see how much space you've used and how much space is available.

Buying more iDisk space

If you notice that you're starting to run low on available space, you can expand your iDisk's storage capacity by clicking on the Buy More button. When you click on this button, you are taken to the Mac.com site in your default web browser, where you will need to enter your member name and password.

After logging in, you will be taken to the Upgrade storage page where you can purchase additional space for your iDisk. The cost of additional iDisk space is detailed in Table 1-1.

Table 1-1. Rate chart for additional iDisk storage space

MB storage	Cost/Year
200 MB	$60
300 MB	$100
500 MB	$180
1000 MB (1 GB)	$350

When you purchase additional space for your iDisk, you will be charged a prorated amount for the remainder of the current year of your membership. After the current year of your .Mac membership is up, you will incur the full annual charge for the additional space.

To purchase additional iDisk storage space, select the amount and click on the Upgrade Now button at the bottom of the page. You will be taken to the Billing Information page where you can enter your credit card and contact information. If you decide that you don't want to upgrade your iDisk, simply click on your browser's Back button and deselect the upgrade option, or close the browser window. To complete the transaction, click on the Buy Now button.

Public folder access

Your iDisk's *Public* folder is what people from the outside world can mount on their system (including Mac OS X, Mac OS 9, and most Windows users) to pick up or place files.

The lower portion of the iDisk pane is used to control access to your iDisk's *Public* folder. The iDisk Utility, which is available on your iDisk (*/Software/Members Only/ dotmac Software/iDisk Utility*), handles many of the same functions of this lower section of the iDisk pane.

For information on how to use the iDisk Utility, see Chapter 3.

Configuring Mail

The information you enter for your .Mac account in the .Mac preference panel (see Figure 1-1) is automatically used by your email client, which by default is set to use Apple's Mail application. This makes it really easy for you to start using your Mac. com email account quickly.

To check Mail's settings, launch the Mail application (/Applications) and select Mail → Preferences (or use its keyboard shortcut, ⌘-,) from the menu bar. When the preferences window opens, you'll see Mail's General settings, as shown in Figure 1-3.

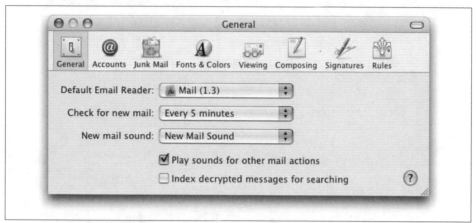

Figure 1-3. Mail's preference pane.

To choose a different email client, click on the pop-up menu next to the heading, Default Email Reader, and choose the Select option. A sheet will slide down from the preference window's titlebar, placing you in the Applications folder, from which you can select another email application.

By default, your .Mac email account is configured to use the Internet Mail Access Protocol, or IMAP, for managing your mail on Apple's email server. The use of IMAP means that your email will be stored on Apple's email servers, making it always available to you, either via the Mail application on your Mac or by using an online version of Mail from the Mac.com web site (more on that in Chapter 4).

If you use IMAP, you should keep in mind that although you're checking email on your computer, your mail is stored Apple's servers, not on your computer. The advantage to this is that your email won't take up a lot of space on your hard drive. The downside is that you need to be diligent about managing the mail stored online, otherwise, you could lose any incoming mail until you either purchase additional email storage (see later) or delete any unwanted messages.

If you decide that you'd rather use POP (Post Office Protocol) to permanently download your .Mac mail to your Mac, there is a way to trick Mail into doing this. Just follow these steps:

1. Launch the Mail application by clicking on its icon in the Dock.

2. Select Mail → Preferences from the menu bar (or use the keyboard shortcut ⌘-,).

3. Click on the Accounts icon near the top of the preference window to see the current settings for your .Mac email account, shown in Figure 1-4.

Figure 1-4. Mail's default settings for your .Mac email account.

4. Just below the Accounts column on the lefthand side of the window, you'll see two buttons: one with a plus sign (+) and the other with a minus sign (–). To add an account, click on the plus sign button; to delete an account, click on the minus sign button. Since we want to trick Mail into using POP for your .Mac email, we're going to add another account, so click on the plus sign button.

5. Now you have a blank slate with which to work. To configure your .Mac account to use POP mail, follow these steps:

   a. From the pop-up menu next to Account Type, select POP.

   b. In the Description field, just type in your .Mac member name; for example, mine is *chuckdude*.

c. In the Email Address field, enter your .Mac email address, which should be your .Mac member name followed by *@mac.com*; for example, mine is *chuckdude@mac.com*.

d. In the Full Name field, enter your first and last name; mine is Chuck Toporek.

e. Set the Incoming Mail Server to *mail.mac.com*. This is the server that Mail checks for any new email messages.

f. Set the User Name field to your .Mac member name (again, mine is *chuckdude*).

g. Type in your .Mac account's password into the Password field. As you enter your password, you won't be able to actually see the characters, since they are hidden by little black round circles, known as *bullets*. If you think you've made a mistake while entering your password, just hit the Delete key to go backwards, and then re-enter the password again.

h. In the Outgoing Mail Server (SMTP) pop-up menu, leave that set to *smtp. mac.com:membername* (mine is set to *smtp.mac.com:chuckdude*).

When you've finished these steps, the Accounts preference window should look similar to Figure 1-5.

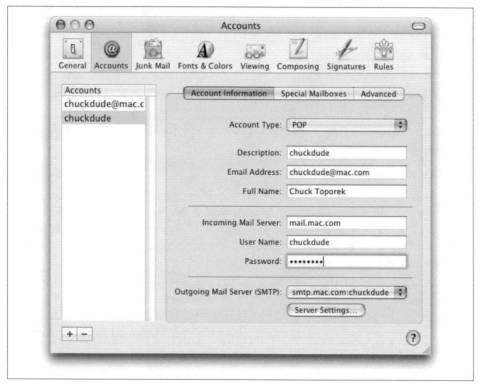

Figure 1-5. Configuring Mail to use POP for getting your .Mac email.

6. Now click on the Advanced tab so you can further define how Mail will handle your .Mac account's email.

7. Make sure that the checkbox next to "Remove mail from server after retrieving a message" is checked, and then select "Right away" from the pop-up menu just beneath that, as shown in Figure 1-6.

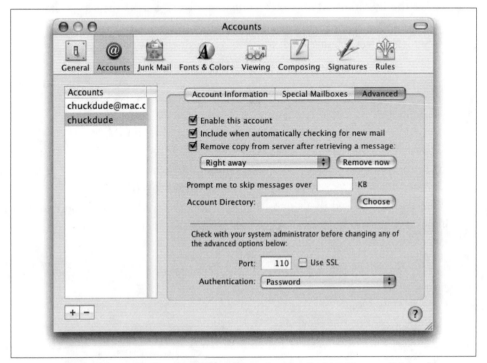

Figure 1-6. In the Advanced tab, set up Mail so that it downloads your .Mac email from the server if there is any new mail waiting for you.

8. Click on the Account Information tab.

9. In the Accounts column to the left, click on your original Mac.com email account (in looking at Figure 1-6, mine would be the top account). When you select that name, the sheet shown in Figure 1-7 slides out of the toolbar, asking you if you want to Save Changes. Click on the Save button to save the POP account you just created.

10. After you click on the Save button, Mail will recognize that you've created another account with the email address of *membername@mac.com*, and will prompt you with the alert window shown in Figure 1-8. Since the account you created is a different type (a POP account), click on the Yes button to continue with the save and dismiss the alert window.

Okay, we're almost there. Now that you've created the POP account in Mail's preferences, it's time to go back and delete the original .Mac email account, which uses

Figure 1-7. Click on the Save button to save the new POP email account you created for receiving your .Mac email.

IMAP. Remember, the difference between POP and IMAP is that POP will download the mail to your Mac and remove the mail from the server. IMAP downloads a copy of the mail to your Mac, but leaves the messages on the server, where you can view them online using a web browser from any computer anywhere. We'll cover the web-based email in Chapter 4.

Now let's get rid of that IMAP account in Mail:

1. With the original Mac.com email address highlighted in the Accounts column, click on the minus sign (–) button, at the lower-left of the window. When you do, Mail pops up an alert window (shown in Figure 1-9) asking you to confirm whether you really want to delete that account.

2. The alert window tells you that deleting the account will erase any mailboxes for the account, but it won't affect any of the messages on the server. The reason why it won't delete the messages on the server is because this account used IMAP to keep the mail on the server and make it readable from anywhere. To erase the account, click on the OK button.

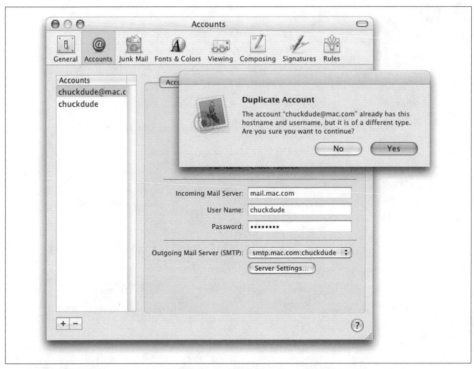

Figure 1-8. Mail tries to be smart, but we know better. Click on the Yes button to continue saving the new account.

Congratulations, you've just learned how to set up Mail to use POP to access to your .Mac email. After you've deleted the IMAP account, Mail's Accounts preference panel should look similar to Figure 1-10.

Notice that the Account Type says POP next to it. The advantage to having Mail configured to use POP for your .Mac email is that when you check mail on your Mac, the email will download off the server and will be stored on your Mac's hard drive (stored in ~/*Library/Mail*). By downloading the mail from the server, you don't have to worry as much about running over your 15 MB email storage limit on the .Mac server. Another advantage to keeping a local copy of your email is that you can use the Backup application to back up your mail.

Also, setting up Mail to use POP for getting at your .Mac email doesn't mean you still can't use IMAP. You can, but just over the Web. If you point Safari (or some other web browser) at *http://www.mac.com/webmail*, you can log in using your .Mac member name and password and use the web-based Mail service. You can read, send, and manage your email online, and the next time you download mail on your Mac using Mail and the POP account, all of your online email will download to your computer. This makes it possible for you to keep a local copy of your email on your Mac, and still be able to read your email when you're away on business or vacation by most modern web browsers, including Safari, Mozilla, and Internet Explorer.

Figure 1-9. Mail asks you to confirm whether you want to remove the account.

Purchasing email-only accounts

By default, every .Mac member receives one Mac.com email account. However, if you wish to purchase additional Mac.com email addresses, you can purchase up to 10 additional email accounts for $10 each per year. The email-only accounts you create are assigned 10 MB of email storage space; this is separate from the 15 MB of storage allotted to your main .Mac email address.

 Unlike your main Mac.com email address, you cannot upgrade the amount of storage space assigned to any email-only account. If you need more than 10 MB of email storage for an email-only account, you will need to upgrade that email account to a full .Mac membership, which gives you 15 MB of storage and is upgradeable to a higher amount (and also all of the other benefits of a .Mac account).

To purchase an additional Mac.com email account, go to System Preferences → .Mac → iDisk, and then click on the Buy More button. (I realize that you're not wishing to purchase additional iDisk space, but this is the quickest way to getting to this option—

Figure 1-10. Your new POP account settings for your .Mac email account.

trust me.) You will be taken to the Mac.com web site, where you'll be prompted for your .Mac member name and password to log in. Once in, you'll be taken to the "Upgrade your .Mac membership" page.

At the top of this page, you will see a section titled Email Accounts, with a drop-down menu that's set to "zero" additional email-only account(s). To purchase an additional email account, click on the drop-down menu and select the number of additional Mac.com email accounts you'd like to purchase, scroll down on the web page (⌘-Down Arrow), and then click on the Continue button.

After verifying or changing your credit card information on the second page, click on the Continue button. After your account information has been verified, you will be taken to a third page, which lets you know how much your credit card will be charged for the additional email account(s). The amount you will be charged for the additional account is prorated for the number of days remaining until your .Mac account is up for renewal. Click on the Buy Now button to complete the transaction.

Once the order has been processed, you will see a page that says "Print your information" at the upper right. This page is your "receipt" for the charge to your credit card for the new email account(s) you've purchased. After you print this page (use ⌘-P), click on the Continue button; you still have a little more work to do.

Next, you'll be taken to a page that says "Your .Mac membership has been successfully upgraded." On that page, you'll see a button labeled Email Account Setup; click on that button to set up the additional email-only accounts. The next page you will see is shown in Figure 1-11.

Figure 1-11. Creating a new email-only account.

Click on the Create New Account button to be taken to the "Create a new email account" page, shown in Figure 1-12.

Enter your first and last name in the Personal Information section, and then enter the Account Information in the spaces provided. Enter the Member Name you'd like to use for your alternate Mac.com email account in the space provided. The name you choose here should be different from your main .Mac member name. After entering the desired Member Name, assign a password for the account and confirm it in the space below. Don't forget what we've said about password security. You should choose a password that's both different from your computer's password and from your main .Mac membership. When you've completed entering the information, click on the Continue button.

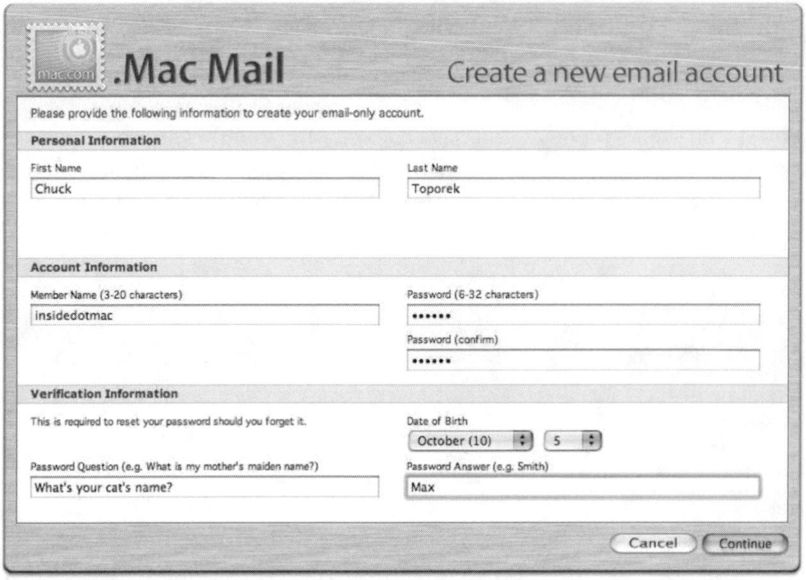

Figure 1-12. Create an extra email account by filling in the blanks.

If the Account Name you've chosen has already been taken (which is highly likely), you will be taken to another page so you can try again. If the Account Name you've chosen is accepted, you will see a page similar to the one shown in Figure 1-13.

You should print this page and file it in a safe place, since it contains both your .Mac Member Name and Password. (Note, the screen you see shows your password in its entirety. The Password in Figure 1-13 has been replaced with bullets to protect the security of this account.)

If you click on the Continue button, you will be taken to the Account management page shown in Figure 1-14.

After the new email account has been set up, you will receive an email at your primary .Mac email address, confirming that you've added another email account to your .Mac membership. This email also provides you with the details you need to configure Mail, including:

- The account member name (for example, *insidedotmac*)
- The account's email address (for example, *insidedotmac@mac.com*)
- Mail server address (*mail.mac.com*)
- SMTP server address (*smtp.mac.com*)

Paperless Security

If you don't want to run the risk of losing a piece of paper with your account information on it, you could take a screenshot of Figure 1-13 instead. To do this, use Shift-⌘-3 to shoot the entire screen, or Shift-⌘-4 to select just that information. If you use Shift-⌘-4, the mouse pointer will change to a set of crosshairs. To take the screenshot, click and hold the mouse button down at the upper-left corner of the web page, and then drag the mouse to the lower-right corner to select the area for the screenshot. When you let go of the mouse button, the screenshot will be taken.

By default, the screenshot will be saved to your Desktop as a PDF file, named something like *Picture 1.pdf*. Since this filename will be easy to confuse with something else, you might want to rename the file and move it to someplace other than your Desktop. To rename the file, follow these steps:

1. Click once on the icon and hit Return.
2. Hit the Left Arrow (←) key to move to the beginning of the filename.
3. Hold down the Shift-Option keys and then press the Right Arrow (→) key three times to select the current filename (but not the period or the file's extension).
4. Enter a new name for the file, such as *xtradotmacmail*.
5. Hit the Return key to accept the new filename. The file will now be named *xtradotmacmail.pdf*.

To keep this file from being viewed by prying eyes, click on the file's icon and select File → Get Info (⌘-I). At the top of the Info window, select the checkbox next to Lock to lock the file. Next, click on the disclosure triangle next to the Ownership & Permissions section. Under Group and Others, select No Access from the drop-down menus. Now if someone logs on to your Mac, they won't be able to view this file without entering your username and password.

Deleting an extra email account

If you decide at a later time that you want to delete one of your additional email accounts (you can't delete your primary Mac.com email account without canceling your membership), you can go to the Mac.com site and follow these steps:

1. Click on the Account button.
2. Enter the member name and password for your primary .Mac account (not for your email-only account).
3. Click on the Email Account Management button near the upper right of the page.
4. In the Account Management section (see Figure 1-14), select the account you'd like to remove and click on the Delete button.

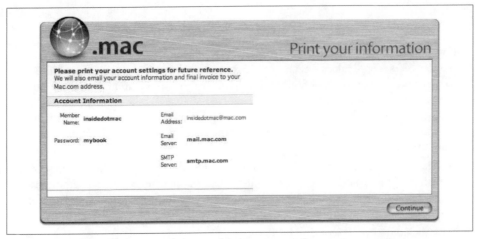

Figure 1-13. Confirm the new member name for the extra email account.

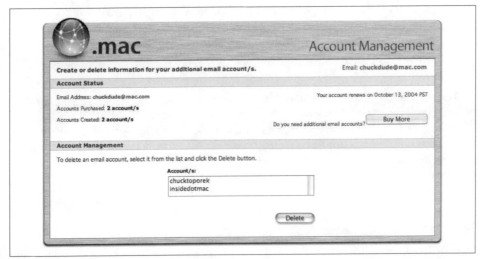

Figure 1-14. The Account management page, showing the primary and any additional email accounts.

Likewise, if you want to change the password for the additional email account, follow the steps detailed here, except click on the Edit button instead of the Delete button.

Buying more email storage space

If you continue to receive messages from Mac.com telling you that you're running out of email space, you have two options: clean up your online email storage (discussed in Chapter 4), or purchase additional space.

To purchase additional email storage space, go to System Preferences → .Mac → iDisk and click on the Buy More button. When you click on this button, you will be taken to the Mac.com site in your default web browser. Before you can enter, though, you will need to enter your .Mac member name and password.

After logging in, you will be taken to the "Upgrade storage" page where you can purchase more storage space for your Mac.com email account(s). The cost of additional Email space is detailed in Table 1-2.

Table 1-2. Rate chart for additional Email storage space

MB storage	Cost/Year
25 MB	$10
50 MB	$30
100 MB	$50
200 MB	$90

As with purchasing additional iDisk space, when you purchase additional space for your Mac.com email, you will be charged a prorated amount for the remainder of the current year of your membership. After the current year of your .Mac membership is up, you will incur the full annual charge for the additional space.

To purchase additional email storage space, select the desired amount and click on the Upgrade Now button at the bottom of the page. You will be taken to the Billing Information page where you can enter your credit card and contact information. If you decide that you don't want to upgrade your email space, simply click on your browser's Back button and deselect the upgrade option, or close the browser window. To complete the transaction, click on the Buy Now button.

Changing Your .Mac Password

When you first set up your .Mac account, you assign a password for accessing your mail, logging on to your iDisk, etc. But what if you decide later that you want to change your .Mac account's password?

At first, you might think that you can change your .Mac password in the System Preferences application, via the .Mac preference panel, but you can't. Instead, you'll need to go to the Mac.com web site and log in to your .Mac account. Once logged in, you'll see a button that contains your .Mac member name at the far right of the .Mac site's navigation bar. Click on this button to be taken to the Account Settings page, as shown in Figure 1-15.

Next, click on the Password Settings button, and you'll be taken to the Password Settings page, shown in Figure 1-16, which you can use to change your .Mac password and/or the password hint.

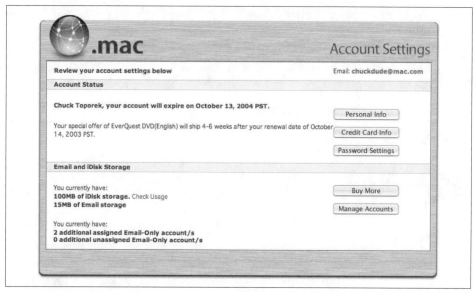

Figure 1-15. The Account Settings page for your .Mac account.

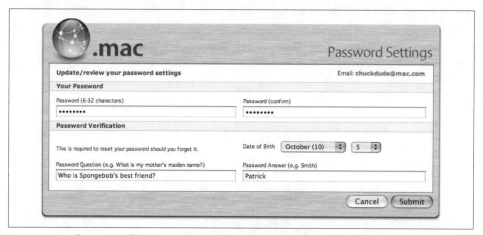

Figure 1-16. The Password Settings page is used to change the password and password hint for your .Mac account.

To change your account's password, just type a new one in the Password field and then tab to the "Password (confirm)" field and re-enter that password. To make your new .Mac password take effect, click on the Submit button.

If you've entered both passwords correctly, you'll be taken back to the Mac.com main page. If one the passwords are entered incorrectly, the page refreshes and you will receive a message that says "Your passwords did not match," prompting you to re-enter the passwords again.

Your .Mac member name and password are used by the iTunes Music Store. If you change your .Mac password, you'll also need to change your password for the iTunes Music Store by clicking on the button containing your account name in iTunes.

Setting an iCal Event to Change Your .Mac Password

If you use iCal (*http://www.apple.com/ical*), you can set up an Event to go off every two or three months to remind you to change your .Mac account's password. If you do use iCal, you can set up this event as follows:

1. Launch iCal by either clicking on its icon in the Dock or by double-clicking on its icon in the *Applications* folder (*/Applications*).

2. Create a new event (File → New Event, or ⌘-N). This places a new Event on today's calendar and opens the Event Info drawer to one side of iCal's window.

3. In the event that was placed on your calendar, type in the name of the event, such as "Change .Mac password".

4. In the drawer, click on the checkbox next to "all-day," since there isn't any specific time of the day that you need to change your .Mac password.

5. On the "from" and "to" lines, change the date for the event. You don't have to, but if you want to set it up so that you change the password on a Friday, you can either drag the event from the day it's currently at to Friday, or change the date on the "from" line.

6. On the "repeat" line, click on the word None to reveal a pop-up menu; from that menu, select Custom and let go of the mouse button.

7. In the window that appears, select Monthly from the Frequency pop-up menu and change the frequency to "Every 3 month(s)".

8. Near the bottom of that window, click on the radio button next to "On the", then select "last" from the first pop-up menu beneath that, and "Friday" from the other popup menu. This will place the Change .Mac Password event on the last Friday of every third month in your calendar. Click the OK button to save these changes and close the window.

9. Switch to the "alarm" section, and then click on None to reveal another pop-up menu, which lets you select how you would like iCal to remind you of this event. There are four options for notifying you of the event: Message, Message with sound, Email, or Open file.

   Of the four options, the first two have a greater chance at getting your attention than playing an alert sound, since it's too easy to confuse an alert sound from iCal with that of any other system event.

10. Quit iCal to save the event.

It isn't necessary for iCal to be running for you to receive alerts. The events you set up with iCal rely on a small application called iCal Helper (*/Applications/iCal/Contents/Resources/iCal Helper.app*) to pick up the events and issue alerts and messages.

Renewing Your .Mac Membership

Your .Mac membership expires one year, to the date, from when it was first activated. The activation date, of course, is when you purchased the .Mac membership and registered it online via the Mac.com web site. To find out when your activation and expiration dates are, log on to the Mac.com web site, and then click on the button in the navigation bar that contains your .Mac member name.

When your .Mac membership is up for renewal, you will receive an email message approximately 30 days before your account will expire, prompting you renew your .Mac account. If your .Mac account is set to renew automatically, your credit card won't be charged until the day that the renewal fee for your .Mac account is due. When it does renew, you will receive an email from Apple, notifying you that your credit card has been charged—and for what amount—and thanking you for renewing your .Mac membership.

You can receive a discount on your annual .Mac membership fee by referring other Mac users to sign up for a .Mac account. When they register their account, there is a space in which they can enter your .Mac member name. You will receive a $10 discount for each new .Mac member you refer to Apple. And since there is no limit to the number of people you can refer in a year, if you refer 10 people to sign up for a .Mac membership, your renewal fee for the coming year will be waived.

Disabling the Auto Renew Option

If you purchased your .Mac membership online, your membership will be set to automatically renew using the credit card information you used to purchase your membership. For most people, having your .Mac account renew automatically is a great convenience; it's one less thing you have to worry about. However, if you prefer to have control over renewing your .Mac membership, you can disable the auto-renew feature, as follows:

1. Go to the Mac.com web site and log in with your .Mac member name and password.

2. In the navigation bar, click on the button that contains your .Mac member name.

3. From the Account Settings page, click on the Billing & Subscription button near the upper right.

4. In the Membership Information section of the Billing & Subscription Settings page, deselect the checkbox beneath Auto Renew.

5. Click on the Update button to save your changes.

Now when it comes time for your .Mac membership to be renewed, you will be notified via email. This notice should arrive in your email box approximately 90 days before your .Mac membership is due to expire.

CHAPTER 2

Inside Mac.com

The Mac.com web site (*http://www.mac.com*) is every .Mac subscriber's home. It's through this site that you can:

- Log in/out of your .Mac account
- Manage and renew your .Mac membership
- Get help through the online Learning Center
- Download the Backup and Virex software packages and other Member's Only specials, such as games and bonus software
- Purchase additional email-only accounts or more space for your iDisk

This short chapter provides you with a quick overview of what you'll find at Apple's hub for .Mac members: the Mac.com web site.

Navigating Mac.com

When you first get to the Mac.com web site (Figure 2-1), you'll see lots of icons and buttons that you can click on. This section provides a quick overview of the buttons and where they'll lead you.

Along the top of the page, as part of the .Mac tab, you will see a navigation bar that contains a set of "buttons," shown in Figure 2-2. These buttons, described as follows, will always be available to you, no matter what page of the Mac.com site you're on. When you click on one of the buttons in the .Mac navigation bar, it will take on a slightly darker gray shading than the other buttons as a way of letting you know where you are.

Home
> Clicking on the Home button (the icon that looks like a house) takes you back to the main Mac.com page (*http://www.mac.com*).

Figure 2-1. The Mac.com web site after you've logged in.

Figure 2-2. Main .Mac site navigation buttons.

Mail

Clicking on this button takes you to .Mac's web-based Mail service (which can also be accessed by going to *http://www.mac.com/webmail*). If you haven't logged in to your .Mac account yet, you will be taken to a page where you can enter your .Mac member name and password before you're taken to the Mail page.

Address Book

If you've used iSync to synchronize your Address Book contacts with your .Mac account, clicking on this button will take you to your online Address Book. You can use the online Address Book to add, remove, and manage your contacts over the Web. For information on how to synchronize your Mac's Address Book with your .Mac account, see Chapters 4 and 9.

Bookmarks

If you've used iSync to synchronize Safari's bookmarks with your .Mac account, clicking on this button opens another browser window from which you can use and manage your bookmarks. For information on how to synchronize and use the web-based Bookmarks window, see Chapter 9.

HomePage

Clicking on this button takes you to the .Mac HomePage building tools (also accessible by pointing your web browser to *http://www.mac.com/homepage*). From here, you can build and manage your .Mac HomePage; see Chapter 7.

iCards

Clicking on this button takes you to the iCards site (*http://www.mac.com/icards*). iCards are a great way for you to keep in touch with friends and family by sending an electronic postcard from the edge. There's an iCard for every occasion, and you can even use your own digital images as iCards to add a personal touch. For more information on using iCards, see Chapter 10.

Help

Clicking on this button takes you to .Mac's Help page. For more information on what you can find at the .Mac Support page, see the section "The .Mac Services Sidebar," later in this chapter.

Log In

When you click on this button, you will be taken to the page shown in Figure 2-3, so you can login to your .Mac account. Just enter your .Mac member name and password, and then click on the Enter button to sign on.

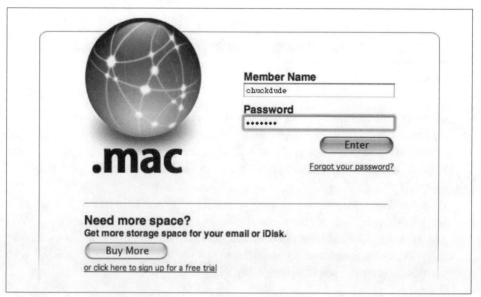

Figure 2-3. The .Mac login screen.

If you've logged on successfully, your .Mac member name appears as a button at the far-right edge of the .Mac navigation bar, as shown in Figure 2-4. Immediately to the left of your account button is a new button, named Log Out. To log out of your .Mac account, simply click on this button.

Figure 2-4. After logging in, your .Mac member name appears as a button on the right edge of the navigation bar.

Managing Your .Mac Account

After logging in successfully, a clickable "account" button appears that bears your .Mac member name. When you click on the account button (shown in Figure 2-4), you can access information about your .Mac account through the Account Settings page, shown in Figure 2-5. The Account Settings page includes details about the current status of your .Mac account, as well as information about the number of Mac.com email addresses you have and how much iDisk space is assigned to your account.

Figure 2-5. The Account Settings page for your .Mac account can be used to update your personal information, change your password, and to manage your accounts.

In looking at Figure 2-5, you can see that there are five buttons on this page that you can click on to take you to other pages that contain information about your account; these include the pages discussed next.

Personal Info

This page contains your name, primary Mac.com email address, and the language used for your account. There's also a checkbox on this page (which is checked by default) for placing you on the .Mac newsletter's email mailing list. If you don't wish to receive this email, uncheck this box and then click on the Submit button after you've made your change.

The .Mac newsletter is sent out weekly to your Mac.com email address. The newsletters are used to inform .Mac members of new member benefits, software updates, software discounts for .Mac members, and important information about changes or additions to the .Mac services.

Credit Card Info

This page contains the credit card information used for your .Mac account, as well as your physical mailing address. If you switch credit cards, or if your current one expires, this is the page you'll need to go to in order to update the information.

Additionally, this page contains the Auto-Renew checkbox, which is checked by default. This means that your .Mac membership (and any extra email addresses or iDisk space) will be renewed automatically when the time comes. If you do not wish for your .Mac account to be renewed automatically, make sure that you uncheck this box.

Your .Mac member name and password are also used as your Apple ID for such things as the iTunes Music Store and the online Apple Store. Any purchases you make through those sources will use the information on the Credit Card Info page to handle your purchases.

Password Settings

This is the page you will need to go to when you want to change your .Mac account's password and/or password hint.

Buy More

This is the page to go to if you want to purchase an additional email account or add storage space for your Mac.com email or to your iDisk. When you add accounts or storage to your .Mac account, you will go through a series of pages to set up the changes before they are actually purchased and assigned to your account.

Manage Accounts

This page, shown in Figure 1-14, is used to manage the email accounts assigned to your .Mac account. You can add and remove email accounts from this page.

Mac.com Navigation Hints

The following is a list of questions and answers to help you get around on the Mac.com web site to perform certain tasks or to find the information you're looking for. The questions here follow on from the form of "How do I...?":

Quickly get back to Mac.com's main page?
Click on the Home button at the top of the page.

View the online help system?
Click on the Help button at the top of the page.

Access the .Mac Learning Center?
Click on the Learning Center icon in the "Inside .Mac" sidebar to the right (see Figure 2-1).

Change the credit card information attached to my .Mac membership?
Account → Credit Card Info

Disable the Auto-Renew feature for my account?
Account → Credit Card Info → uncheck the checkbox next to Auto-Renew

Change my mailing address?
Account → Credit Card Info

Get the list of names for the extra .Mac email addresses you've purchased?
Account → Manage Accounts

Change my language settings?
Account → Personal Info

Delete an extra .Mac email account that you're not using or no longer want?
Account → Manage Accounts → select the email account name → Delete

Change my password hint?
Account → Password Settings

Increase or decrease the amount of storage space for your .Mac email account or for your iDisk?
Account → Buy More

Forget Your Password?

If you're like me, you have many passwords you need to remember, so it can be easy to forget the ones you don't use frequently. If it's been a while since you last logged in to your .Mac account, you can click on the "Forgot your password" link shown in Figure 2-3. This begins a three-step process to getting a new password.

1. Enter your .Mac Member Name and your Birth Date, as shown in Figure 2-6.

2. Answer the password hint question you set up when you created your .Mac membership; you will see a screen similar to the one shown in Figure 2-7.

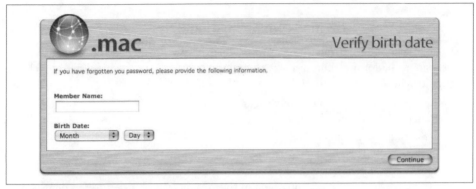

Figure 2-6. Step 1 to getting your password back: verify your birth date.

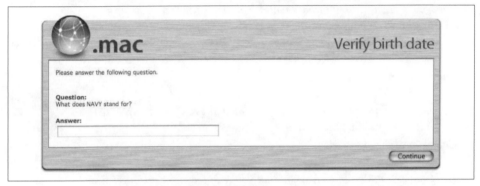

Figure 2-7. Answer the question for your password hint.

3. Instead of taking you to a page that displays the password to your .Mac account, you will be asked to assign a new password to your account, as shown in Figure 2-8.

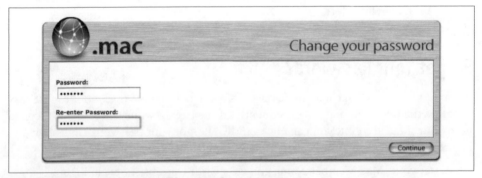

Figure 2-8. Enter a new password for your .Mac account.

Click on the Continue button after entering the new password (in both fields) to assign the password to your .Mac account. You will be taken back to the .Mac Log

In page, shown in Figure 2-3. Now use your Member Name and the new password you've created to log in (and write that new password down somewhere so you remember it).

Another option for getting your .Mac account's password, without having to change it to something else, is to find the password in Keychain Access (*/Applications/ Utilities*). To get the password for your .Mac account, follow these steps:

1. Launch Keychain Access.
2. In the Kind column, look for an item labeled ".Mac password"; click on it.

 Rather than scrolling through the list of items in your keychain, click on the Kind column heading. This sorts the keychains by the name in the Kind column, causing the ".Mac password" item to bubble up to the top of the list.

3. Beneath the listing of keys, you will see two tabbed panes.
4. In the Attributes pane, you will see an empty text field beneath the label "Show password," which has an empty checkbox next to it.
5. Click on the checkbox next to "Show password"; the password for your .Mac account will appear in the text field below.
6. Click on the Copy Password to Clipboard button. This copies the password for your .Mac account into the clipboard (the equivalent of selecting the password and hitting ⌘-C).
7. Deselect the checkbox next to "Show password"; the text field will go blank, hiding your password once again.
8. Quit Keychain Access (⌘-Q).
9. Go back to your web browser and paste (⌘-V) your .Mac account's password in the appropriate field to log in.

It just goes to show that there's more than one way to skin a cat. (Not that I'd recommend doing that, but I think you get my point.)

The .Mac Services Sidebar

After you log on to the .Mac site, you will see a sidebar that contains icons for the services and applications available to every .Mac member. This sidebar, shown in Figure 2-9, is very similar to the Finder's Sidebar in that clicking on any of these icons takes you to a page that contains additional information about the application or service, or it takes you to a login page, where you'll be challenged for your .Mac member name and password.

The icons you'll find in the .Mac Services Sidebar include those discussed in the following list.

Auto-Fill Your .Mac Password

If you are using Safari as your web browser, you can enable it to automatically fill in the .Mac member name and password fields so you don't have to lift a finger. To do this, follow these steps:

1. Launch Safari.
2. Select Safari → Preferences (⌘-,) from the menu bar
3. In the preference window's toolbar, click on the AutoFill icon
4. Place a checkmark in the checkbox next to the second item, "User names and passwords" by clicking on the checkbox (if there's already a checkmark there, skip this step)
5. Close Safari's preferences window by either clicking on the red close window button or by using the standard keyboard shortcut, ⌘-W

Now every time you need to enter your .Mac password, Safari automatically places your .Mac member name and password in the appropriate fields; all you'll have to do is click on the Enter button or hit Return to accept the field values.

Mail

> Formerly known as Webmail, clicking on the Mail icon will let you access your Mac.com email account using your default web browser. Mail is described in greater detail in Chapter 4.

Address Book

> This takes you to a page that contains all of the contacts stored in your .Mac account's Address Book. If you have iSync installed on your system, you can sync your Mac's Address Book with your .Mac account. This means that the information stored in your computer's Address Book will be available for use online, and you can sync its data back and forth. Use of the Address Book will be discussed further in Chapter 4.

Bookmarks

> If you use iSync to synchronize Safari's bookmarks with your iDisk, clicking on this link takes you to a page that gives you access to your bookmarks online. This means that wherever you are, your bookmarks are always available to you if you have an Internet connection. For more information about Bookmark syncing, see Chapter 9.

iCards

> Clicking this icon takes you to the iCards page, from which you can send electronic postcards to your friends using a variety of images provided by Apple, or images you store in your iDisk's *Pictures* folder. iCards are discussed further in Chapter 10.

HomePage

> Clicking this icon takes you to the HomePage building page, described further in Chapter 7.

Figure 2-9. .Mac's services and applications sidebar.

iDisk

    This page provides you with general information about iDisks, and nothing pertaining to your actual iDisk. This is more of a Help page for iDisk users, which contains information about what information to store (and where) on your iDisk, how to open and share your iDisk, and information for using the iDisk Utility, which can be downloaded from Apple, at *http://www.mac.com/1/ idiskutility_download.html*. For more information about iDisks, see Chapter 3.

iSync

    This link takes you to a page where you can learn more about how to use iSync with your .Mac account. There's also a link on this page for downloading iSync; however, if you are running Panther on your Mac, iSync should have been installed by default and can be found in the *Applications* folder. For more information on how to use iSync, see Chapter 9.

iCal

Like the iSync link, when you click on the iCal link, you are taken to a page where you can learn more about how iCal can be used with your .Mac Home-Page. iCal is installed by default on Panther and can be found in the *Applications* folder.

Backup

This page provides you with basic information about the Backup application available to every .Mac member. If you didn't purchase the boxed set for a .Mac membership, which includes a CD containing the Backup application, you can come to this page to download your copy of Backup. Use of the Backup application will be covered in Chapter 6.

Virex

This link takes you to Mac.com's Virex page, where you can find out more information about Virex, as well as download the software and anti-virus updates. A complete overview and guide to using Virex can be found in Chapter 5.

Support

This page, shown in Figure 2-10, gives you easy access to .Mac's support network. From this main page, you can access separate pages for each of the .Mac services (Mail, iDisk, Backup, etc.).

Each of the service Support pages contain a Frequently Asked Questions (FAQ) section so you can quickly find an answer or solution to a problem you might have. If you can't find the answer to your question in the FAQ, you can jump into the .Mac Discussion Boards or click on the .Mac Feedback link to send an email to the .Mac team at Apple.

The main Support page also displays information about .Mac's System and Network Status, and provides you with access to the following:

Search the AppleCare Knowledge Base

The search field at the top of the Support pages let you search through the AppleCare Knowledge Base (if you're hip, just refer to it as the "KB") for .Mac-related articles. The KB is a vast repository of technical documents you can search through to find answers to tough questions you might have.

.Mac Discussion Boards

The Discussion Boards are a place where you can share information with and ask questions from other .Mac members. If you're having a problem trying to figure something out, this is a good place to go for more information.

.Mac Feedback

This page provides you with a way to send feedback to .Mac's engineering team at Apple.

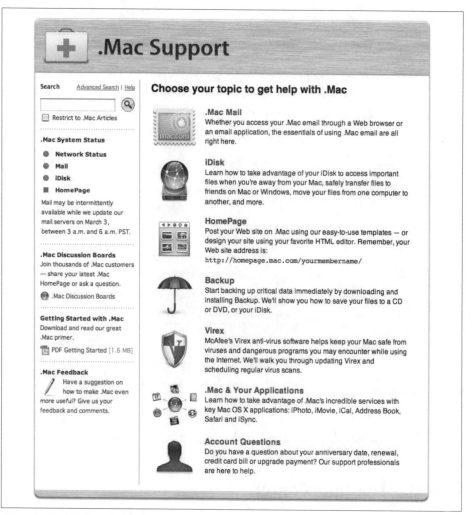

Figure 2-10. .Mac's main Support page.

If you click on one of the topic links, you'll be taken to support page that contains detailed information about that particular service or application. For example, the Mail support page (shown in Figure 2-11) includes lots of useful tips for using and troubleshooting Mail. At the bottom of the support pages, you'll also see a "Still having trouble?" section; use the links found here to join the .Mac Discussion Boards or to send email directly to the .Mac support team to receive prompt answers to your questions.

Account

When you click on this button in the Sidebar, you'll be taken to the Account Settings page, shown earlier in Figure 2-5, which you can use to manage your .Mac account (described earlier in "Managing Your .Mac Account").

Figure 2-11. .Mac Mail's Support page.

The .Mac Learning Center

One of the most recent additions to the .Mac services is the Learning Center, which you can access by clicking on the Learning Center icon in the Inside .Mac Sidebar, located on the right side of the Mac.com web site after you've logged in (see Figure 2-1). The Learning Center offers training and tutorials for learning more about the .Mac services, Mac OS X and the iLife '04 applications (iMovie, iPhoto, iTunes, iDVD, and GarageBand). The Learning Center also offers QuickTime training movies to help you learn your way around your Mac.

The Learning Center, shown in Figure 2-12, gives you access to online tutorials and QuickTime movies to help you learn more about the .Mac services and Mac OS X and its applications.

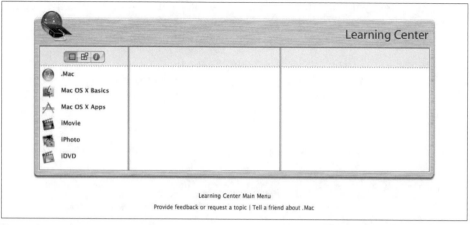

Figure 2-12. The new .Mac Learning Center.

At the top of the first column to the left in Figure 2-12, you'll see three simple buttons. The first button (a square) lists the Learning Center's categories as follows:

- The .Mac services and applications
- Mac OS X Basics
- Mac OS X Applications
- iMovie
- iPhoto
- iDVD

When you go to the Learning Center, the first page that will load in is the Getting Started with .Mac tutorial. This tutorial gives you a quick overview of the .Mac services and applications and is a great aid for new .Mac members who want to quickly see what's available.

The second button, which looks like four smaller squares with the upper-right one slightly askew, lists the Learning Center's contents by the following topics:

- New Mac User
- The Internet
- Digital Photography
- Movies and DVDs
- Getting Organized
- Security

These Learning Center modules provide you with useful tips on such things as how to manage your .Mac Mail or use your digital camera.

The third button, with the little "i" in it, is the Information button. When you click on this, you'll get access to all of the Learning Center's training modules, listed in alphabetical order.

To use the Learning Center, select a category in the first column, and then one of the learning modules in the middle column. When you select one of the learning modules, you'll see a brief introduction to the module in the right column; just click on the Start Learning button in this column to go on to the tutorial, as shown in Figure 2-13.

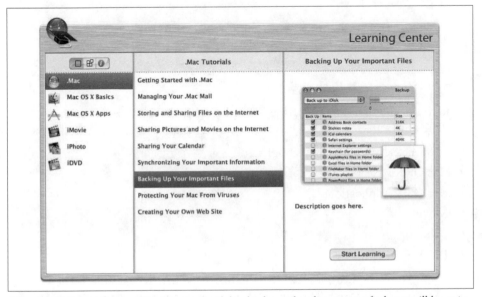

Figure 2-13. Selecting one of the learning modules displays a brief overview of what you'll learn in the right column.

Once in a learning module, you can use the pop-up menu in the upper-left corner (see Figure 2-14) to see and quickly go to the topics of the module, or use the Previous and Next buttons to the right to go back and forward through the module, respectively.

At the bottom of the learning module's window, you'll see two more buttons: Play the Movie and Learn More. If you click on the Play the Movie button, a new window opens, which plays a QuickTime movie of the full learning module. Clicking on the Learn More button expands the module's display to give you some additional tips for the topic page you're viewing, as shown in Figure 2-15.

The Learning Center is a great addition to the .Mac services, especially for new Mac users who need to get up to speed on their Mac and everything they can do with it. The Learning Center modules provide a wealth of information, even if you're a seasoned MacHead.

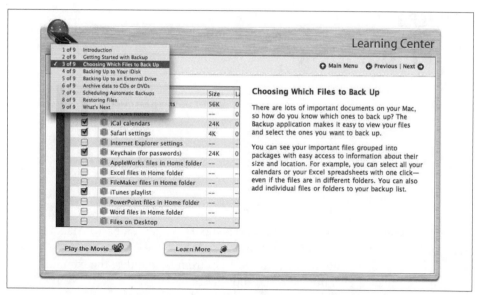

Figure 2-14. *Navigating your way through the learning modules is a snap.*

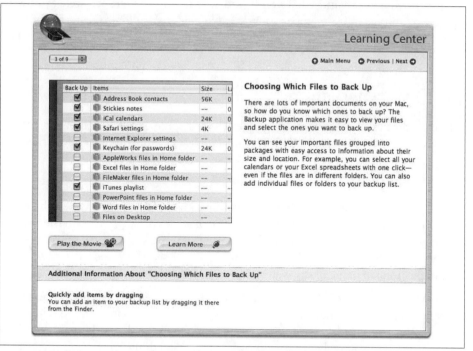

Figure 2-15. *Clicking on the Learn More button reveals some great tips.*

CHAPTER 3

Using Your iDisk

The cornerstone of your .Mac membership is the iDisk. With a basic .Mac membership, the iDisk provides you with 100 MB of storage space on one of Apple's .Mac servers, which you can mount on your Desktop from the Finder, the command line using the Terminal application, and via AppleScript.

This chapter provides an in-depth view of your iDisk, including details on how to connect to your iDisk and what you'll find when you get there, as well as how to connect to another .Mac member's iDisk *Public* folder. You'll also learn about what allows your Mac to connect to an iDisk: a wonderful piece of technology, called WebDAV.

The iDisk's Filesystem

Before we dive in and start mounting your iDisk or some other .Mac member's iDisk *Public* folder, let's take a quick look at what an iDisk is, and what you'll find there.

What Is an iDisk?

The technology behind your iDisk is something known as WebDAV, which stands for *Web-based Distributed Authoring and Versioning*. WebDAV is an extension to the HTTP protocol, which we all know is the protocol that's used over the Web. Any time you type in a URL into a web browser, you'll see the standard *http://* prefix behind the domain name of the web site you want to browse.

WebDAV uses HTTP to allow you to access folders on a web server. Since these folders reside on a server, they are often referred to as a *share*, since the folder shares space on the server with other folders. Without going into a long, drawn-out technical discussion, all you really need to know are these two things:

- Your iDisk is nothing more than a folder that lives on Apple's server (located at *idisk.mac.com*)
- Your .Mac member name is the name of your WebDAV folder on that server

When you put the two together, you end up with a URL that looks something like this:

```
http://idisk.mac.com/membername
```

But don't try entering that URL into a web browser, because you'll get an error. Instead, the easiest way to mount your iDisk is with the Finder or the iDisk Utility, which we'll cover later in this chapter.

What's on the iDisk?

So now that we know that an iDisk is a folder that lives on a web server, let's take a look at what's on your iDisk. To start out, every iDisk has a default set of folders, as shown in Figure 3-1.

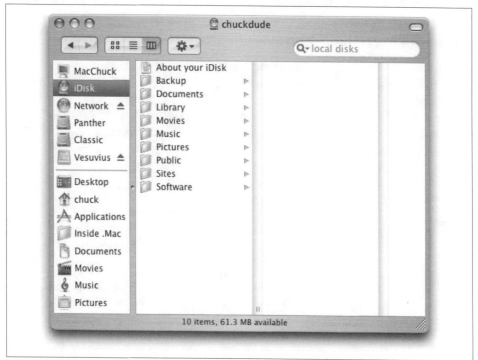

Figure 3-1. Your iDisk, as viewed from the Finder.

But in reality, there's a lot more going on behind the scenes with your iDisk. For example, if your iDisk is mounted, open up the Terminal (*/Applications/Utilities*) and issue the following command:

```
$ ls -lapR /Volumes/dotMacMemberName
```

You'll see a long stream of files and folder names go by, since this command lists everything on your iDisk. To save you the pain of watching the contents of your iDisk flash before your eyes, I've watered this down a bit to show you the basic filesystem structure of your iDisk in Figure 3-2.

As you start to use other utilities, such as Backup and iSync, directories to support their services are added; for example:

- In the case of Backup, a *Backup* directory is added
- iSync adds a *Library* directory to your iDisk, which contains the calendar data from iCal, the contacts in your Address Book, and your bookmark information from Safari
- If you've published any Photo Albums from iPhoto to your iDisk, they appear in */Pictures/Photo Album Pictures*
- If you've created a .Mac Slide Show (more commonly known as a screensaver), the images and data for the Slide Show are saved in */Pictures/Slide Shows/Public*

A Place for Everything, and Everything in Its Place

Each folder on your iDisk has a specific purpose. For example, you'll notice folders with similar names to those that appear in your *Home* directory, such as *Documents*, *Library*, *Movies*, *Music*, *Pictures*, *Public*, and *Sites*. While it might seem odd to have a *Documents* folder on your iDisk, the reason is somewhat opaque, yet clear. Apple chose to use the same name for folders in your *Home* folder with those on your iDisk so you would know where to place files.

> You cannot change the names for the default set of folders on your iDisk. The reason is because the .Mac services and some of the iApps (such as iPhoto, iMovie, and iSync) are programmed to store information in specifically named folders on your iDisk. If you try to change the name of a folder, an alert window pops up telling you that you don't have sufficient permissions to do so.
>
> Your iDisk, and the default set of folders within, is nothing more than a folder on Apple's server that gets shared to you via WebDAV. Since Apple is serving the iDisk folders, only Apple can change the name of any of the default folders.
>
> You can, however, change the names of any folders you add to your iDisk, or place within any of the default folders.

Now let's take a quick run through the folders on your iDisk to see what's there and what their intended purpose is:

Backup
  This folder is created by the Backup application (see Chapter 6) when you back up data to your iDisk. The data you back up gets stored in two places: */Backup/ Catalog* and */Backup/membername/Library*. This folder is used exclusively by the Backup application; nothing else—not even you—can save files to the *Backup* folder.

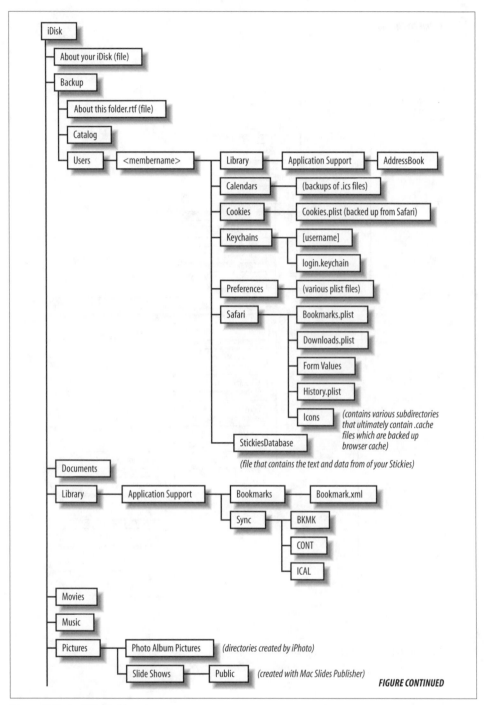

Figure 3-2. An iDisk's filesystem.

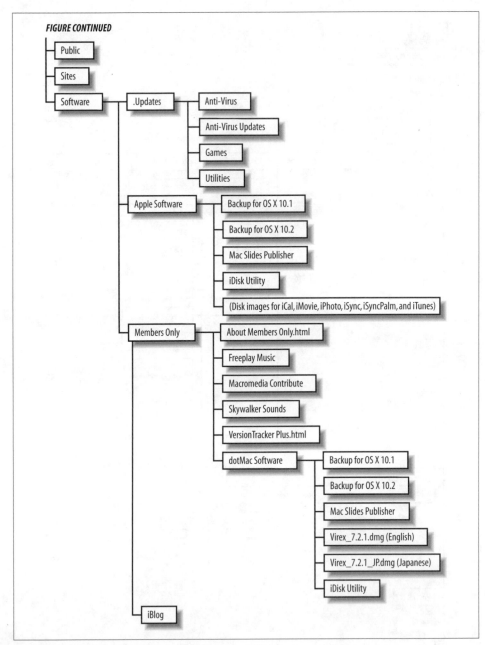

FIGURE CONTINUED

- Public
- Sites
- Software
  - .Updates
    - Anti-Virus
    - Anti-Virus Updates
    - Games
    - Utilities
  - Apple Software
    - Backup for OS X 10.1
    - Backup for OS X 10.2
    - Mac Slides Publisher
    - iDisk Utility
    - (Disk images for iCal, iMovie, iPhoto, iSync, iSyncPalm, and iTunes)
  - Members Only
    - About Members Only.html
    - Freeplay Music
    - Macromedia Contribute
    - Skywalker Sounds
    - VersionTracker Plus.html
    - dotMac Software
      - Backup for OS X 10.1
      - Backup for OS X 10.2
      - Mac Slides Publisher
      - Virex_7.2.1.dmg (English)
      - Virex_7.2.1_JP.dmg (Japanese)
      - iDisk Utility
- iBlog

Figure 3-2. An iDisk's filesystem. (continued)

Documents

This directory can be used to store miscellaneous files.

Library

This folder is created by iSync (see Chapter 9) if you've synchronized data from your Mac to your iDisk. This directory houses data from your Address Book, iCal, and Safari's bookmarks.

Movies

This is a place were you can store movie files (QuickTime or otherwise). If you plan to show off your iMovies on your .Mac HomePage (see Chapter 7), you will need to place the QuickTime movie files in this folder. If you've installed iLife '04 on your Mac, iMovie 4 has a new Share feature that you can use to upload movies to your iDisk and then create a web page so others can view your iMovie over the Web. For more information on how this feature of iMovie 4 works, see Chapter 7.

Music

This is a place where you can store music and sound files.

Pictures

As its name implies, this folder should be used to store image files. These images can be used as part of your .Mac HomePage (see Chapter 7), or for use in creating personalized iCards. iPhoto also uses this folder to store the images for any Photo Album pages you create for your .Mac HomePage. Additionally, if you create a Public Slide Show (or screensaver) with iPhoto or the Mac Slides Publisher, the slide show's images are saved here as well.

Public

Unless someone knows your .Mac password, this will be the only directory from your iDisk that can be mounted on another computer. Depending on how you've set the *Public* folder's preferences (System Preferences → .Mac → iDisk), your *Public* folder may be read-only (the default) or read-write. You can also password-protect your *Public* folder, which adds another level of security to the files within. See the later section "Configuring Your iDisk's Public Folder" for more information on setting a password for your *Public* folder.

 If you change the privileges on your iDisk's *Public* folder to read-write, you should password-protect the folder. The reason for this is that anyone who mounts your *Public* folder can just start dumping files there for their own use, quickly taking up precious iDisk space.

Sites

This is where the files for your .Mac HomePage will be served. If you haven't built a HomePage yet, this directory will be empty. You can drag and drop files into your iDisk's *Sites* folder to make them available for download over the Web. For example, if you save a file named *myphotos.zip* in the *Sites* folder, you could send the following link to your friends via email so they can download the Zip archive to their computer:

http://homepage.mac.com/membername/myphotos.zip

In this link, replace *membername* with your .Mac member name.

Software

The *Software* folder is something that's available to all .Mac members. Apple provides this space "free of charge," meaning, its contents don't count against your allotted 100 MB of iDisk storage space. As such, this isn't a place where you can store files, and any attempt to do so will result in a warning message popping up telling you that you don't have sufficient privileges to copy files there.

The *Software* directory has three main subdirectories:

.Updates

Because this folder's name starts with a period, the *.Updates* folder is hidden from view in the Finder. To view the contents of this folder, you will need to use the Terminal application, and change directories to */Volumes/ iDiskName/.Updates*. This folder contains virus updates for Virex (see Chapter 5) and other .Mac utilities.

Apple Software

This directory contains Apple-created software for your Mac OS X system. Here you'll find such things as updates for AppleWorks, disk images for Backup, iCal, iSync, iSyncPalm (for use with Palm devices), iTunes, iDisk Utility, and Mac Slides Publisher.

 The software you find in this directory is packaged as disk images (*.dmg* files). To install something, you can either drag the disk image to your Desktop to install it from there, or you can double-click on the disk image on the iDisk and mount it that way.

Members Only

This folder contains software and audio tracks that are only available to full .Mac members (i.e., non-Trial members). Here you'll find exclusive software demos, updates for .Mac applications, and more. Here's just a sample of what you'll find:

- Look inside the dotMac Software folder for updates to applications like Backup, Virex, iDisk Utility, and Mac Slides Publisher.

- Exclusive sound effects from Skywalker Sound, which you can use in your iMovie projects.

- The Freeplay Music folder contains hundreds of AAC-encoded music files that you can use as background tracks for your iMovies, or DVDs you create with iDVD. The Freeplay Music clips are provided as a member benefit and can be used for noncommercial purposes (i.e., for personal use). Each clip is available in six different durations, ranging from 10-, 15-, 20-, 30-, and 60-second sound bites, as well as a full-length clip, most of which are around two minutes in length.

 If you were to purchase the Freeplay Music tracks from another source, you could end up paying more than what you paid for your annual .Mac membership. If you're creating iMovies, the audio clips available in the Freeplay Music directory are invaluable.

- Themes for use with Apple's Keynote application (*http://www.apple.com/keynote*).
- Demos of software available only to .Mac members, including games and other utilities
- This folder contains software and audio tracks that are only available to .Mac subscribers who have a full membership (i.e., non-Trial memberships). Here you'll find demos of software available only to .Mac members, as well as loads of free audio clips in the Freeplay Music folder.

Now that you know what's available on your iDisk, let's mount that thing and get working with it.

Trial .Mac Members: Your iDisk Will Vary

If you signed up for a free, 60-day trial .Mac membership, your iDisk will only have one-fifth of the storage of a basic .Mac membership (in other words, only 20 MB of storage space).

When you look in the *Software* folder of your iDisk, you won't see folders that contain disk images for the Backup application. However, you can still download Backup from the Mac.com site. When using Backup, you can only backup data to your iDisk, not to CDs, DVDs, or external disks. For that privilege, you'll need a full .Mac membership. In order to use Backup, you need a .Mac membership of some kind, Trial or full. When Backup launches, it probes the .Mac preferences (System Preferences → .Mac) to look for a .Mac member name and password. If it doesn't find one, you can't use Backup.

You also won't have access to any of the Freeplay Music audio files or other software in the *Members Only* folder.

Membership has its privileges.

Mounting the iDisk

In order to use your iDisk, you must first be connected to the Internet, either via PPP or an Ethernet connection. If you're not connected to the Internet, you won't be able to mount the iDisk on your Mac. The reason why you need to be connected to the Net is because all iDisks use a protocol known as WebDAV for mounting shares hosted at Apple (actually, hosted off of the main IP address of 17.250.248.77).

If you have a Finder window open, the quickest way to mount your iDisk is by simply clicking on the iDisk icon, located in the upper section of the Finder window's Sidebar. When you click on the iDisk icon, the Finder collects your .Mac member name and password that you've set in the .Mac preferences panel (System Preferences → .Mac → .Mac) and sends that information off to Apple's server. If the .Mac member name and password matches the information stored on Apple's side, your iDisk mounts on your Desktop and the contents of your iDisk become viewable in the Finder window, as shown in Figure 3-3.

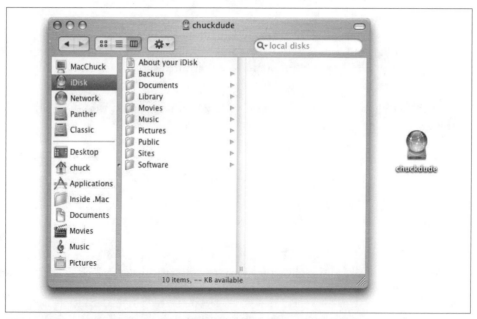

Figure 3-3. An iDisk's Finder window is displayed in Icon View when mounted.

 If your Finder is set to show connected servers on the Desktop (Finder → Preferences → Show these items on the Desktop), the iDisk icon shown at the right of Figure 3-3 appears on your Desktop.

Another way to mount your iDisk is from the Finder's Go menu, as shown in Figure 3-4. If you select Go → iDisk, a submenu appears to the right of the Go menu, giving you options for connecting to your iDisk, to another .Mac member's iDisk, or to another .Mac member's *Public* folder. (iDisk *Public* folders and how they're used is discussed later in this chapter.)

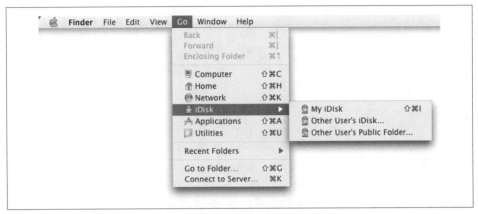

Figure 3-4. The Finder's Go window can also be used for mounting iDisks.

If you try to connect to your iDisk and haven't entered your .Mac Member Name and Password in the .Mac preference panel, or if you select Go → iDisk → Other User's iDisk from the menu bar, the window shown in Figure 3-5 appears.

Figure 3-5. The Connect To iDisk window.

To connect to the iDisk, enter the .Mac Member name and Password and click on the Connect button. Again, the information you enter in these fields will be validated against Apple's servers. If what you enter passes muster, the iDisk mounts on the Desktop and in the Finder.

The Connect To iDisk window (shown in Figure 3-4) appears any time you try connecting to an iDisk from a Mac that doesn't have the .Mac Member Name and Password set in the .Mac preference panel. This can be useful for connecting to your iDisk from another person's Mac who doesn't have a .Mac account. (Of course, you could give someone your Member Name and Password so they could connect and use your iDisk as well, but that would be cheating, right?)

Mounting Your iDisk at Login

If you have a broadband connection to the Internet (either via cable, DSL, or T1 access at work) you can mount your iDisk automatically when you log on to your Mac. Getting your iDisk to mount automatically whenever you log on to your Mac is actually pretty simple; just follow these steps:

1. If your iDisk isn't currently mounted on your Mac, you can mount it quickly from the Finder by using the keyboard shortcut, Shift-⌘-I.

2. Once the iDisk appears on your Desktop, launch the System Preferences application by clicking on its icon in the Dock.

3. Click on the icon for the Accounts panel in the System section.

4. On the left side of the Accounts panel, you'll see a list of all of the user accounts on your Mac. Click on the one that says My Account in gray text above your username.

5. On the right side of the Accounts panel, click on the Startup Items tab. This switches the window's view to show you the applications that will start up automatically when you log on to your account.

6. Click on the titlebar of the System Preferences window and move it to the side so you can see the iDisk icon on your Desktop, as shown in Figure 3-6. Once you've moved the window, let go of the mouse button.

7. Now click on the iDisk icon and drag it into the Startup Items pane. When you see the ghostly image of your iDisk, as shown in Figure 3-7, let go of the mouse button to add the iDisk to your list of Startup Items.

8. Quit the System Preferences application by either clicking on the red close window button, or using either the ⌘-W or ⌘-Q keyboard shortcuts.

To test this out, log out of your account by holding down the Option key and selecting the Log Out option from the bottom of the Apple menu (⌘ → Log Out *Your Account Name*). When you log back in, the Startup Items you've placed in your Account are loaded, which means that your iDisk should mount if you have an Internet connection.

Figure 3-6. A view of the Startup Items pane in the Accounts preference panel with my iDisk waiting in the wings.

iDisk Public Folders

One of the great things about having an iDisk is its *Public* folder. The *Public* folder is a place where you can store files that you want to share with other people or that other people want to share with you.

This section shows you how to configure the settings for your *Public* folder, and also how to connect to other .Mac members' *Public* folders. You'll also learn a bit more about how to tell whether someone has added password-protection to their *Public* folder.

Configuring Your iDisk's Public Folder

As mentioned earlier, all iDisk *Public* folders can have their permissions set to one of two options:

Read-Only
> If you select this option, other users can mount your iDisk's *Public* folder on their computer and view and download its contents; they cannot place files in the *Public* folder. The Read-Only option is selected by default.

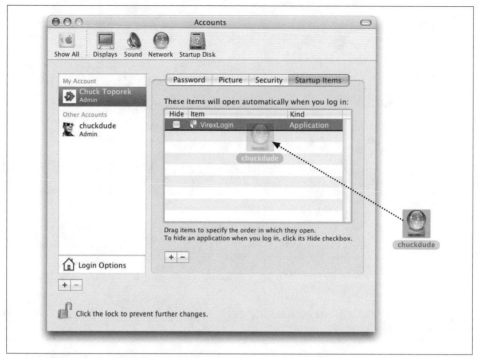

Figure 3-7. Drag and drop your iDisk into the Startup Items pane.

Read-Write

> Selecting this option allows others to mount your iDisk's *Public* folder, view and download its contents, as well as upload (or place) files on your iDisk.

If you want to change your *Public* folder's permissions to read-write so other people can save files there, go to System Preferences → .Mac → iDisk and click on the radio button next to Read & Write in the Your Public Folder section, as shown in Figure 3-8.

You can also assign a password to control access to your *Public* folder by clicking on the Set Password button near the bottom of this window. When you do, a sheet slides out at the top of the window, in which you can assign a password (as shown in Figure 3-9). The password you choose must be between 6–8 alphanumeric characters.

 You cannot use your .Mac member name as the password for your iDisk's *Public* folder. For example, I cannot use *chuckdude* as the password for my *Public* folder because that's my .Mac member name.

Also, you shouldn't use the same password for your *Public* folder as what you're using for your .Mac account; if you do, anyone who knows your *Public* folder's password will be able to access your .Mac email and any vital information (such as your credit card number and expiration date) stored in your Account information section.

Figure 3-8. To allow others to upload files to your iDisk's Public folder, simply click on the radio button next to Read & Write.

If you plan to enable Read & Write access privileges, you should assign a password to protect your *Public* folder. If you don't password-protect your *Public* folder, any malcontent could come along and drop files into it, quickly taking up precious space on your iDisk. The first rule of thumb should be: protect yourself.

You can also enable password-protection for your iDisk's *Public* folder if it's "Read only". While that may seem a little extreme, since nobody will be able to write files there, it does protect prying eyes from viewing and downloading your *Public* folder's contents unless they have the proper password.

Connecting to Public Folders

Depending on your situation, there may come a time when you'll want or need to connect to another .Mac member's *Public* folder. This section shows you the various ways you can make the same connection from Mac OS X, including:

- From the Address Book
- From the Go menu
- Using the iDisk Utility

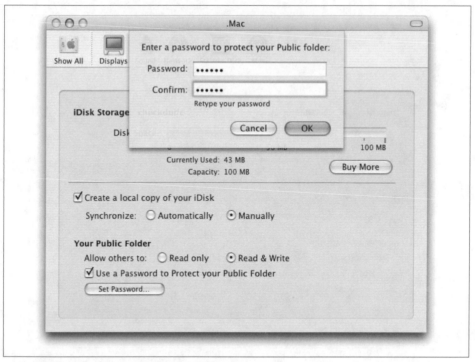

Figure 3-9. Assigning a password to your iDisk's Public folder.

Since the iDisk Utility is covered later in the chapter, we'll just cover the first two ways in the subsections that follow.

 If you are using Mac OS 9, you will need to use an application called Goliath to access your iDisk. For information on where to get and how to use Goliath, see the section "Mounting an iDisk on a Mac OS 9 System," later in this chapter.

From the Address Book

To connect to another .Mac member's iDisk from the Address Book, follow these steps:

1. Select the .Mac member's record in your Address Book.
2. Click on their Mac.com email address and select Open iDisk from the menu that appears (as shown in Figure 3-10).

After selecting the Open iDisk option, the .Mac member's *Public* folder will mount on your Desktop and a Finder window will open, revealing its contents.

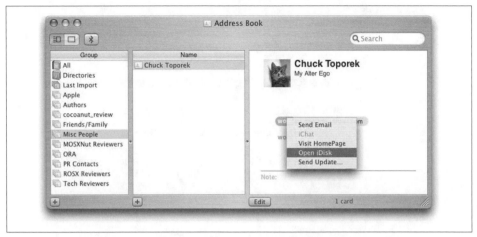

Figure 3-10. Connecting to another .Mac member's iDisk from their Address Book record.

From the Go menu

There are two ways you can connect to another .Mac member's *Public* folder from the Go menu:

- From Go → iDisk → Other User's Public Folder
- From Go → Connect to Server

When you select Go → iDisk → Other User's Public Folder from the menu bar, the window shown in Figure 3-11 appears.

Figure 3-11. Connecting to a .Mac member's Public folder from the Go menu.

Simply type in the .Mac member name for the person whose *Public* folder you need access to, and then click on the Connect button. If the *Public* folder isn't password-protected, it will mount on your Desktop, and a Finder window will pop open revealing its contents. However, if the *Public* folder is password-protected, you will be challenged for a password, as shown in Figure 3-12.

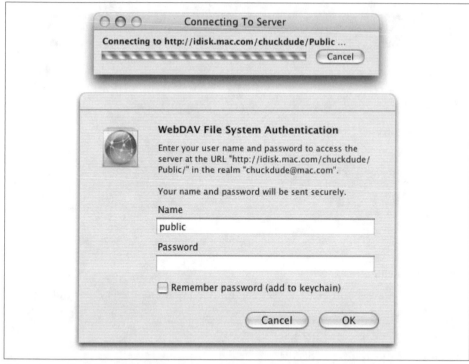

Figure 3-12. If a Public folder is password-protected, you'll be challenged for a password.

If you will be connecting to this user's *Public* folder regularly, you should click on the checkbox next to "Remember password (add to keychain)" so the next time you need to connect, the iDisk *Public* folder will automatically mount on your system without challenging you for a password.

Using the Go menu is the easiest way to mount another user's iDisk or iDisk Public folder, but it's not the only way. You can also select Connect to Server (⌘-K) from the Go menu. In the Connect to Server window (shown in Figure 3-13), enter the URL for the *Public* folder you need access to in the form of:

   http://idisk.mac.com/membername-Public

If the .Mac member's *Public* folder is password-protected, the window shown in Figure 3-11 will pop up. Enter the proper password to mount the *Public* folder and don't forget to select the checkbox next to "Remember password (add to keychain)" so you'll never have to enter the password again.

Public Folders and Permissions

Once you've mounted a *Public* folder, you'll see them pop up in the Finder and on your Desktop. We all know by now that *Public* folders are read-only by default, but there's an easy way to tell for sure once they're mounted.

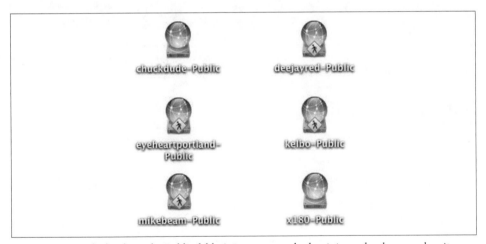

Figure 3-13. Using the Connect to Server window to connect to a .Mac member's Public folder.

The first way is by just looking at the *Public* folder's icon on your Desktop. Most *Public* folders have a yellow sign attached to them, which looks like the pedestrian crosswalk signs here in the States. However, if you look closely at Figure 3-14, you'll see some *Public* folders that are missing the crosswalk sign.

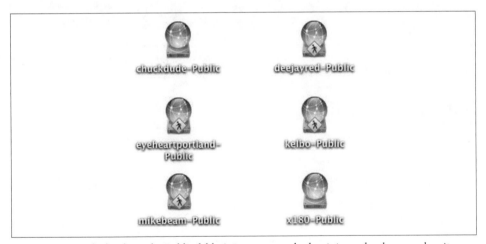

Figure 3-14. Look closely at the Public folder's icon to see whether it is read-only or read-write.

The *Public* folders with the yellow crosswalk symbol attached to them are read-only, and the ones without are read-write. The way to confirm this is to select one of the *Public* folders in the Finder's Sidebar. If you look at the bottom of the Finder window, you'll see a little pencil symbol that's crossed out, as shown in Figure 3-15.

This is yet another queue to let you know that the *Public* folder is read-only.

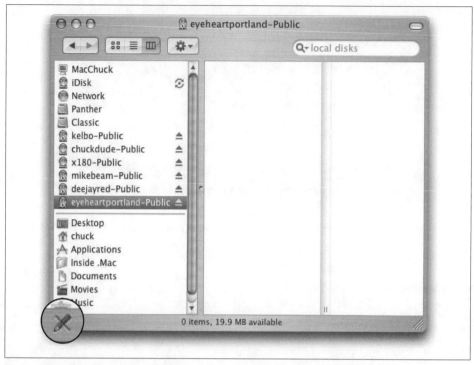

Figure 3-15. If you see a crossed-out pencil at the lower-left corner the Finder window, you cannot save files to this Public folder.

Unmounting an iDisk

Unmounting an iDisk is pretty easy. Once you've had enough of your iDisk, you can:

- Drag the iDisk icon to the Trash.
- Click on the iDisk's icon and hit ⌘-E; this is the same as selecting File → Eject from within the Finder.
- Open a Finder window, hit Shift-⌘-C (for "Computer"), select the iDisk, and hit ⌘-E; again, this ejects the iDisk from your system.

> Unlike other mounted disks, the iDisk does not have an eject icon next to it in the Finder's Sidebar when it is mounted. This is unfortunate, because when you're looking at a Finder window, there really isn't a way to know that your iDisk is mounted unless you physically click on its icon (and even then, if your iDisk isn't mounted, it soon will be if you're connected to the Internet).

Mounting an iDisk on a Mac OS 9 System

Not everyone has access to a Mac OS X system. Lots of people are still waiting for critical software to be carbonized to run on Mac OS X, while others are holding on to their legacy machines because they still function quite nicely. However, as time goes by, legacy Macs running Mac OS 9 are being left in the dust; meanwhile, the .Mac services are moving ahead full-steam.

Fortunately, if you're still clinging on to Mac OS 9, you can use an application called Goliath (*http://www.webdav.org/goliath*) to access iDisks via WebDAV. Goliath can not only be used to access your own iDisk, but to access the *Public* folders on other .Mac members' iDisks as well.

 There is a version of Goliath for Mac OS X, but it hasn't been updated recently for Panther. If you decide to download and use the Mac OS X version on Panther, do so at your own risk.

Using Goliath to Connect to an iDisk

To use Goliath to mount your own iDisk on a Mac OS 9 system, follow these steps:

1. Launch Goliath.
2. Go to File → Open iDisk Connection from the menu bar.
3. Enter your .Mac member name in the User Name field and your password in the Password field, as shown in Figure 3-16.

Figure 3-16. Connecting to your iDisk using Goliath.

4. Click on the OK button to mount your iDisk. When Goliath connects to your iDisk, you won't see a disk icon on your Desktop. Instead, you'll only see a window open up, revealing the contents of your iDisk, as shown in Figure 3-17.

Once connected to your iDisk, you can double-click on folders to open windows, or click on the disclosure triangles to the left of a folder name to reveal its contents. You can drag and drop files and folders into the various iDisk folders as well, just as you could before.

To disconnect from your iDisk, just close the window with ⌘-W.

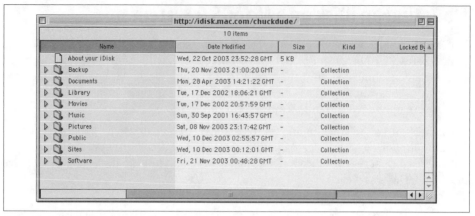

Figure 3-17. Goliath, connected to an iDisk.

Using Goliath to Connect to an iDisk Public Folder

To use Goliath to connect to another .Mac member's *Public* folder, follow these steps:

1. Select File → New Connection (⌘-N) from the menu bar.

2. In the window that appears, enter the following information (also shown in Figure 3-18):

    a. In the URL field, type in the address of for the .Mac member's iDisk that you'd like to connect to, using the form of:

    http://idisk.mac.com/membername-Public

    where *membername* is the .Mac member name; for example, mine would be *http://idisk.mac.com/chuckdude-Public*.

    b. Tab down to the User Name field and type in the word **public** in lowercase letters.

    c. Tab to the Password field. If the .Mac member's iDisk *Public* folder is password-protected, you should enter the password in this field. If the iDisk *Public* folder is not password-protected, leave this field blank.

    d. Click on the OK button to make the connection.

Once Goliath connects, a window pops up showing you the contents of the .Mac member's *Public* folder, as shown in Figure 3-19.

Depending on how the .Mac member has configured their settings, the *Public* folder will either be read-only or read-write. If the *Public* folder is read-only, you can download files from the iDisk by dragging them to your Desktop or to another Finder window, but you cannot upload files to the member's iDisk. If the member's *Public* folder has read-write privileges, you can download and upload files to their iDisk.

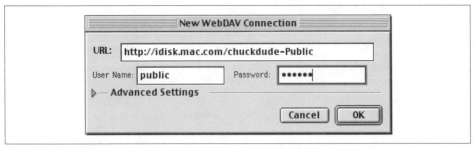

Figure 3-18. Connecting to an iDisk Public folder.

Figure 3-19. The view of my iDisk's Public folder.

By default, all iDisk *Public* folders are read-only; the .Mac member must enable read-write access in the iDisk preference pane (System Preferences → .Mac → iDisk) or with the iDisk Utility.

Unfortunately, there is no way for you to find out whether a *Public* folder is read-only or read-write; you'll have to obtain this information from the .Mac member before you connect.

To unmount an iDisk *Public* folder from Goliath, simply close the window with ⌘-W.

The iDisk Utility

For managing your iDisk or gaining access to another .Mac member's *Public* folder, Apple has provided a small application called the iDisk Utility. The iDisk Utility can be downloaded from your iDisk (*/Software/Apple Software/iDisk Utility* or */Software/ Members Only/dotMac Software/iDisk Utility*) and is also available on the CD that came with the boxed .Mac membership sold in stores.

With Mac OS X Panther, the iDisk Utility really isn't necessary because you can use the Go → iDisk menu to mount iDisks and *Public* folders, and the iDisk preference pane (System Preferences → .Mac → iDisk) actually works for setting and changing the password for your iDisk's *Public* folder.

That said, the iDisk Utility does have some nice features, so rather than spending a lot of time talking about how to use it, we'll just show off what's best about it. If you find yourself using the iDisk Utility frequently, you should consider adding it to your Dock by dragging its icon there from the Finder.

Installing the iDisk Utility

To install the iDisk Utility, follow these steps:

1. Drag the *iDisk_Utility.dmg* file to your Desktop
2. Double-click on the disk image to mount it on your computer
3. Double-click on the *iDisk_Utility.pkg* to start the installation process; just follow along through the installation screens and enter your password when prompted to complete the install

The iDisk Utility will be installed in the *Utilities* folder (*/Applications/Utilities*) on your Mac. After it has successfully installed, unmount the disk image and drag the *iDisk_Utility.dmg* file to the Trash.

Using the iDisk Utility

To launch the iDisk Utility, make your way to the *Utilities* folder in the Finder (or use the keyboard shortcut Shift-⌘-U), and then double-click on the iDisk Utility. As you can see from Figure 3-20, the iDisk Utility has a fairly simple interface.

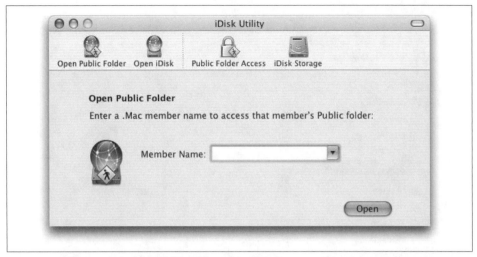

Figure 3-20. The iDisk Utility's Open Public Folder view.

Along the top of the iDisk Utility's window is a toolbar with a series of self-explanatory icons used for gaining access to or managing an iDisk. Each button changes the iDisk Utility's view, similar to how clicking on an icon in the System Preferences application will take you to one of the various panels for configuring your system. The four views of the iDisk Utility are described in the following sections.

Open Public Folder

When you launch iDisk Utility, the application starts at the Open Public Folder view. This view, shown in Figure 3-20, is used when you want to connect to another .Mac member's *Public* folder.

One thing to keep in mind is that, by default, all iDisk *Public* folders are read-only. This means that you can only view its contents and retrieve items stored in another member's *Public* folder. You cannot place items in another member's *Public* folder unless they specifically change its settings to read-write in the iDisk preference pane (System Preferences → .Mac → iDisk) or within the iDisk Utility's Public Folder Access view, described later.

To mount another member's *Public* folder, simply enter their .Mac member name in the text field and click on the Open button. After a short while (depending on the speed of your Internet connection), the member's *Public* folder will mount on your Desktop and appear in the Finder's Sidebar, as shown in Figure 3-21.

One handy feature of the iDisk Utility is that it keeps track of the last five *Public* folders you've mounted, as shown in Figure 3-22. The next time you need to access someone's *Public* folder, all you need to do is click on the pull-down menu, select the name, and then click on the Open button.

Figure 3-21. When mounted, .Mac Public folders appear at the top part of the Finder's Sidebar.

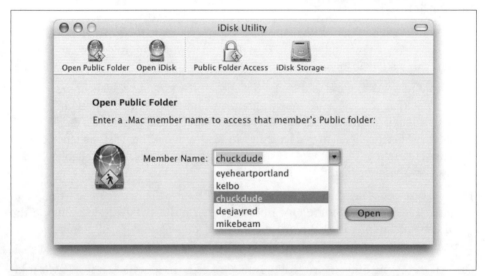

Figure 3-22. The iDisk Utility maintains a listing of recently accessed Public folders for quick access.

If a .Mac member has their *Public* folder password-protected, you will be prompted to enter a password, as shown in Figure 3-23. If the password you enter is incorrect, you will be prompted to retry the password again until you get it right. (There is no cut-off on the number of times you can try entering a password to gain access to a password-protected *Public* folder.)

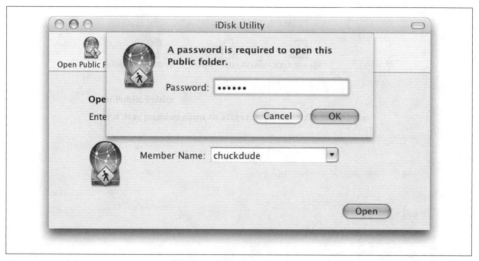

Figure 3-23. If you run across a Public folder that's password-protected, the iDisk Utility prompts you for the passwords.

Open iDisk

The Open iDisk view, shown in Figure 3-24, can be used to open any .Mac member's iDisk. The only rule that applies is that you need to know both the .Mac member name and the password.

By default, the iDisk Utility enters the .Mac member name and password it finds in the .Mac preference panel (System Preferences → .Mac). However, you don't really need this view to open your iDisk, since you can quickly mount it by clicking on the iDisk icon in the Finder's Sidebar or by pressing the keyboard shortcut, Shift-⌘-I.

 You don't need to have a Finder window open to do this. You can click once on the Desktop (say, on either side of the Dock), and then issue the keyboard shortcut to mount your iDisk (Shift-⌘-I).

Public folder access

As mentioned earlier, the tabbed iDisk pane of the Internet preferences panel (System Preferences → .Mac → iDisk) lets you set the access privileges for your iDisk's *Public* folder. However, you can also use the iDisk Utility's Public Folder Access view, shown in Figure 3-25.

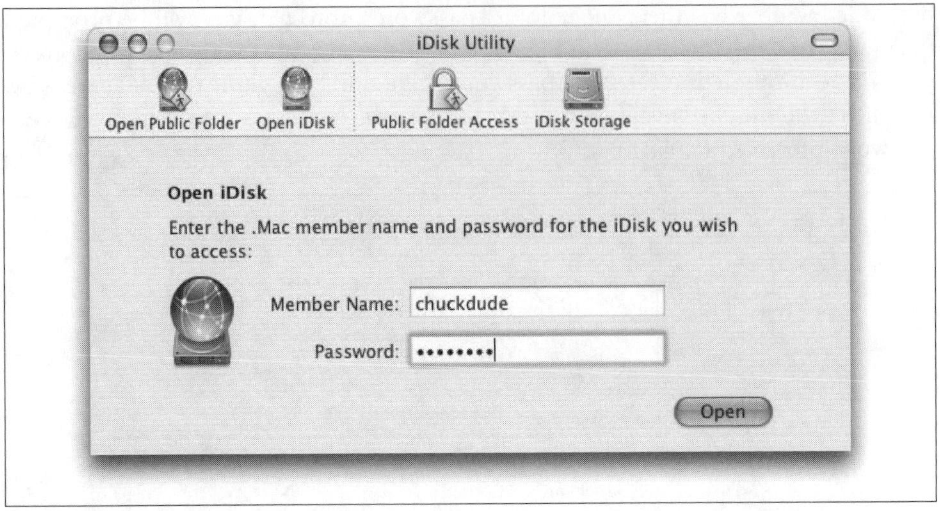

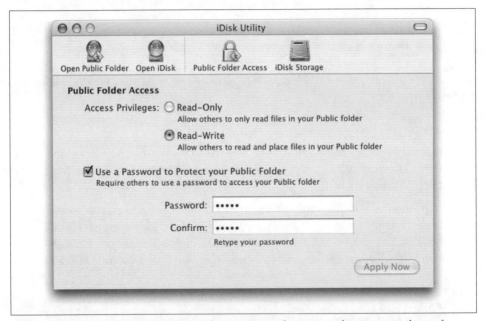

Figure 3-24. *The iDisk Utility's Open iDisk view.*

Figure 3-25. *The iDisk Utility's Public Folder Access view lets you set the access privileges of your iDisk's Public folder.*

iDisk storage

The iDisk Storage view of the iDisk Utility, shown in Figure 3-26, is very similar to the top portion of the iDisk preferences pane (System Preferences → .Mac → iDisk).

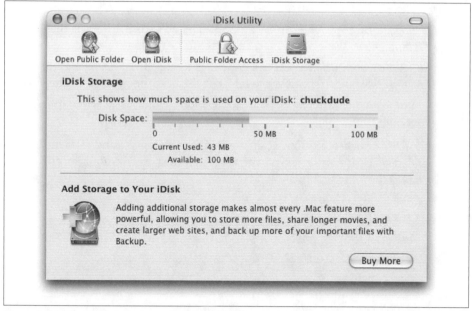

Figure 3-26. The iDisk Storage view of the iDisk Utility.

The iDisk Storage view shows how much space is used/available on your iDisk. This view also has a Buy More button that, when clicked, takes you to a link on Apple's site to purchase additional storage space for your iDisk. When you click on the Buy More button, it opens the page *http://www.apple.com/mac/redirects/idiskutility/ buystorage*, in your default web browser. This in turn takes you to a .Mac login page (shown in Figure 2-3). After logging in, you'll find yourself at the Add Storage page, from which you can purchase additional Email and iDisk storage space.

For more information about purchasing additional iDisk space, see Chapter 1.

iDisk Synchronization

One of the features added to Mac OS X Panther is iDisk synchronization, which allows you to keep a copy of everything that you've stored on your iDisk on your Mac. This includes your .Mac HomePage, any Photo Albums you've created with iPhoto or the HomePage tools, and anything else you've uploaded to your iDisk. The only rule that applies here is that you need to reserve as much drive space as your iDisk can handle. So, with the basic .Mac membership, you will need at least 100 MB of spare drive space to sync your iDisk.

 The items in the *Backup*, *Library*, and *Software* folders will not be synchronized to your Mac; these items remain on your iDisk.

Reasons you should consider enabling iDisk synchronization include:

- By having a local copy, you can back up the data on your iDisk using the Backup application.
- If you tend to work offline, you can copy files to your local iDisk, and then synchronize your local copy with your real iDisk the next time you go online.
- So you can save files directly from an application to your iDisk without first having to mount it.

To enable iDisk synchronization, open the iDisk preference pane (System Preferences → .Mac → iDisk), and click on the checkbox next to "Create a local copy of your iDisk", as shown in Figure 3-27.

Figure 3-27. Click on the checkbox in the iDisk preference pane to create a local copy of your iDisk.

Automatic or Manual iDisk Syncing?

In looking at Figure 3-27, you'll notice that there are two options for synchronization: Automatically (the default) and Manually. If you have iDisk synchronization set to Automatically, your local iDisk will sync with your online iDisk any time you make a change to the contents of the local copy. For example, if you drag a couple image files to the *Pictures* folder on your local iDisk, as soon as the save is complete, your iDisks will synchronize, making the images available from your iDisk's *Picture* folder.

If you set your iDisk synchronization to Manually, you can add and remove files or add and remove subdirectories to the existing folders as much as you want. However, in order to synchronize the local copy with your iDisk on Apple's servers, you will need to manually click on the button next to the iDisk name in the Finder's Sidebar (see Figure 3-28), or Control-click on the iDisk icon on your Desktop and select Sync Now from the contextual menu (shown in Figure 3-29).

Figure 3-28. To manually synchronize your iDisk, click on the sync icon to the right of the iDisk in the Finder's Sidebar, or...

If you look closely at the sync icon in Figure 3-28, you'll see that it has a small dot in the center of it. This dot is an indicator to let you know that you have set iDisk synchronization to Manually in the iDisk preference pane.

Synchronizing the iDisks

After you enable iDisk synchronization, you'll notice that nothing happens right away. However, if you have left synchronization set to Automatically, the second you click on the .Mac tab or close the System Preferences window, your iDisk will start to synchronize with your Mac. You'll know the synchronization is taking place because the alert window shown in Figure 3-30 appears.

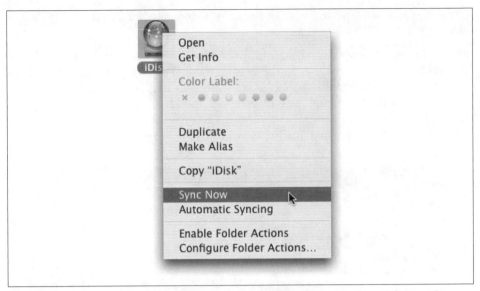

Figure 3-29. ...Control-click on the iDisk icon on your Desktop and select Sync Now from the contextual menu.

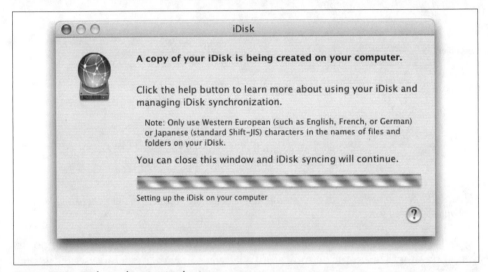

Figure 3-30. iDisk synchronization begins.

When the synchronization process begins, you'll see an iDisk icon appear on your Desktop, with just the plain name of "iDisk", as shown to the right of Figure 3-31.

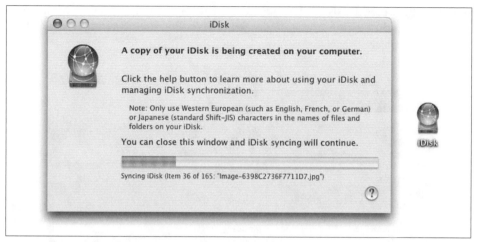

Figure 3-31. Your local iDisk, simply named iDisk, is created on your Desktop, while the progress meter keeps track of what's being synced.

The progress meter lets you know how far along you are in the synchronization process, while messages appear below the progress meter to let you know:

- How many files there are to synchronize
- How many files have been synchronized
- The name of the file currently being transferred

When your iDisk has finished synchronizing, the window shown in Figure 3-32 appears to let you know that everything transferred okay.

Figure 3-32. Look to the right of the iDisk name for the synchronization icon.

Now that your iDisk has successfully synchronized to your Desktop, you'll notice a couple of changes in the Finder. First off, when you open a Finder window, you'll see a little synchronization icon to the right of the iDisk in the Finder's Sidebar, as shown in Figure 3-33. Also, when you select the iDisk in the Sidebar, you'll see a message along the bottom of the Finder window, telling you when the last synchronization took place.

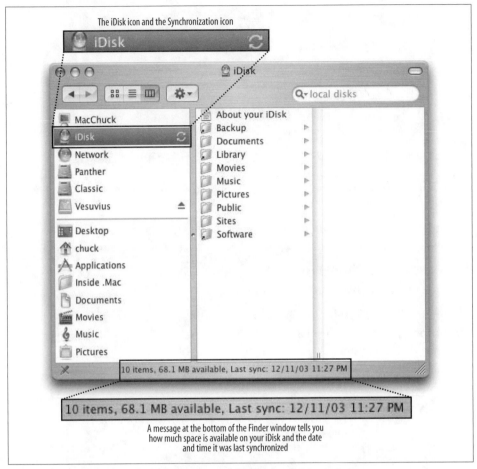

Figure 3-33. Look to the right of the iDisk name for the synchronization icon.

There are a couple ways you can synchronize your iDisk, but a lot of this depends on how you set up synchronization in the first place.

Whenever you synchronize your iDisk, the sync icon rotates until the synchronization has completed, and the message at the bottom of the window changes to a progress meter, as shown in Figure 3-34. If you have iDisk synchronization set to

Automatically, the sync icon will spin periodically, or when you save something new to your local iDisk, to ensure your iDisks are in sync.

Figure 3-34. When synchronizing, a progress meter appears at the bottom of the Finder window.

Turning off iDisk Synchronization

If you later decide that you don't want iDisk synchronization, you can always turn it off by going back to the iDisk preference pane and unchecking the checkbox next to "Create a local copy of your iDisk". When you go to close the System Preferences window (or click on the .Mac tab or any of the icons in System Preferences' toolbar), the alert sheet shown in Figure 3-35 appears.

Just click on the "Turn off local iDisk" button if you really want to disable iDisk synchronization. When you do, the iDisk folder that was on your Desktop gets converted to a disk image named "Previous local iDisk for *membername.dmg*" (for

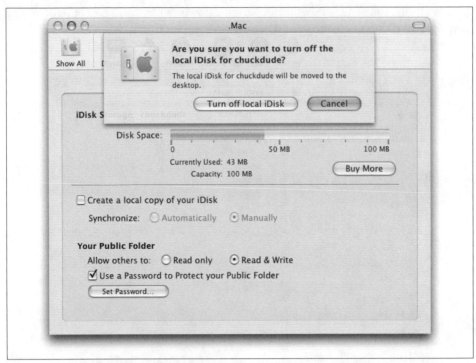

Figure 3-35. Turning off iDisk synchronization.

example, mine would be named "Previous local iDisk for *chuckdude.dmg*"). You can do one of two things with this: burn it to CD and then dump it to trash, or just dump it to trash; either way, you'll get some disk space back.

CHAPTER 4

.Mac Mail

Next to cell phones and instant messaging, email is probably the most popular form of communication today. Seems hard to believe, but 10 years ago, very few but the geek elite knew about email, and now its hard to meet someone who doesn't have an email address or two. Heck, even my parents have an email account (although they don't have a Mac, but I'll forgive them for that).

Every .Mac membership comes with a personalized Mac.com email address. Whether you use this as your primary or secondary email account, it's a distinctive way to let people know "Hey, I'm a Mac user."

Because email clients can vary, this chapter will not cover how to configure individual mail clients such as Mac OS X's Mail application. Instead, this chapter focuses on showing you how to use .Mac's web-based Mail service, which you can access from any standard browser, including Safari, Camino, Mozilla Firebird, and even Internet Explorer.

Two Ways to Check Your .Mac Mail

One of the best parts of having a Mac.com email address is that you have two options for checking your mail: you can either configure your mail client (such as Mail.app, Entourage, Mailsmith, or Eudora) to check and download your mail, or you can opt to check your mail on the Web via Mac.com's Mail service (formerly known as WebMail).

The .Mac email servers use the Internet Mail Access Protocol (IMAP) for managing access to your email. Without getting technical, IMAP keeps your email on the server, which makes it easy to get at from anywhere, including from Windows or other Unix-based systems. All of your mail stays on the server, even after you've moved an email message to the trash. This means that you need to manage your email carefully to ensure that you don't exceed the mail storage limit of 15 MB that comes standard with every .Mac account.

The other option is that you can configure your email application (such as Mail, Entourage, Mailsmith, or Eudora) to download your email from the .Mac mail servers using the Post-Office Protocol, more commonly known as POP. When you use POP, all of the email will download to your computer when you check mail. Basically, you will be using the .Mac servers as a go-between for sending and receiving mail, rather than storing the mail on the server side.

IMAP Versus POP — Which Is Best for Me?

As you can see, it appears that you have only two options for checking your .Mac Mail: IMAP or POP. But how do you know what's best for you?

The advantage to using IMAP is that your mail is always available from one central location: the .Mac mail servers. Your mail is automatically backed up by Apple, and you don't have to worry about the mail taking up huge amounts of space on your hard drive.

POP on the other hand, downloads the mail to your computer and stores it on your hard drive. That means that your mail is always on your system when you need it, but it also means that you'll need to allow for drive space to store your mail, and that you will need to back up your mail on a regular basis. The one advantage POP has over IMAP is that your .Mac mail will download from Apple's servers onto your computer, which helps you keep under that 15 MB email storage limit.

Which solution you choose—IMAP or POP—is really up to you, and you should seriously consider your options. I use a combination of both IMAP and POP. Since I spend most of my day working in email from work, I have my PowerBook configured to use my work email address (*chuck@oreilly.com*) as my primary email account, and my PowerMac at home configured to use my .Mac email account (*chuckdude@mac.com*) as a POP account. Of course, this means that I can't get at a message I've already downloaded to my Mac at home, but that's the choice I've made and the price I've paid.

 Refer back to Chapter 1 for instructions on how to configure Mac OS X's Mail application to use POP for accessing your .Mac email.

Using .Mac's Web-Based Mail

The web interface for accessing your .Mac email (formerly known as WebMail) is pretty intuitive; there's not much guesswork as to which button performs which function, and so forth. But like all email clients, there are some things you'll need to know to configure your settings.

The first thing you need to know is the quick link to getting to Mail. Sure, you can go to the Mac.com web site and then click on the Mail button, but an easier route is to just point your browser at *http://www.mac.com/webmail*; this takes you to Mail's login page. All you need to do is enter your Member Name and Password in the appropriate fields, and click on the Connect button.

 If you're using Safari, Camino, Mozilla Firebird, or Internet Explorer, you might want to enable their auto-fill feature for web forms. Why? Well, these browsers will store your .Mac Member Name and Password in your Keychains file so that when you come back to this site again, the browser will automatically enter the info for the fields. All you'll need to do then is either hit the Return key or click on the Connect button to accept the values and log in.

Understanding the Interface

.Mac's web-based Mail service is a bit quirky to use, but once you understand its interface and learn your way around, you'll be sending and receiving messages like a pro in no time at all.

Once you've successfully logged on to check your .Mac Mail, you'll be taken to your Inbox, as shown in Figure 4-1.

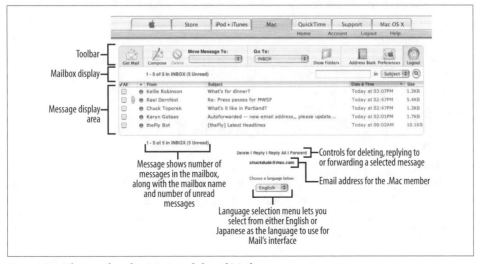

Figure 4-1. The interface for .Mac's web-based Mail.

As noted in Figure 4-1, Mail's interface has three main areas:

- A toolbar along the top
- A display area that relays messages to you about the mailbox you're in, any actions you have performed (such as moving messages from one mailbox to another) and that also includes a search field
- The message display area, which either shows you a list of the messages in a mailbox, or, when a message is clicked, the contents of an email message

Mail's toolbar

Mail's toolbar (shown in Figure 4-2) has the following buttons, which allow you to manage your .Mac email:

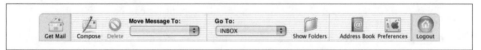

Figure 4-2. Mail's toolbar.

Get Mail
> Clicking this button checks the .Mac mail server for any incoming mail. If there are new messages waiting in the queue, they will show up in the display after the web page refreshes.

Compose
> Clicking this button creates and sends a new email message.

Delete
> This button is only activated when you've selected a checkbox next to one of the messages in the display window. If an email message has a checkmark next to it, the Delete button becomes active; when clicked, the selected message(s) is sent to the *Deleted Messages* folder.

Move Message To:
> If an email message has a checkmark next to it, this pop-up menu allows you to transfer a message(s) to another folder you've created, as well as to the *Deleted Messages* and *Trash* folders.

Go To:
> This pop-up menu let's you switch to another email folder so you can view its contents.

Show Folders
> This button takes you to a display that shows all of your email folders. The page you're taken to also lets you add or delete folders, rename folders, or trash a folder's contents with a single click. Also available on this page is a progress bar that tells you how much email storage space you have left.

Address Book
> This button displays any contacts you may have stored online in your Address Book. If you've used iSync to synchronize your Mac with your .Mac account, all of the contacts from your computer will be stored online where you can get at them quickly. For more information on using iSync to synchronize your Address Book contacts, see Chapter 9.

Preferences
> Clicking this button takes you to a page where you can tweak the settings for your .Mac Mail account. Here you can add a picture to your email and set up a "signature" that gets tacked on to the end of your email messages.

Logout

Clicking this button logs you out of Mail and takes you back to the Mac.com site (*http://www.mac.com*).

The mailbox display

The area below the toolbar, shown in Figure 4-3, is used to display information about the mailbox you're currently in, as well as to search for messages within that mailbox.

Figure 4-3. The mailbox display area.

This area of the interface provides you with details about the mailbox you're currently viewing, and any actions you take from there (such as deleting or moving messages to another mailbox). By default, the message display area shows only 15 messages when viewing the contents of a mail folder. On the left side of the mailbox display shown in Figure 4-3, you'll see two buttons that you can click on to page up or down (respectively) through the list of messages in a mailbox. Immediately to the right of these two buttons is a message that tells you which messages are being displayed and in which message folder you are currently.

On the right side of the mailbox display area is a Search field. You can search for messages in the selected mailbox based on their Subject, From, To, or CC lines. For example, if I wanted to search for messages that had the word "Max" in the subject line, I would type that into the search field, select Subject from the pop-up menu, and then click on the search button (the one with the little magnifying glass on it). If any messages are found that have "Max" in the subject line, two things will happen, as described here and shown in Figure 4-4:

• A message will appear in the mailbox display area in bold text, telling me how many messages have been found (if any) that meet the search criteria.

• Any email messages that have been found will show up in the message display area.

If no messages are found to meet your search criteria, you will see a message in bold text telling you that no messages were found.

The message display area

Below the toolbar, you'll see a message that tells you how many email messages are in that particular folder (including how many messages are unread) and a text entry field for searching through messages in the folder. When it comes to searching, you can search through messages based on information found in the Subject or based on an email address in the From, To, or CC (carbon copy) field. To search, simply enter

Figure 4-4. Searching for messages is easy.

the search criteria in the text field, select one of the items from the pop-up menu, and click on the search button; the results of the search will be displayed in the message viewing area.

Messages are displayed in a column view, shown in Figure 4-5, similar to the Finder's List View. Above the list of incoming messages is another row of controls. These controls are used for selecting all of the messages in a folder or for sorting how the messages appear in the display.

✓ All	•	From	Subject	Date & Time ▼	Size
☐	●	Kellie Robinson	What's for dinner?	Today at 03:07PM	1.3KB
☐ 📎	●	Rael Dornfest	Re: Press passes for MWSF	Today at 02:47PM	5.4KB
☐	●	Chuck Toporek	What's it like in Portland?	Today at 02:47PM	1.3KB
☐	●	Karyn Gotaas	Autoforwarded -- new email address,, please update...	Today at 02:01PM	1.7KB
☐	●	theFly Bot	[theFly] Latest Headlines	Today at 09:02AM	10.1KB

Figure 4-5. The incoming mail display lets you sort messages by clicking on the column headings.

When you click on a column heading, that portion of the heading will turn gray as a way of letting you know that that's how the messages are being sorted. You will also notice a black triangle that's either pointing up or down at the right edge of the column heading. These triangles indicate the sorting order for that item. The column headings are described in the following list:

✓ *All*

Clicking on this column heading will place a checkmark in the boxes next to all of the messages in the display. This is handy to keep in mind when you want to delete the messages in the display or to move all of the messages to another folder.

(Blank)

This column is used to indicate whether an email message has an attachment. If you see a paper clip in this column (as shown in Figure 4-5), it means the message has an attachment.

• *(a dot)*

If a message has a blue dot in this column, it means that the message is new and hasn't been read (or viewed) yet. If you click on this column heading, the messages in the window will either be sorted by messages that haven't been read (i.e., new, incoming messages), or by messages that have already been read. (There is no black triangle on this column head to indicate the sorting order.)

From

Clicking on this column heading sorts the messages in the folder by the sender. If the triangle is pointing down, message senders are sorted A–Z; if it's pointing upward, messages are sorted Z–A.

Subject

Sorts messages by their subject line. If the triangle is pointing down, subjects are sorted A–Z; if it's pointing upward, subjects are sorted Z–A.

Date & Time

Sorts messages by the day and time they were received. If the triangle is pointing down, messages are sorted by most recently received message to the oldest; if the arrow is pointing upward, messages are sorted with the older messages appearing first.

Size

Sorts messages by their file size. If the triangle is pointing down, messages are sorted from biggest to smallest, and vice versa if the triangle is pointing upward.

By default, incoming messages are sorted in the order in which they are received, with the most recently received message showing up at the top of the list. To change the sort order, simply click on one of the other column headings.

Setting Mail's Preferences

Now that you know your way around the web interface a bit, let's configure your preferences for using .Mac's web-based mail. In the Mail toolbar, click on the Preferences icon (the one that looks like the System Preferences icon in the Dock).

When the Mail Preferences page loads, you'll see your .Mac email address in the mailbox display area, along with a little status bar to the right that shows how much storage space you've used. By looking at the status bar, you can quickly find out how much email storage space you've used and how much you have waiting at the ready for incoming email. There's also a Buy More button, which when clicked, takes you to a page where you can purchase additional storage space.

Mail's Preferences page is divided into three sections:

- Composing
- Viewing
- Account

The sections that follow contain details on Mail's preference panes.

Gotchas of .Mac Mail

As mentioned in Chapter 1, the basic .Mac membership comes with 15 MB of space for storing email on Apple's servers. However, there are some gotchas to sending and receiving Mac.com mail that you may not be aware of, including:

- The maximum size for incoming and outgoing messages through the Mac.com servers is 3 MB. Be careful with this limit, though, since it means that people can also send you large files as attachments. With 15 MB of email storage, it won't be hard for someone to clog your mailbox with one or two raw JPEG images taken from a 6-megapixel digital camera.

- If you need to send something larger than 3 MB, you can upload the file to the *Sites* folder on your iDisk and then send an email containing a URL to the file's location so it can be downloaded. For example, if I have a 20-MB Zip archive (named *randompics.zip*) that contains a bunch of digital photos, I could mount my iDisk and place the Zip file in the *Sites* folder, and then send an email with the following URL:

  http://homepage.mac.com/chuckdude/randompics.zip

  When the recipient of that email clicks on the link, the *randompics.zip* file automatically downloads to their computer.

- Likewise, if someone is trying to send you a file larger than 3 MB (or if your inbox runneth over), that message will bounce to the sender. To solve the problem, you might want to ask the sender to mount and upload the file to your iDisk's *Public* folder (see Chapter 3), and then send you a message telling you which file it is you need to grab.

- You can send up to 200 messages a day, or mail to 400 recipients a day, whichever comes first. For example, if you send 100 messages a day, and each message goes to four people, you'll hit your limit.

- The maximum number of recipients to a single email message is 100.

Keep in mind that .Mac mail is intended more for personal use, rather than for bulk mail purposes. Additional terms are detailed in the .Mac Membership Agreement and Acceptable Use Policy found at *http://www.mac.com/1/membership_terms.html*, and also in a TechNote at *http://docs.info.apple.com/article.html?artnum=25301*.

 When you make any changes to your Mail preferences, make sure you scroll down to the bottom of the web page and click on the Save button. If you don't, the changes you've applied won't take effect.

Composing

This section, shown in Figure 4-6, lets you configure Mail for how it handles the email messages you send.

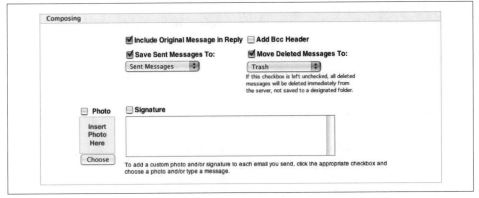

Figure 4-6. The Composing pane of Mail's Preferences page.

The top part of this section has a series of checkboxes that you can check or uncheck, depending on your needs. These include:

Include Original Message in Reply
With this option selected, the contents of the original email message will be displayed in the message body area (described later) when you reply to an email.

This works only if the person who has sent you an email is sending their mail as *plain text*. This means that their message cannot contain any special formatting. If it does and you click on the Reply button, the original message will be sent back along with your reply as an attachment. This can be really annoying, because you have no way of seeing what you were replying to unless you go back, select, and copy all of the message text with the mouse, and then paste their message text into your reply.

Add Bcc Header
The Bcc header, which stands for Blind Carbon Copy, lets you copy someone on the message, and Mail will hide that person's email address from everyone else who received the message. This feature is convenient for when you want to send an email message to a group of people, but want to hide the list of recipients from everyone else. For example, if you type in the addresses for 20 different people into the Bcc header field, each person will see the message with only their name and/or email address in the To: field; they won't see everyone else's. Bcc headers are also great for copying someone on a message when you don't want the person whose address you've typed into the To: field to know that you're copying someone else. This option is unchecked by default.

Save Sent Messages To
If this option is selected, a copy of the messages that you send from Mail will be saved to the folder you select from the pop-up menu. This option is unchecked by default.

Move Deleted Messages To

Select this checkbox if you want to keep copies of the messages you've deleted, or to have them placed in a different mail folder (such as the *Deleted Messages* folder). If this option is unchecked, any messages that you delete will be removed from the server immediately. This is helpful for keeping the size of your .Mac mailbox under control.

If you leave this box checked, you can delete all of the messages from the .Mac server by doing the following:

1. From Mail's toolbar, select Go To → Show All Folders.

2. Click on the Empty Now link next to the *Trash* folder.

If there are still messages in your *Deleted Messages* folder that you want to get rid of, do the following:

1. Select Go To → Deleted Messages from Mail's toolbar.

2. Select all of the messages by clicking on the All column heading. This places a checkmark next to all of the messages in the view.

3. In Mail's toolbar, select Move Message To → Trash to move the messages to the *Trash* folder. If there is more than one screen of messages here to trash, repeat this step until no more messages show up in the *Deleted Messages* folder.

4. In Mail's toolbar, select Go To → Show All Folders.

5. Click on the Empty Now link next to the *Trash* folder to remove the messages from the server.

Adding a photo to your .Mac email messages

While it isn't a requirement, you can also attach a photo of yourself (or some other goofy image) to the email messages you send from your .Mac account.

To add a photo to your .Mac record, follow these steps:

1. Click on the checkbox next to the word Photo and place a checkmark in this box to enable this feature.

2. Click on the Choose button below where your image will be to select an image to use. The web page will change to that shown in Figure 4-7.

3. Click on the Choose File button under Step 1. As the message says, you can only use a GIF or JPEG image; don't worry about the size of the image, we'll get to that in a moment.

   A Finder sheet (shown in Figure 4-8) slides out of the browser's titlebar, from which you can locate a picture to use. If you're like me and you store your images in your *Pictures* folder, select that from the Sidebar of the sheet, locate the picture you want to use on the right side, and then click on the Choose button.

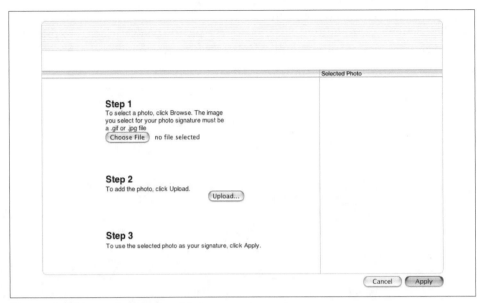

Figure 4-7. Adding a photo to your .Mac messages.

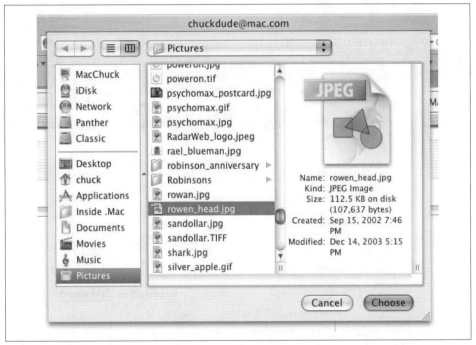

Figure 4-8. Locate the picture you want to use, and then click on the Choose button.

4. After you have selected the picture to use, proceed to Step 2 in the window and click on the Upload button; this uploads the picture you've selected to the .Mac server. Once the picture has uploaded to the server, you will see it displayed to the right in the Selected Photo section, as shown in Figure 4-9.

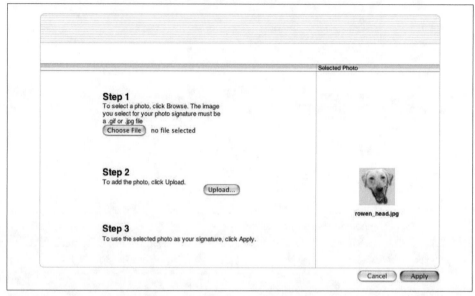

Figure 4-9. Once uploaded, your picture will appear on the right.

5. Click on the Apply button (shown at the bottom right of Figure 4-9). This applies the photo you've selected to your .Mac account, and takes you back to the Composing preferences page to show you the photo you've selected, as shown in Figure 4-10.

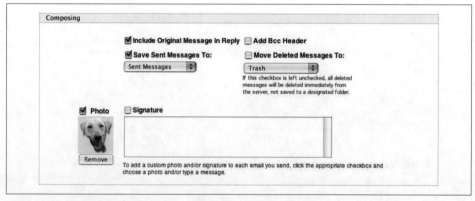

Figure 4-10. Your photo has now been added to your .Mac account.

6. If you're okay with the photo you've added, click on the Save button.

Adding a signature to your emails

If you want to include a signature a the bottom of your email messages, click on the checkbox next to Signature, and then type something in the text field below.

Your email signature can be anything, such as your name and email address:

> Chuck Toporek
> Editor, Author, Speaker
> chuckdude@mac.com

or something that includes a URL:

> Chuck Toporek
> Author of "Inside .Mac" (http://www.oreilly.com/catalog/indotmac)
> chuckdude@mac.com

In the case of the last example, I've placed a URL in parenthesis, which points to O'Reilly's web site for this book. When an email message is delivered with my signature attached, the URL turns into a link; when clicked, the recipient is taken to this page.

 The URL actually gets processed as a redirect. When you place your mouse over a link in someone's email message or signature, you can see a URL similar to the following show up in Safari's status bar (if you have it enabled):

```
http://www.mac.com/webmail/redirect/http://www.oreilly.com/↵
catalog/indotmac
```

To enable Safari's status bar, select View → Status Bar, or use its keyboard shortcut (⌘-/).

What you put in your signature is really up to you, but word to the wise: don't include your phone number or any other personal information in your signature. If you really need to give someone your phone number, it's best to do that on a case-by-case basis, rather than to include it as part of your email's signature.

Viewing

This section of Mail's Preferences, shown in Figure 4-11, has the following three options for controlling how Mail displays the messages in your inbox:

Time Zone
> This is the time zone in which you live or from where you are sending email messages. When you send an email, the current date and time are attached to your messages based on what you've selected from the pop-up menu.

Messages Per Page
> By clicking on the pop-up menu, you can opt to have 10 (the default), 15, 20, 25, 30, or 50 messages display in the message list when you're viewing the messages in a mail folder. The option you select here applies to all of your message folders.

Show "All Headers" Option
> This option is unchecked by default; however, if you want the ability to view all of the headers on an email message (which is mostly gibberish that one mail server uses to send email to another mail server), click on this checkbox. With this option enabled, a Show All Headers button will appear at the top of each email message you view online.
>
> For the most part, you should never have to look at a message's headers; however, there are times when they do come in handy. For an example, see the sidebar titled, "Dealing with Spam," located in the next section.

Figure 4-11. The Viewing pane lets you specify how the messages appear in the display.

Account

If you thought having an image on your .Mac email or being able to view message headers was fun, just wait until you hit the Accounts section of the preferences page, shown in Figure 4-12.

From this part of the Mail preferences page, you can:

- Specify an address to forward your Mac.com email to
- Set up an auto-reply message
- Check the email for a POP email account using your .Mac account

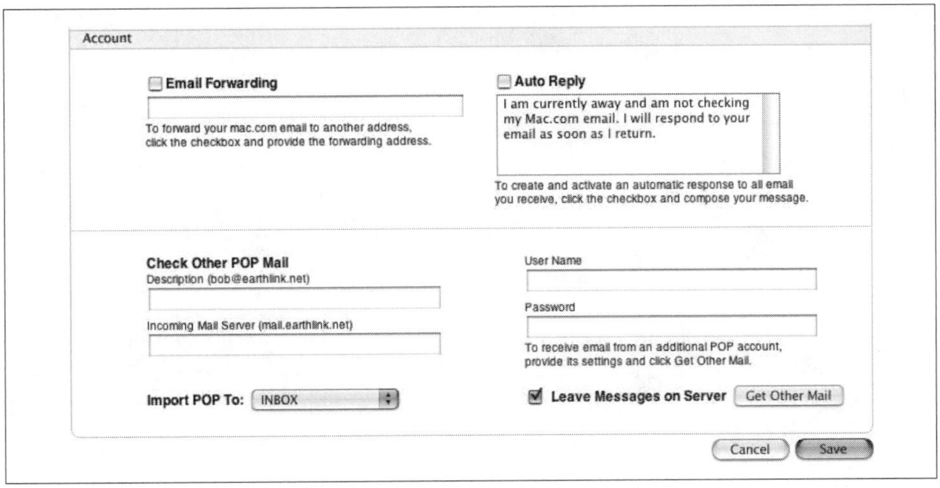

Figure 4-12. The Account preferences pane.

Dealing with Spam

No, I'm not talking about the gelled lunch meat that comes in a can, but the dreadful email messages you might receive for no reason. If you find that you're getting a lot of spam to your Mac.com email address, there are some things you can do to head them off at the pass:

1. If you're reading your Mac.com email with Mac OS X's Mail application, you can set up the Junk Mail filtering to look for suspected spam and automatically delete it. To do this, go to Mail → Junk Mail and (at first) enable Training mode. Once you're sure that the messages Mail is flagging as Junk are actually junk, you can flip the switch and put Junk Mail into Automatic mode so you don't have to do anything.

2. Forward the offending spam message, including its message headers, to *spam@mac.com*. To reveal the message headers, go to *http://www.mac.com/ webmail* and log in using your .Mac member name and password. Click on the Account button in the Sidebar (or your named button in the navigation bar), and then enable the checkbox next to the Show All Headers option. Go back to the spam message and click on the Show All Headers button, and then forward the message to *spam@mac.com*.

It's worth noting that Apple does a fair amount of spam filtering on the server side that .Mac users never see. However, on those occasions when one does slip through, it's nice to know there's something you can do to help solve the problem.

The first two of these are fairly self-explanatory, but there's a bit more to setting up the third option. The three options you'll find in the Account section include:

Email Forwarding

If you want to have your .Mac email forwarded to another email address, click on the checkbox to place a checkmark there, and then type in the email address to where you want your .Mac mail forwarded. After clicking on the Save button at the bottom of the page, your .Mac mail will be sent on to the email address you've specified.

Auto-Reply

If you are going to be away on business or vacation, but want to let people know that their message has been received, click on the checkbox next to Auto-Reply. You can opt to use the default message (shown in Figure 4-12), or you can delete that and type in something different.

 If you enable Email Forwarding or Auto Reply, just remember to come back here and disable these options when you no longer need them.

Check Other POP Mail

If you have a POP email account (say through your ISP or from work), you can configure .Mac's Mail to pick up this mail, making it viewable on the Web. This is particularly handy for when you go on vacation, but don't want to drag your expensive PowerBook or iBook along. If you find yourself someplace that offers Internet access, you can go on the Web and read all of your email online.

To set this up, however, involves a little bit more work, but if you follow along closely, you shouldn't have any problems:

1. Exit out of Mail's preferences by clicking on the Save button at the bottom of the web page. This should take you back to the main Mail page, showing you the messages in your Inbox.

2. In the toolbar, click on the Show Folders button. This takes you to a page that lists all of your email folders, as shown in Figure 4-13.

3. On this page's toolbar, click on the New icon to create a new email folder. You will see a new folder appear at the top of the list of folders, with a blank field next to it. Type in something that will let you quickly identify that folder with the POP account; for example "Work Mail" or "My ISP", as shown in Figure 4-14. After entering the name for the folder, click on the Save button at the lower right of the page. The page will refresh, showing you the new folder you've created.

4. Now click on the Mail icon at the far left of the toolbar; this will take you to your main Mail page.

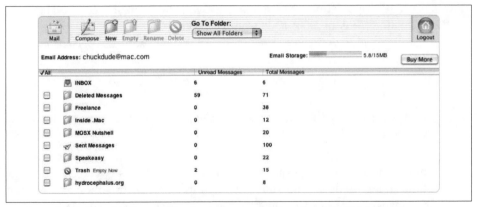

Figure 4-13. Click on the Show Folders button to see a listing of your Mail folders, shown here.

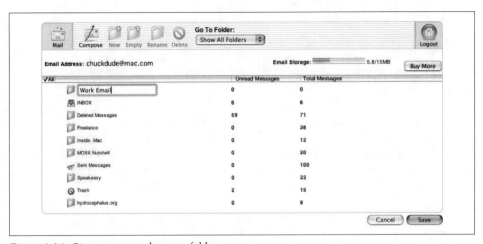

Figure 4-14. Give a name to that new folder.

5. In the toolbar, click on the Preferences icon to go back to the Mail preferences page; once there, scroll back down to the Check other POP Mail section.

6. In the fields for this section, enter the following information:

- *Description:* Enter something simple such as your work email address (for example, mine would be *chuck@oreilly.com*), or something easy, such as "My Work Email".

- *Incoming Mail Server:* Type in the name of your incoming mail server; you should obtain this from your ISP or from your system administrator at work.

- *User Name:* Enter the username for your POP email account. The user-name for your POP mail account appears before the @ symbol in the email address. For example, if my work email address is *chuck@oreilly. com*, my username is *chuck*.

- *Password:* Enter the password you use to access your email from the POP server.

7. In the pop-up menu next to Import POP To, select the name of the folder you created earlier (for example, Work Mail or My ISP).

8. And the all-important step: make sure that there is a checkmark in the box next to Leave Messages on Server. The reason for this is because the next time you go to download your POP mail from wherever you mainly do, the messages you've been reading through the .Mac web-based Mail interface will still be there to download to your computer.

9. Click on the Save button to save your changes.

 If you have more than one POP account that you'd like to check as well, click on the Get Other Mail button and repeat all of the steps listed here. Don't forget to create a folder to filter the POP mail in to.

Now the next time you check for new messages, your POP mail will download along with your .Mac mail, and the POP mail will filter its way into the folder you created for it. (It's just a shame that you can't set up rules or filters for other incoming messages so you could automatically redirect them to other email folders. For this, you'll have to rely on the Mail application that ships with Mac OS X instead.)

 If you receive a lot of mail with lots of attachments at one or more of your POP accounts, be warned that you can quickly exceed .Mac's base email storage of 15 MB. Use this feature judiciously, or plan to watch the meter on your email account quickly go into the red.

If you decide at a later time that you want to disable POP mail forwarding, go back to Mail's preferences page, delete the entries from the fields, and then click the Save button to save the changes.

Working with Mail

Now that you've learned your way around Mail's web-based interface, and you have all of your preferences set, it's time to start sending and receiving email.

Sending Mail

To create and send a new email message, follow these simple steps:

1. Click on the Compose icon in the toolbar; you will be taken to a new page, which you can use to write and send your email.

 To quickly move from one field to the next, use the Tab key rather than moving the mouse and clicking in each individual field.

2. In the To: field, type in the email address of the person you want to send the message to; likewise for the Cc: field if you want to copy someone on the message.

3. Type something into the Subject field (your messages should always contain a subject, even if it's just "Hi there").

4. Type in whatever it is that you want to say in the message body area (shown in Figure 4-15).

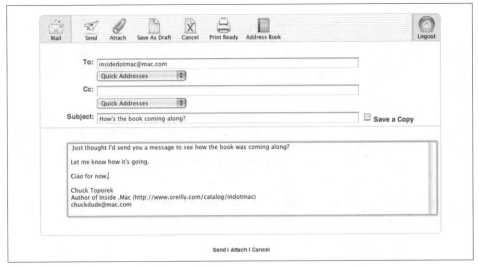

Figure 4-15. Sending a new email message.

5. Click on the Send icon in the toolbar or on the Send link below the message body area.

That's pretty much all it takes to send an email. However, there's a lot more to it than that. For example, what if you want to send the message to more than one person or to include an attachment?

Sending Messages to Multiple Recipients

If you want to send the same message to more than one person, you don't have to send each message individually. To send a message to more than one person, all you

Let Safari Check Your Spelling

There's nothing worse than getting an email message that's full of spelling errors. At the very least, you should read through your email to ensure that you've spelled everything correctly. Or, if you're lazy (like me), you can let Safari check your spelling as you're typing.

To turn on spell-checking in Safari, do the following:

- When you're in the message body area (before you start typing), select Edit → Spelling → Check Spelling As You Type.

That's it. Just one simple step (okay, two if you consider tabbing to the message body field as a step).

Now as you're typing along, any misspelled words will have a red squiggle line beneath them. You can either go back to correct the spelling yourself, or you can Control-click on the misspelled word and select the correct spelling from the pop-up menu that appears.

need to do is place a comma (followed by a space) between each email address; for example:

```
insidedotmac@mac.com, eyeheartportland@mac.com
```

When the message gets sent, the mail server will see the comma, and if it finds another email address after that, the message will be sent to the next address as well. As noted earlier, you can have up to 100 recipients on each email message you send (that's the total between the To:, Cc:, and Bcc: fields).

Of course, your fingers would fall off if you had to manually type in all 100 email addresses. Fortunately, you can set up a pseudogroup that contains multiple email addresses in your Address Book, and then insert the name of the pseudogroup into the To:, Cc:, or Bcc: field.

Why am I calling this a "pseudogroup"? Well, because the .Mac Address Book (accessible by clicking on the Address Book icon in Mail's toolbar or from Mac. com's main page) doesn't allow you to set up email groups like the real Address Book application that ships with Mac OS X. But you can trick the .Mac Address Book into letting you set up a group by doing the following:

1. Click on the Address Book icon in Mail's toolbar; the web page will change, taking you to your online Address Book.

2. Click on the New icon in the Address Book's toolbar.

3. In the First Name field, enter a name for the group you want to create (such as "MyFamily," "MyFriends," etc.).

4. Click in the Home Email field and type in the email addresses for everyone you want to include in your group (remember, you can only have up to 100 people copied on a single message, so use that as your limit).

5. When you've typed in all of the email addresses, scroll down the page and then click on the Save button.

Ta-da! You've just duped the .Mac Address Book into letting you create a group without it knowing.

To send an email message to the group (or to anyone else listed in your .Mac Address Book), follow these steps:

1. Click on the Compose icon to start creating a new email message.

2. In the message window's titlebar (see Figure 4-15), click on the Address Book icon.

3. Search for the name of your group by typing its name in the Search field and clicking on the magnifying glass button.

4. When the page reloads, you should see the name of your group in the results, as shown in Figure 4-16.

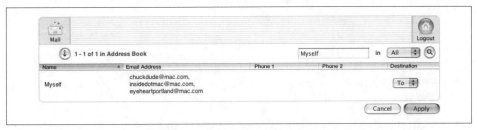

Figure 4-16. Search for the name of your "Group," and then choose its Destination.

5. In the Destination column, select either To, Cc, or Bcc from the pop-up menu, and then click on the Apply button; this places the Name of the group and the email addresses in the appropriate field of the email message, as shown in Figure 4-17.

6. Now type in your email message in the message body area and click on the Send icon.

7. When you click on the Send button, you'll get a fairly quick error message back, telling you that the addresses you've typed in the To: field aren't valid. If you look closely at Figure 4-18, you can see that the email messages have angle brackets on either side, plus the name you assigned to the group.

All you need to do is delete these from the To: line and you should be okay. To quickly delete these items:

a. Click the mouse just to the right of first angle bracket (<), and then hit the Delete key until the cursor has erased the bracket and the name of the group.

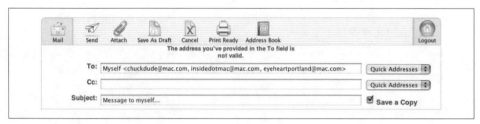

Figure 4-17. The group email addresses have now been added to the To: line.

Figure 4-18. Houston, we have a problem…delete the group name and the angle brackets from the To: line and your message should send.

b. Hit the Down Arrow key on your keyboard to move the cursor to the very end of the To: line. You should see another angle bracket there (>); hit the Delete key to remove this bracket.

8. Now click on the Send icon and the message will send without fail.

Okay, now you can celebrate, knowing that you have indeed successfully tricked .Mac's Mail to let you create and use a group.

Attachments

One of the reasons you have an email account is so you can send and receive stuff from the people you know. The most important thing to keep in mind when sending and receiving attachments is file size. Emails containing attachments can be no bigger than 3 MB, either incoming or outgoing. Keep in mind that this not only includes the file size of the attachment, but also of the text of the email message itself. So, if you've got a 3-MB image file you're trying to send, the message will most definitely bounce back with an error because the message itself will be at least a few kilobytes in size. If you're sending an attachment that's close to 3 MB in size, you should keep your message short and sweet (*kurz and gut*), just to be on the safe side.

Sending attachments

To attach a file (or multiple files) to an email, simply click on the Attach icon in the toolbar; it's the one with the paper clip, as shown in Figure 4-19.

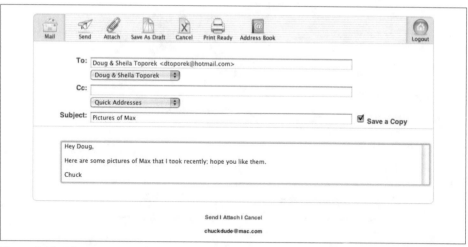

Figure 4-19. After you've typed in the message, click on the Attach button to start the process of attaching files to an email.

After clicking on the Attach icon, you'll be taken to another page (shown in Figure 4-20) that lets you select and attach files to your email message. It's a simple three-step process that goes as follows:

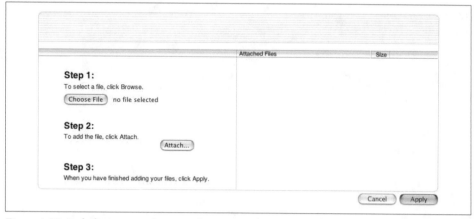

Figure 4-20. Including an attachment with your email is easy; just follow the steps.

1. Select a file by clicking on the Choose File button. A sheet slides out of the browser's titlebar (as shown in Figure 4-21) with a dialog box that lets you select a file to attach. Simply move around in the column view as you would with the Finder, select the file to attach by clicking on it once, and then click on the Choose button.

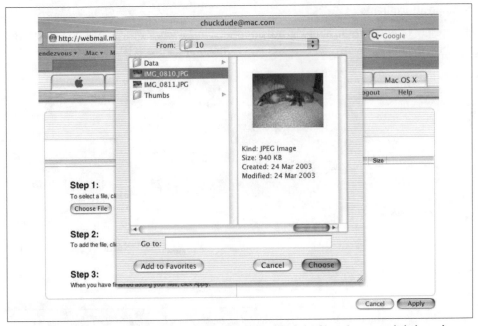

Figure 4-21. Selecting an attachment is pretty simple, just find the file, select it, and click on the Choose button.

2. After clicking on the Choose button, the sheet will slide back up into the browser's titlebar, and you'll see an icon for the file, along with its filename, next to the Choose File button as shown in Figure 4-22.

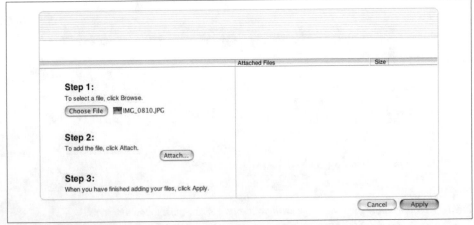

Figure 4-22. Click on the Attach button in Step 2 to attach the file to your email.

Now before you try attaching more files, don't click on the Choose File button just yet because the first file hasn't really been "attached." Once you've chosen a file to attach, you need to proceed to Step 2 in the window and click on the Attach button; this actually attaches the file to your message.

After the file has attached itself, you'll see the file listed in the right side of the window, as shown in Figure 4-23. Notice that the right pane shows the filename and its file size in kilobytes, and also has a Remove button next to it, just in case you change your mind about attaching that file.

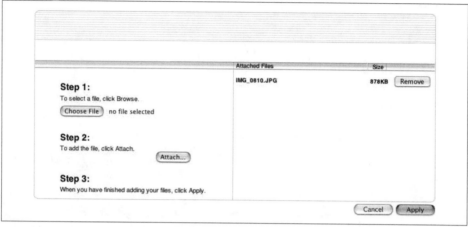

Figure 4-23. Now the file is attached (sort of).

 It's worth noting that the right pane of the page doesn't calculate the total size of the attachments you've applied to a message. If you're uncertain about how close you are to hitting the 3-MB limit, you'll need to add up the file sizes yourself. Since the file sizes are shown in kilobytes (KB), keep in mind that there are a 1000 KB to a megabyte (MB). If the total of your attachments is nearing 2900 KB, you might want to cut it short and send any additional files with a separate email message.

3. If you have more files to attach to your message, go back and repeat the first two steps. When you're certain that all of the files you want to attach are there, click on the Apply button at the bottom of the page. After you do this, the attachments are applied to the message, and you're returned to the Compose message view, as shown in Figure 4-24.

If you look below the Subject line, you'll see an additional header to the message: an Attachments line. To view additional information about the attachments, click on the black disclosure triangle (next to "Attachments:"). The triangle will point downward (Figure 4-25), and you'll see the attachments listed showing their filename, size, and MIME type, along with a Remove button so you can drop one or all of the attachments if you've changed your mind.

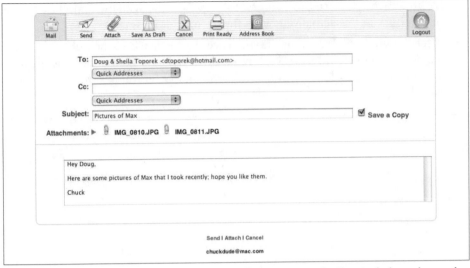

Figure 4-24. Only after clicking the Apply button will the messages finally attach themselves to the message.

Figure 4-25. Click on the disclosure triangle to reveal an email's attachments.

If everything looks right (meaning the files you want to send are there), click on the Send button to send the message with the attachments. If you need to attach additional files, you can go back and click on the Attach button and repeat Steps 1–3 again.

What the Heck Is a MIME Type?

As you can see from Figure 4-25, the Attachments line displays the MIME type for any attachments. But what the heck is a MIME type?

MIME, which stands for Multipurpose Internet Mail Extensions (and not the goofy white-faced, stripe-wearing freaks found in parks of large metropolitan areas), is a way of indicating what type the file is, what icon to apply to it, which applications can open it, and so forth. In the case of the attachments in Figure 4-25, you can see that their MIME type is listed as "image/jpeg", which lets you know that these are, well, JPEG images.

MIME types are assigned by the Internet Assigned Numbers Authority (IANA; *http://www.iana.org*). A complete listing of MIME types is available on through their web site at *http://www.iana.org/assignments/media-types*.

Receiving attachments

When you receive a message that contains attachments, you'll see a little paper clip in the column that's sandwiched between the checkbox and the column that contains the blue dots that indicate an unread message, as shown in Figure 4-26.

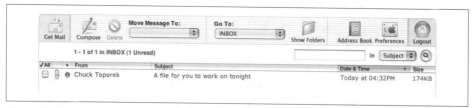

Figure 4-26. A paper clip icon in a message is an indicator that the message has an attachment.

Before you can download the attachment from the .Mac email server to your Mac, you first need to view the message by either clicking on the sender's name in the From column or on the subject line in the Subject column. You'll notice that the word "Attachments" is highlighted in blue, and you can see the filename of the attachment next to a paper clip and a black disclosure triangle. If you click on either "Attachments" or on the disclosure triangle, the triangle will flip downward, revealing the details for the attachment as shown in Figure 4-27.

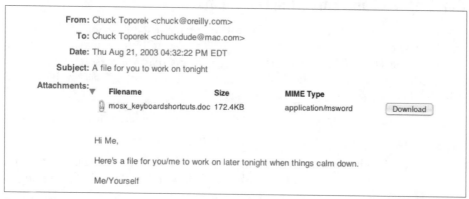

Figure 4-27. Viewing the attachment (at least in the email message) is as simple as clicking on the disclosure triangle.

As with outgoing attachments, you can see the attachment's filename, size (in KB), and MIME type. In the case of this attachment, the MIME type (application/msword) tells us that the file can be opened using Microsoft Word. To download the attachment from the .Mac email server to your Mac, click on the Download button. Another browser window opens as the file downloads to your Mac, after which you can just close that window by clicking on the link provided.

The attachment will download to wherever you have specified downloaded files to be saved on your Mac. For example, I have Safari set up so that any files I download from the Internet are saved in a *Downloads* folder on my Desktop. By default, Safari is configured to save downloaded files to your Desktop; however, if you want to create your own *Downloads* folder, follow these steps:

1. From the menu bar, go to Safari → Preferences (⌘-,)
2. Click on the General icon in the preference window's toolbar
3. In the pop-up menu next to "Save downloaded files to", select "Other..."; a sheet will slide out of the preference window's titlebar
4. Click on Desktop in the sheet's sidebar
5. Click on the New Folder button beneath the sidebar
6. In the window that appears, enter "Downloads" as the name of the new folder
7. Click on the Create button to create the *Downloads* folder on your Desktop
8. Click on the Select button to select the *Downloads* folder and close the sheet
9. Close Safari's preferences window with ⌘-W (or click on the red close window button)

Now the next time you save an attachment from .Mac's web-based Mail or download something from the Internet, the file will be saved in your *Downloads* folder.

Deleting Mail and Emptying the Trash

One thing that's slightly confusing is the role of the *Deleted Messages* and *Trash* folders. After selecting a message and clicking on the Delete button, that message gets moved to the *Deleted Messages* folder, which means that the message will still be around, taking up space. Only messages that are moved to the *Trash* folder will be deleted when you log out.

To clear out the messages sitting in the *Deleted Messages* folder, follow these steps:

1. Select Go To → Deleted Messages from Mail's toolbar.
2. Since you've already moved these messages to the *Deleted Messages* folder, you know you want to get rid of all of these. Click on the ✓ All column heading to place a checkmark next to all of the messages in the view, and then select Move Messages To → Trash from the toolbar (as shown in Figure 4-28).

    Repeat this step until all of the messages in your *Deleted Messages* folder have been moved to the *Trash* folder.
3. Click on the Show Folders icon in the toolbar; this will take you to the page shown in Figure 4-29, which lists all of your email folders.
4. To permanently delete the messages in the *Trash* folder from the .Mac mail servers, click on the Empty Now link next to the name of the *Trash* folder.

The page will refresh, and you should see that there are no messages sitting in your *Trash* folder. In addition, take a look at the Email Storage meter to see how much email space you just recovered.

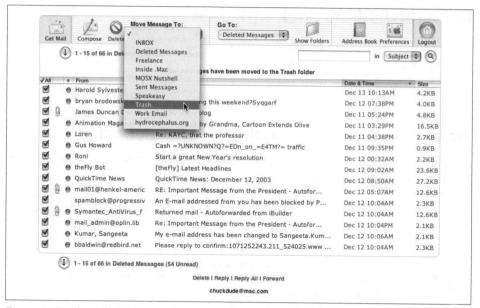

Figure 4-28. Select all of the messages you want to permanently delete, and then move them to the Trash folder.

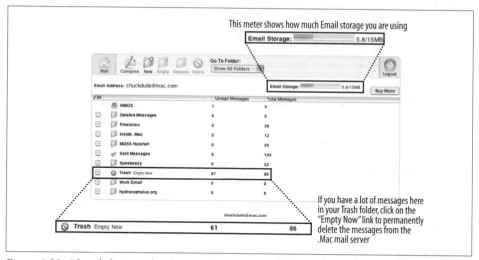

Figure 4-29. After clicking on the Show Folders icon, you'll see a listing of your email folders.

Of course, the one way around all of this is to click on the Preferences icon in the toolbar and uncheck the box next to "Move Deleted Messages To" in the Composing pane. Since you won't be moving deleted messages to any particular folder, they will be removed from the server as soon as you click on the Delete icon.

Using the Address Book with .Mac

If you use Mac OS X's Address Book application for storing and managing your contacts, you can make them available for use with .Mac's web-based Mail as well. All you need to do is use iSync to synchronize your Address Book data to your iDisk, which instantly makes your contacts available for use with Mail.

Syncing Your Mac's Address Book with Your .Mac Account

Of course, it isn't necessary to maintain an Address Book online, but it sure makes it easier when you're on the road and you can't remember someone's phone number or email address. If you have used iSync to synchronize data from your Mac to your iDisk (see Chapter 9), one thing you can do is pair up the contacts you have stored in the Address Book application on your Mac with the online Address Book.

 If you haven't already used iSync to synchronize data on your Mac with your iDisk, you might want to skip ahead to Chapter 9 to learn more about iSync, and then come back here.

Once your Address Book data has been synced to your iDisk, you'll need to flip the proverbial switch to make it all work seamlessly. To do this, log in to your .Mac account and follow these steps:

1. Click on the Address Book icon on the Mac.com site.

2. Log in using your .Mac member name and password.

3. Click on the Turn On Syncing button, as shown in Figure 4-30.

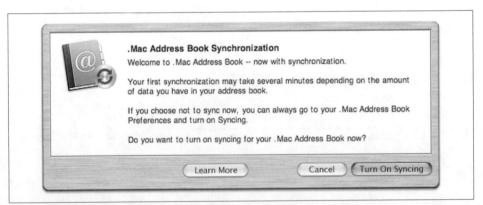

Figure 4-30. Before the Address Books can be synced, this message will be displayed.

As the message states, it could take a few minutes to create your online Address Book the first time you sync your Address Books. This is because the data stored on your iDisk (in */Library/Application Support/Sync/CONT*) needs to be pulled out and formatted as a viewable/usable contact list. As the information in your Address

Books sync, the message shown in Figure 4-31 is displayed. Apple even went as far as creating an animated GIF that has iSync's icon spinning around, just as it does in the Dock when iSync is in progress.

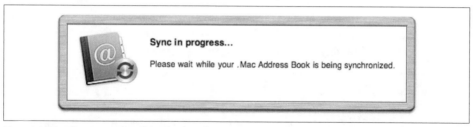

Figure 4-31. *This message will be displayed as the data stored on your iDisk gets formatted into an online Address Book.*

Once the synchronization process has completed, you can now use your Address Book contacts online with .Mac's web-based Mail.

Adding an Address to an Email

Once your Address Book contacts have been synchronized with the .Mac servers, you can pull addresses from your online Address Book rather quickly. The first step is to click on the Compose icon in the toolbar to bring up a blank message, as shown in Figure 4-32.

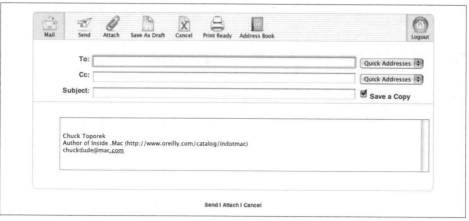

Figure 4-32. *A blank email message...your slate is clean.*

Now just follow these steps:

1. Click on the Address Book icon in the message's toolbar; this takes you to a page that shows all of your Address Book contacts in list form.

2. Depending on how many contacts you have in your Address Book, you may only have a page or two to look through to find the person for whom you're looking. One easy way to find a contact is to use the Search field. Type some information that you know will turn up a result, and then select an option from the pop-up menu. By default, this is set to All, but you can also search based on Name, Email, and Phone. Once you've set your search criteria (shown in Figure 4-33), click on the magnifying glass button to start your search.

Figure 4-33. Use the Address Book's Search field to quickly find the person you want to email.

3. After a quick search through your contacts, the results appear in a new page, as shown in Figure 4-34.

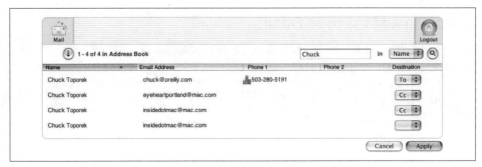

Figure 4-34. Use the search results page to select the right person to email.

On the right side of the search results page, you will see an empty pop-up menu for each contact entry. Use these pop-up menus to select the address line of the email on which you would like the person's email address to appear. Your options are To, Cc, Bcc, or blank. For example, if someone's address showed up in the search results and you didn't want to include them on the message, leave the pop-up menu blank.

4. Once you've selected where you would like their email address to appear on the message, click on the Apply button. This takes you back to the message you were composing, as shown in Figure 4-35.

5. Now all you need to do is type in your message and then click on the Send button.

If you look closely at how the multiple email addresses are listed in the Cc: line, you'll see that they take the form of:

```
FirstName LastName <email_address>, FirstName LastName <email_address>
```

Figure 4-35. With the addresses inserted, just type your message and send it on its way.

with the person's email address placed between angle brackets, followed by a comma and a space before the next address. Keep this in mind for times when you want to type this in manually.

Setting Up Quick Addresses

Wouldn't it be great if there were a way you could quickly pop in an address for someone you email frequently? Well, there is. If you look off to the right of the To: and Cc: lines when you go to Compose a new email message (see Figure 4-32), you'll see pop-up menus next to these fields that say Quick Addresses on them.

The Quick Addresses menus can contain up to 10 email addresses, which you can then use to quickly insert names and their associated email addresses in the To:, Cc:, and Bcc: fields.

To configure the Quick Addresses menus, follow these steps:

1. From the .Mac web page, click on the Address Book link.

2. Log in with your .Mac member name and password.

3. Locate the person (or persons) whose address you want to add to the Quick Addresses menu and select the checkbox to the right of their name in the Quick Addresses column, as shown in Figure 4-36.

4. Click on the Save button to place these folks into your Quick Addresses menus.

You cannot have separate Quick Address lists for the To:, Cc:, or Bcc: fields; the 10 people whose names you selected will appear in all of the Quick Address menus, as shown in Figure 4-37.

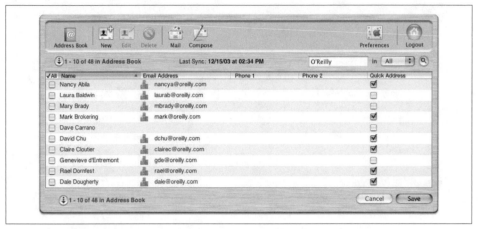

Figure 4-36. Select the names of the people you want to add to the Quick Addresses menu.

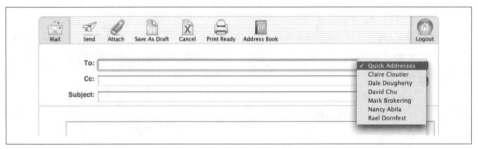

Figure 4-37. Use the Quick Addresses menu to insert names and email addresses into the To:, Cc:, and Bcc: fields.

To remove a name from your Quick Addresses menu, simply go back into your online Address Book, search for the name of the person, and then uncheck the box in the Quick Address column next to their name.

 If you have enabled Safari's auto-fill feature (Safari → Preferences → AutoFill), Safari will auto-complete an email address that you've previously entered, just like with Mac OS X's Mail application. This almost reduces your need to add names to the Quick Address menus, but they can be useful for people you email less frequently.

Creating a New Address Book Record Online

Even though you've synced your Address Book contacts to your iDisk, you can still add new contacts to your Address Book online. To create a new contact for your online Address Book, follow these steps:

1. From the Mac.com home page, click on the Address Book icon

2. Log in using your .Mac member name and password

3. In the toolbar, click on the New icon

4. Fill in the blanks that you have information for or want to include in the record

5. Click on the Save button to save the changes

Then, the next time you use iSync on your Mac, the new contact you've added will get merged with the contacts on your Mac.

PART II

Protecting Your Mac

As I mentioned earlier, my Mac is my life, and if something were to happen to it—be it a hard drive crash or a virus infestation, or something worse such as someone breaking in and walking off with my cherished PowerBook—there are some things I can do to protect it Mac and the data upon it. And right there with me are two key components of the .Mac service: Virex and Backup. These two little programs can be used to back up critical data and to detect and eliminate viruses from your Mac.

The chapters included in this part of the book include:

- Chapter 5, *Using Virex*
- Chapter 6, *Using Backup*

Using Virex

Viruses are the bane of the Internet. They typically get started by some punk who has nothing better to do with their time than to waste everybody else's. When a virus gets onto your system, they can create a living Hell for you, particularly if the virus is a worm that exploits your mailbox. Fortunately, Macs seem to be safe from most viruses, but every now and then, one will slip through, and when one does, you need to be prepared to deal with it.

.Mac members have access to Virex anti-virus software from McAfee Software. Once installed, you can use Virex to periodically scan your system for viruses; it can also be used to scan email attachments and as a command-line utility from the Terminal application (*/Applications/Utilities*).

 At the time of this writing, Virex hasn't been localized to support languages other than English and Japanese.

Finding and Installing Virex

If you purchased the boxed set for your .Mac membership, you can find a package for installing Virex on the CD. However, if you registered your .Mac membership online, you can download the Virex package from the Mac.com web site by clicking on the Virex shield icon on the .Mac site's sidebar.

The Virex Download page, shown in Figure 5-1, is where you can download the latest version of Virex and updates to the virus data files (described later).

The version of Virex we'll be working with in this chapter is Virex 7.2, which was released in February 2003. A fix, Virex 7.2.1, was released in April 2003, which corrected some problems that affected people who run the Fink package utility (*http://fink.sourceforge.net*). If you are still running Virex 7.1 or an earlier version, you should download and install Virex 7.2.1 from the Mac.com site.

If a newer version of Virex is available, you should download that version and check the book's web site (*http://homepage.mac.com/chuckdude/insidedotmac*) for an update of the information.

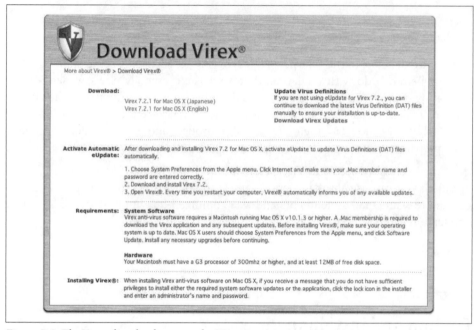

Figure 5-1. The Virex download page on the Mac.com site.

When Virex is installed (in */Applications/Virex 7*), the *.VirexLogin* process is added to your Startup Items preferences pane (System Preferences → Accounts → *yourAccount* → Startup Items). This process causes Virex to launch automatically when you start up and log in to your Mac.

When you log in, Virex launches automatically and checks the files in your *Home* directory for viruses. If you don't want Virex to perform this task when you log in, you can change this setting in Virex's preferences or by removing the *.VirexLogin* process from the Login Items panel.

What Is the .VirexLogin Process?

In case you're wondering, the *.VirexLogin* process is an application in itself. Since this process is an application, its real filename is *.VirexLogin.app*, and it can be found in the */Applications/Virex 7* directory along with the real Virex application. The reason you can't see it in the Finder is because its filename begins with a period, or *dot*, which is hidden from users by default.

Dot files can be anything from a regular text file that holds information used by other parts of the operating system (such as the *.Trash* file located in your home directory) or scripts or other low-level applications. To view the dot files in a directory, you can use the Terminal application and issue the *ls –la* command to list all of the files, including hidden dot files, within that directory.

Running Virex

The first time you run Virex 7.2, you will instantly be prompted to enter an administrator's password to invoke eUpdate, as shown in Figure 5-2.

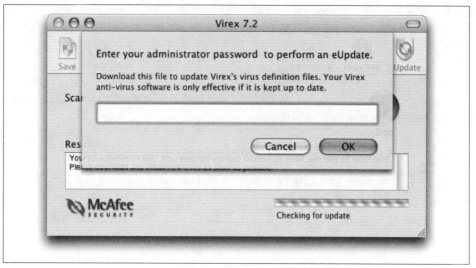

Figure 5-2. eUpdate helps to keep Virex 7.2's virus definition files up to date.

eUpdate is a small script that automatically looks for updates to Virex 7.2's virus definition files, or DAT files. If you enter your password and click OK, eUpdate looks in the */Software/.Updates/Anti-Virus Updates* directory on your iDisk and compares the DAT file Virex is currently running against any DAT files it finds on your iDisk. If the DAT file on your iDisk is more recent, the update will download and install on your Mac before Virex runs. When the eUpdate has downloaded, Virex 7.2's Results window will look similar to that shown in Figure 5-3.

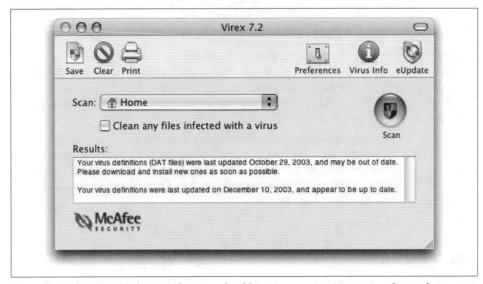

Figure 5-3. After downloading eUpdate, you should see a message in Virex's Results window saying that your virus definitions are up to date.

By default, Virex is configured to scan the files in your *Home* directory (*/Users/ username*), as shown in Figure 5-3. To scan for viruses, simply click on the Scan button and Virex will search through all of the files in your *Home* directory on its quest for infected files.

Another way to scan files is to drag one or more files (or folders) onto the Scan button from the Finder. If you drag a folder onto the Scan button, the contents of any folders within will also be scanned for viruses.

 One fairly standard Mac keyboard shortcut that isn't available in Virex is a Cancel command, typically ⌘-. (Command-period). If you've started to scan a file or directory and decide that you want to cancel that operation, you will need to click on the Stop button. However, if you are scanning files using the *vscanx* command-line utility (see the later section, "Virus Scanning from the Terminal"), either Control-C or ⌘-. can be used to cancel a scanning operation.

Preferences and Configuring Virex

To configure Virex's preferences, select Virex 7.2 → Preferences, and a sheet will slide down from the Virex window's titlebar, as shown in Figure 5-4.

The options available in Virex's preferences sheet include:

Scan
> The following options determine what to scan when Virex is used; by default, all three of these options are selected:

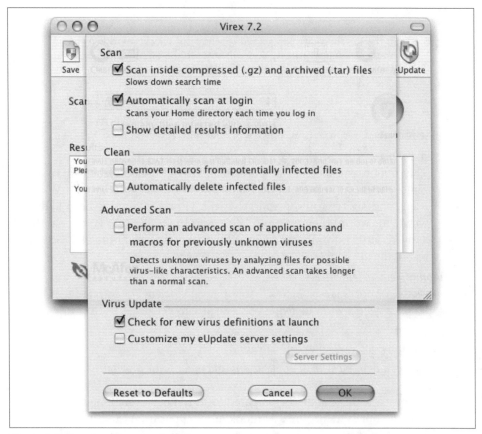

Figure 5-4. Virex's preferences sheet.

Scan inside compressed (.gz) and archived (.tar) files

> If you select this option, Virex will look inside compressed and archived files to see if something within contains a virus. While the option says that it will only look at *.gz* and *.tar* files, it will also search within other compressed files, including *.sit*, *.zip*, and *.hqx* files.

Automatically scan at login

> Selecting this option will force Virex to launch automatically and scan the files in your *Home* directory for viruses. Note that this scan could take a while, since Virex will look at every file and folder in your *Home* directory. You can run other applications and work on files while Virex performs this scan, but it's been my experience that this could slow things down a bit. Instead, you might want to login and let Virex run while you head off for a cup of coffee.

Show detailed results information

> This option will show detailed results in the Results view. As Virex scans through the files and directories on your system, its results will be displayed in this view.

Since it takes time for Virex to print (not literally) the results of its scan in the Results view, you should deselect this checkbox to help speed up the scanning process. You will still see the Summary report; you just won't be able to see all of the files scrolling by as they're being checked.

Clean

These options determine how Virex will deal with infected files:

Remove macros from potentially infected files

This option will look for any known macro viruses attached to a file and remove them from the file. Macro viruses are usually the crux of Windows users, and are typically spread via email. However, they've been known to wiggle (or worm) their way into Word and Excel files that land on a Mac. If a macro virus is found, the macro will be removed from the file, leaving the rest of the file intact.

Automatically delete infected files

As this option states, Virex will automatically delete any infected files it finds on your system without giving you a chance to decide on its disposition.

Advanced Scan

There is only one option in this category:

Perform an advanced scan of applications and macros for previously unknown viruses

If you select this option, be prepared for it to take a very long time for Virex to scan your system. Virex will look at all applications and files in the path you select from the Scan pull-down menu and analyze them for an unknown, or yet-to-be-discovered, virus. To do this, Virex looks for certain characteristics typically found in known viruses, and flags any file it finds that might contain a virus.

Virus Update

This section gives you options for deciding if and how Virex will check for updates to the virus definition files:

Check for new virus definitions at launch

This item, which is selected by default, will automatically check for updates to the virus definition files when you launch Virex. Selecting this option will help keep some of the guesswork out of when you should check for an update. Updates to the DAT files do come out monthly, but a special update could be released if a particularly nasty virus hits the street.

Customize my eUpdate server settings

Selecting this option enables the Server Settings button, which allows you to specify whether eUpdate will gather updates via HTTP or FTP. See the section, "eUpdate Server Settings," later in this chapter.

When you've finished selecting the preference options you would like Virex to use, click on the OK button, or click on Cancel to close the sheet and ignore any changes you have made. At any time, you can click on the Reset to Defaults button, which will check all three items in the Scan category and uncheck the remaining options.

Deciding what to scan

As mentioned earlier, Virex will scan your *Home* directory by default. However, if you want to change what and where Virex scans, click on the Scan pull-down menu, as shown in Figure 5-5.

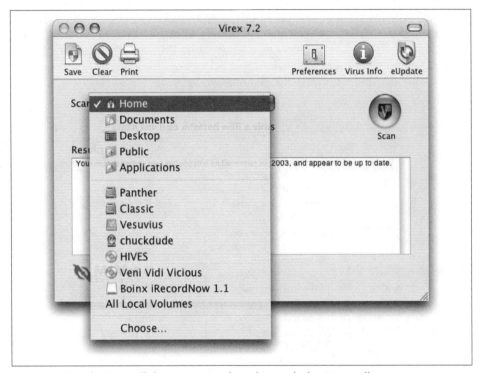

Figure 5-5. Use the Scan pull-down menu to select where and what Virex will scan.

Although they're not labeled as such, the Scan menu is divided into the following three sections:

Directories
> The top five items are directories that Virex assumes you will want to scan most often. These include the Home, Documents, Desktop, Public, and Applications directories. If you select Home from this menu, the items found in Documents, Desktop, and Public will be scanned since these are subdirectories within your *Home* directory.

Volumes

Virex will list any mounted volumes as possible sources to scan. A volume can include internal and external hard drives, network drives (including your iDisk or an SMB share), disk images, and CDs and DVDs. If you select the final option in this section, you can opt to scan "All Local Volumes," which scans the files on every volume mounted on your Mac.

Choose

The final option in the Scan menu is Choose. Selecting this option will open a window, similar to the Open window.

After selecting Choose from the pull-down menu, the "Select a file or folder to Scan" window pops up, as shown in Figure 5-6. This window is very similar to an Open dialog, in that you move around the view to select the folder or file you'd like to scan for viruses. Once you've found the item to be scanned, click once on its name and then click on the Select Location button. Virex scans the selected item and reports back its findings in the Results window.

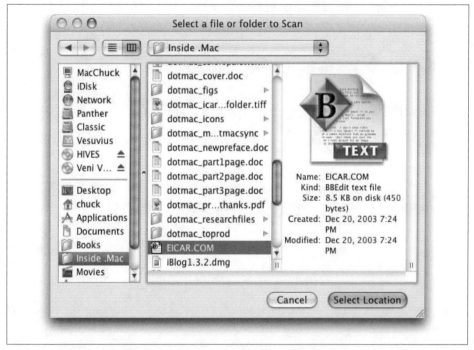

Figure 5-6. Virex's Scan pull-down menu offers a Choose option, which lets you select individual folders or files to scan for viruses.

Virex's Toolbar

One thing you may have noticed is that the Virex application window has a toolbar. If you Option-⌘-click on the toolbar button, the Customize Toolbar sheet shown in Figure 5-7 will be displayed.

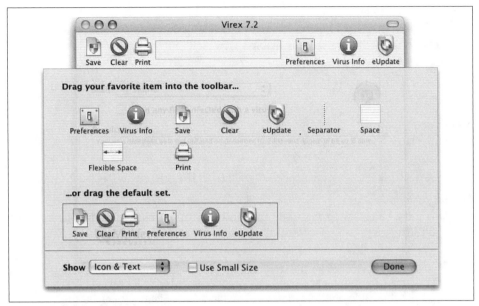

Figure 5-7. Virex's Customize Toolbar sheet.

The default items in Virex's toolbar include:

Save
Clicking this icon saves the information from the latest scan (shown in the Results window) to a rich text file with a *.rtfd* extension. This file can help you keep track of your scans or refer to infected files.

Clear
Clicking this icon clears the information in the Results window.

Print
Clicking this icon sends the information in the Results window to the printer.

Preferences
Clicking this icon opens Virex's Preferences sheet, shown in Figure 5-4.

Virus Info
Clicking this icon will take you to McAfee Software's Virus Information Library in your default web browser. This requires you to be connected to the Internet. Your default web browser will be launched automatically if it isn't running when you click on the Virus Info icon.

The Virus Information Library contains detailed information about the known viruses, including where they came from, which systems they will affect, how they infect your system, and how to remove them. If Virex detects a virus on your Mac, you will need to come here to find out more information about the virus it has found.

eUpdate

Clicking this icon will check for any available updates to Virex's virus definition files. If any updates are available, they will be downloaded and installed automatically.

In addition to the default items, there are three additional items you can select from that aren't in the toolbar:

Separator

This places a vertical bar between items.

Space

This places a space, equivalent to the width of the other icons, between items.

Flexible Space

This places a rather long space between items in the toolbar, although its name is deceiving.

> With a name like "Flexible Space," you would think that there would be a way to adjust the width of this space, but there isn't. Holding down the Shift, Option, or Command keys—and any combination thereof—offers no way for you to actually adjust the width of this space.

Testing Virex

After installing Virex, there is a simple test you can run to make sure that it's working properly; just follow these steps:

1. In the Virex 7 folder (installed in */Applications*), double-click on the *Update.rtf* file; this opens the file in TextEdit.

2. To find the section you need, select Edit → Find → Find (⌘-F); this opens a window from which you can search through the contents of the file.

3. In the Find field, enter "Testing Your Installation" (without the quotes), and click on the Next button twice. You should read through this entire section before going on to the next step.

4. Triple-click on the line, similar to the one shown below, and copy it to the pasteboard by selecting Edit → Copy (⌘-C):

   ```
   X50!P%@AP[4\PZX54(P^)7CC)7}$EICAR-STANDARD-ANTIVIRUS-TEST-FILE!$H+H*
   ```

5. With the line selected in TextEdit, go to the menu bar and select TextEdit → Services → TextEdit → New Window Containing Selection. When you select this option, the line you selected in the *Update.rtf* file gets copied to a new TextEdit file.

6. In the new file, select Format → Make Plain Text (Shift-⌘-T); this changes the format of the file from TextEdit's default format (Rich Text Format, *.rtf*) to plain text without any special formatting.

7. A sheet slides out of the window's titlebar with the note "Convert document to plain text?". Click OK to accept this change.

8. Select File → Save (⌘-S) to save the file.

9. In the "Save as" field, enter *EICAR.COM* as the filename. Be sure to remove the *.txt* extension from the file.

10. From the Where drop-down menu, select Desktop (⌘-D).

11. Click on the Save button.

12. Another warning note will pop up, saying "Save Plain Text: Document name EICAR.COM already seems to have an extension. Append '.txt' anyway?" Since Virex will look for a file named *EICAR.COM* when we run the test, we don't want the file to have a *.txt* extension; click on the Don't Append button to save the file.

13. Quit TextEdit (⌘-Q).

 It's important to note that the *EICAR.COM* file does not contain a virus, so you don't have to worry about it exploding and infecting files on your Mac. Instead, this file contains a string of characters similar to patterns found in some viruses. Virex searches through this file and flags it as one that's possibly infected. The name of the file is derived from the organization that helped to develop the test file, the European Institute for Computer Anti-Virus Research. For more information about EICAR or the test file, visit their web site at *http://www.eicar.com*.

Now we're ready to test our installation of Virex to make sure that it will detect an infected file. To complete the test of Virex, follow these steps:

1. Launch Virex (*/Applications/Virex* 7) by double-clicking on its icon in the Finder.

2. From the Scan drop-down menu, select Desktop.

3. Make sure that the box next to "Clean any files infected with a virus" has a checkmark in it.

4. Click on the Scan & Clean button.

Virex will scan through the files on your Desktop and check them against any known viruses using the virus definition (*.dat*) files on your system (*/usr/local/vscanx*). When Virex completes its scan, the results will look similar to that shown in Figure 5-8.

As you can see from Figure 5-8, Virex found the *EICAR.COM* file on the Desktop. The file was labeled as a "test file," and not a virus. However, because this is a virus test, the file was renamed as *EICAR.vOM*. By changing the file extension to *.vOM*, the file has been flagged as "Possibly Infected" in the "Summary report" section.

With the test complete, you can move the *EICAR.vOM* file into the Trash and delete it from your system.

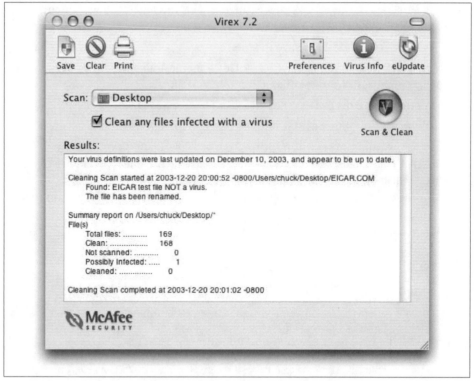

Figure 5-8. Look in Virex's Results window to see the outcome of your quest for infected files.

Virex's DAT files

As mentioned in the previous section, when Virex runs, it uses the *.dat* files found in */usr/local/vscanx* to check for viruses on your system. These data files are supplied and updated regularly by McAfee Software, and are made available to you by Apple on the Mac.com web site as a bundled package. The *.dat* files you'll find on your Mac include:

clean.dat
    This file contains the code used by Virex to clean an infected file.

license.dat
    This file contains the license information for the Virex software.

messages.dat
    This file contains the messages that Virex displays in its Results window.

names.dat
    This file contains the names of any known viruses.

scan.dat
    This file contains the data that Virex uses to scan for possible viruses, based on strings found in other viruses.

When you install an update for Virex, typically only the *clean.dat*, *names.dat*, and *scan.dat* files will change.

Tips for Using Virex

The following tips will help use Virex more effectively:

- Minimize the Virex window to speed up scans
- Reduce the number of folders you scan daily (scanning an entire drive or partition can take longer)
- Deselect the "Show detailed results information" checkbox in Virex's preferences
- Deselect the "Scan inside compressed (.gz) and archived (.tar) files" checkbox in Virex's preferences as this slows down the scan time
- If you use StuffIt Expander (*/Applications*) to uncompress archived files (*.zip*, *.sit*, *.hqx*, etc.), you can set StuffIt's preferences to have Virex automatically scan the files before it expands the archive

---

Dealing with Infected Files

If Virex discovers an infected file, you should take the following precautions:

- Do not attempt to open the file by double-clicking on it; doing so could launch the virus and then who knows what will happen.

- If someone you know sent you a file that contains a virus, you should call or email them and let them know that they sent you an infected file.

- If Virex tells you what sort of virus it is, relay this information to your network administrator or ISP to let them know you've received a file that contains a virus.

- If your Mac isn't in a network environment (i.e., not at work), you should move the infected file to the Trash and delete it as soon as possible. However, if your Mac is on a network, you should Zip or tar up the infected file and contact your network administrator immediately; they may want to look on at the file on a secure machine to see what sort of damage it could do.

 You can change Virex's preferences so that it automatically deletes infected files from your system; however, I wouldn't recommend doing this. Ultimately, you will want to delete that infected file from your Mac, but it's wise to keep it around if your ISP, or network or systems administrator wants to review the file. Once you get the all-clear from whoever it is you reported the infected file to, then you should delete the file.

eUpdate Server Settings

If you selected the "Customize my eUpdate server settings" checkbox in Virex's preferences (see Figure 5-4), the Server Settings button will be enabled. If you click on that button, the eUpdate Server Settings window, shown in Figure 5-9, will pop-up.

Figure 5-9. Virex's eUpdate Server Settings window.

From the eUpdate Server Settings window, you can select either HTTP or FTP from the Type pull-down menu.

eUpdate via HTTP

By default, Virex is configured to use HTTP and query Apple's servers to check for updates to Virex. Virex will use your .Mac member name and password for the Username and Password fields shown in Figure 5-9, so you won't have to fill in these blanks. The HTTP link that Virex will check by default is:

configuration.apple.com/configurations/internetservices/virex/1/virexdatinfo.txt

> To download a copy of the *virexdatinfo.txt* file, open the Terminal, switch to your Desktop, and enter the following command:
>
> ```
> curl -O http://configuration.apple.com/configurations/⏎
> internetservices/virex/1/virexdatinfo.txt
> ```
>
> The file will quickly download to your Desktop, after which you can view its contents with the command *more virexdatinfo.txt*.

This "link" is a simple text file used by Virex to look in a little-known directory on your iDisk to check for updates. The *virexdatinfo.txt* file uses your .Mac member

Proxy Problems?

If you're behind a proxy server and you're having troubles downloading updates to Virex or accessing any other .Mac services, you might want to download Authoxy from HRSoftWorks (*http://wpool.com/hrsw/Products.html*).

After downloading, follow these steps to install Authoxy:

1. Double-click on the *.dmg* file to mount the disk image on your Desktop.
2. Double-click on the Authoxy disk image to view its contents in the Finder (this is Finder window #1).
3. Double-click on the *ReadMe.rtf* file; this will open the file in TextEdit. Read through this file carefully and follow its directions.
4. Open a new Finder window (File → New Finder Window, or ⌘-N) and position the two Finder windows so you can see the contents of both windows (this is Finder window #2).
5. In Finder window #2, click on Home → Library → PreferencePanes.
6. Switch to Finder window #1 and drag the *Authoxy.prefPane* folder into the PreferencePanes view of Finder window #2. This will copy Authoxy onto your system and make it available in the System Preferences application.
7. Close both Finder windows.
8. Unmount the Authoxy disk image by clicking on the Desktop icon and dragging it to the Trash (or by pressing F12 or ⌘-E).
9. Launch the System Preferences from the Dock and look in the Other section for Authoxy. (If the System Preferences application is already running, you will need to quit and then restart it to see the Authoxy pane.)

Be sure to read the *ReadMe.rtf* file; it contains some important information about how to configure Authoxy on your system.

---

name to look for Virex updates on your iDisk in */Software/.Updates/Anti-Virus Updates*. The *.Updates* directory is hidden from view in the Finder. To view items in this directory, you must either use the Terminal application (*/Applications/Utilities*), or enable the Finder to view hidden items using TinkerTool (*http://www.bresink.de/osx/TinkerTool.html*) or by tweaking the *com.apple.finder.plist* file (*~/Library/Preferences*).

When a new update is available, Apple changes the name of the package in the *virexdatinfo.txt* file that will be downloaded and installed by Virex when it checks for an eUpdate. For example, the current Virex update (as of December 2003) is *V7031210.gz*, so the *virexdatinfo.txt* file will look similar to this:

idisk.mac.com/membername/Software/.Updates/Anti-Virus Updates/V7031210.gz

where *membername* is where your .Mac member name is inserted.

The filename for the Virex update, *V7031210.gz*, also reveals details about the update. The first part of the filename, *V7*, shows that this is an update for Virex Version 7. The second part of the filename, *031210*, is the date of the update in YYMMDD format (in this case, 2003 December 10). The file extension, *.gz*, simply means that the Virex update has been compressed using *gzip*.

eUpdate via FTP

The other Type option for the eUpdate Server Settings is FTP. When you select FTP from the Type pull-down menu, the window changes to that shown in Figure 5-10.

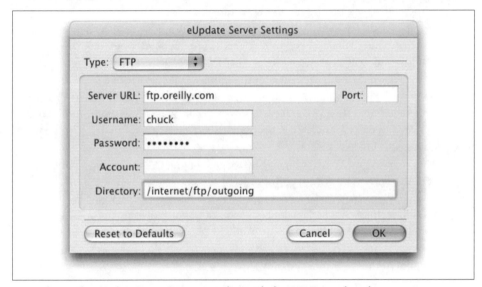

Figure 5-10. The eUpdate Server Settings window with the FTP Type selected.

 Theoretically, you should be able to use this panel to check for Virex updates hosted on another HTTP or FTP server. This can be particularly helpful if your Mac is behind a corporate firewall, or for system administrators who want to provide an easy way of maintaining users' systems. However, the version of Virex that comes with your .Mac membership doesn't allow you to connect to another HTTP or FTP server to check for updates. Instead, you're restricted to getting updates from the *.Updates* directory on your iDisk. At the time of this writing, this might just be a bug, so we're hoping it will be fixed in a future release.

Scanning Attachments in Mail

The easiest way for a virus to land on your computer is as a *Trojan horse*, typically in the way of an email attachment. By Trojan horse, we mean that the virus is introduced to your computer in what would otherwise be a harmless way. Some viruses are embedded as macros in Microsoft Office files since they're the easiest to exploit.

If a friend of yours forwards an email attachment to you, and you are unsure of its origin, you should *always* scan that file for a virus before opening or double-clicking it. With Virex installed on your Mac, however, this process can be really easy, particularly if you're using Mail.app.

To scan an attachment to an email message, hold down the Control key and click on the attachment to reveal the context menu shown in Figure 5-11.

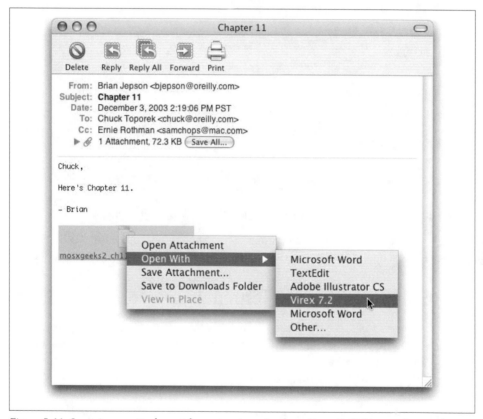

Figure 5-11. Scanning an attachment for a virus is as simple as Control-clicking on the attachment and selecting Virex from the Open With submenu.

After selecting Virex from the Open With submenu, Virex will launch and scan the file for any known viruses. After the file has been scanned, Virex will report its results back to you, as shown in Figure 5-12.

As you can see from the Results, this file is clean and okay to open. If Virex reports back and says that the attachment is infected, you should consider deleting the email

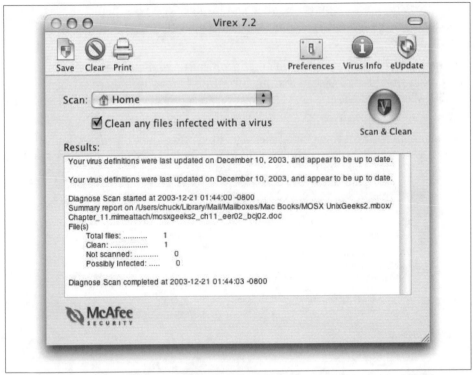

Figure 5-12. Once the attachment has been scanned, Virex will report back with its results.

message and its attachment immediately. The other thing you should do is send a message to its sender to let that person know that the file they sent to you is infected.

Virus Scanning from the Terminal

Believe it or not, Virex comes with a command-line utility that allows you to scan files for viruses from the Terminal application (*/Applications/Utilities*). Virex's utility, *vscanx*, can be found in */usr/local/vscanx* on your system. This program has the same functionality as Virex does, if not more.

Adding vscanx to the Command Path

Before you can use *vscanx*, there is one important step you need to take: adding *vscanx* to the Terminal's command path.

To do this, you will need to launch the Terminal application, which is located in */Applications/Utilities*, and follow along closely:

1. With the Terminal window open, enter the following command:

   ```
   $ ls .bash*
   ```

If you see a file named *.bash_profile* in the output, you can proceed to the next step, but know that you'll be editing an existing *.bash_profile* file instead of creating a new file. If you don't see this file, proceed to the next step to create one of your very own.

2. At the command prompt, enter the following and hit the Return key:

```
$ vi .bash_profile
```

This command creates the *.bash_profile* in your *Home* directory and opens the vi editor in the Terminal. We will use vi here to enter the contents of the *.bash_profile* file, which is used by the Terminal every time it launches.

3. Once in the file, hit the "i" key. This puts the vi editor into insert mode.

4. Type the following line:

```
export PATH=$PATH:/usr/local/vscanx
```

This command basically tells the bash shell which paths to search when it tries to invoke a command. In this case, we're telling the shell to use its default paths (as denoted by $PATH), and to then also search in /usr/local/vscanx for any commands that might reside there. The colon between them is used to tell the shell to use both entries.

5. Hit the Escape key, which is labeled "Esc", and is located at the upper-left corner of your keyboard. This takes the vi editor out of insert mode and places it in command mode.

6. Type in the following:

```
:wq
```

You will see these characters appear toward the bottom of the Terminal window. Each character of this command has a purpose:

- The colon (:) lets the vi editor know that you're going to issue a command.
- The w tells vi to write what you just typed to the file (in this case, to the *.bash_profile* file).
- The q tells vi to quit.

After you type in those three characters, hit the Return key to invoke them in succession. The vi editor will write the changes to the file and quit in one fell swoop, after which you are returned to the command line.

Okay, now you're ready to run *vscanx* from the command line without any problems. Had you not changed the command path, any time you tried to issue the *vscanx* command the Terminal would spit an error back at you saying that it couldn't find that command.

Virex's Command-line Cousin: vscanx

When you installed Virex on your Mac, it was placed in the Virex 7 folder in the *Applications* folder (*/Applications/Virex 7*). Within the Virex 7 folder, however, you will see a couple extra files in addition to Virex itself. One file of particular interest to you is the *Virex 7.2 Product Guide.pdf* file. This PDF document contains a detailed overview of how to use *vscanx* on the command line in the Terminal. You should take the time to read this file or *vscanx*'s manpage in the Terminal (*man vscanx*) to learn about all of its possible options.

The following is a simple listing of *vscanx*'s command syntax.

vscanx

Syntax

```
vscanx [options] [directory | file]
```

Description

Used to scan files and directories for possible viruses.

Options

The following options can be used with the *vscanx* command:

`--analyze, --analyse`
: Use a set of heuristics to check clean files for possible viruses.

`-c, --clean`
: Attempt to remove any viruses found from an infected file.

`--delete`
: Delete any infected files discovered during the scan.

`-h, --help`
: Display the help file for *vscanx*.

`-m <directory>, --move <directory>`
: Move any infected files to a specified *directory*. This option is useful for cordoning off infected files so you can analyze them later.

`-r, --recursive, --sub`
: Recursively scan through any subdirectories in the scan location. Note: if you attempt to recursively scan a directory with a lot of files, you could encounter a Segmentation Fault error. If you see this error message, try scanning the subdirectories individually.

`-s, --selected`
: Scan only executable files, such as *.bat*, *.com*, *.exe*, and more.

`--summary`
: Display a summary of the results, similar to what is shown in Virex's Results window if you uncheck the "Show detailed results information" checkbox in its Preferences.

-v, --verbose

   Display detailed information about the performed scan.

--version

   Display Virex's version number.

Again, these are only a few of *vscanx*'s options; please consult its manpage for a complete listing and detailed descriptions.

Examples

The following examples will show you various uses of *vscanx*:

Display a list of all of the viruses that Virex can detect:

```
$ vscanx --virus-list
Virus names stored in /usr/local/vscanx/extra.dat:
Virus names stored in /usr/local/vscanx/names.dat:
Aardvark,            ABCD,               ABCD.b,
Aircop,              Aircop.e,           Alar.mp,
Alcon,               Alfa.mp.3072,       Alive,
Alla.mp,             Altex.mp,           Amjads,
Ancev,               Andrew,             Andris,
Andropinis.mp.518,   Anticad.1,          Anticad.mp.4096,
Anticad.mp,          Anticmos,           Anticmos.e,
Anticmos.f,          Antiexe,            AntiWin95,
Exebug,              AP,                 APE.mp,
April,               Aragon,             Daboys,
...
```

Scan all of the files located in the Documents folder:

```
$ vscanx -r --summary ~/Documents

Summary report on /Users/chuck/Documents/*
File(s)
        Total files: ...........   5525
        Clean: ................    5525
        Not scanned: ..........       0
        Possibly Infected: .....      0
```

The output shows the location of the file in the filesystem, and gives you a report on the files found in the directory, similar to that found in the graphical Virex application.

Scan the files on my Desktop and place any infected files in a folder named infected:

```
$ vscanx --summary -m ~/infected ~/Desktop
/Users/chuck/Desktop/EICAR.COM
        Found: EICAR test file NOT a virus.
        File has been relocated.

Summary report on /Users/chuck/Desktop/*
File(s)
        Total files: ...........     15
        Clean: ................      14
        Not scanned: ..........       0
```

```
          Possibly Infected: .....      1
               Moved: ................      1
MacChuck:~ chuck$ cd infected
MacChuck:~/infected chuck$ ls
Users
MacChuck:~/infected chuck$ cd Users
MacChuck:~/infected/Users chuck$ ls
chuck
MacChuck:~/infected/Users chuck$ cd chuck
MacChuck:~/infected/Users/chuck chuck$ ls
Desktop
MacChuck:~/infected/Users/chuck chuck$ cd Desktop
MacChuck:~/infected/Users/chuck/Desktop chuck$ ls
EICAR.COM
```

In the case of this example, *vscanx* discovered the *EICAR.COM* test file on my Desktop and flagged it as a file that was possibly infected, and then moved the file to the *~/infected* directory. You can see that *vscanx* also recreated the path to the infected file within the *~/infected* directory, as noted by all the *ls* and *cd* commands issued. Eventually, the *EICAR.COM* file ended up in *~/infected/Users/ chuck/Desktop*.

If I had added the *–c* option to the previous command, the *EICAR. COM* file would have been renamed as *EICAR.vOM* and moved into the *~/infected* directory.

Running vscanx as a cron Job

By default, Virex runs only when you tell it to, which can be one of three ways:

- When you first log in and the *.VirexLogin* process runs, causing Virex to launch
- When you manually double-click on the Virex application
- When you run *vscanx* on the command line

These options don't help much if you want to regularly have your system checked for viruses every day on a system you rarely shut down. However, since *vscanx* is a command-line process, you can make it run whenever you'd like, with the help of *cron*. (If you're new to Unix, *cron* is a program that you can use to have commands run at specified times.)

For example, to schedule *vscanx* to run every day at 12:15 p.m., follow these steps:

1. Launch the Terminal application (*/Applications/Utilities*).
2. At the prompt, enter the following command:

   ```
   $ crontab -e
   ```

   This command opens your *crontab* file in edit mode (thus the *–e* option).

---

3. If you haven't edited your *crontab* file before, you will see an empty file in the Terminal window. Also, if you haven't changed your default editor, you will be using vi (as described earlier) to edit the *crontab* file.

4. Type the letter "i" (without the quotation marks) to place vi in Insert mode (you should see the word INSERT displayed at the bottom of the Terminal window).

5. Now type in the following line:

```
15 12 * * * /usr/local/vscanx -v -r -m ~/infected --summary > ~/Desktop/↵
vscanxreport.txt /Users/username
```

Make sure this is all on one line without any line breaks (meaning, don't hit Return to carry this over to another line). There's a lot going on in that line, so let's break it apart into smaller chunks to help you understand exactly what the command will do:

- The first part of the entry `15 12 * * *` tells *cron* what time and day to run the command. In this case, we haven't specified a day, only the time (15 minutes after the 12th hour, so 12:15 p.m.).

- Next, we tell *cron* to issue the *vscanx* command by giving *cron* its entire path: `/usr/local/vscanx`.

- Next, some options: `-v` for verbose output; `-r` to scan recursively through directories and subdirectories; `-m ~/infected` to tell *vscanx* to place any infected files into the *~/infected* directory; and, `--summary` to issue a summary report for the scan.

- The next part, `> ~/Desktop/vscanxreport.txt`, uses a redirect (the > symbol) and tells *vscanx* to take all of its output and summary, and save that to a file named *vscanxreport.txt* on the Desktop. That way, when *vscanx* completes its task, you can look for this file on your Desktop and see how the virus scan went.

6. After you have entered all of that command on one line, hit the Escape key (Esc) to take the vi editor out of Insert mode. (You should see the word INSERT disappear from the bottom of the Terminal window.)

7. Now save the changes to your *crontab* file by typing the command **:wq** and hitting the Return key. As described earlier, the colon (:) is used to place vi into Command mode, the w tells vi to write (or save) the file, and the q tells vi to quit.

8. After you hit the Return key, the changes are saved to your *crontab* file.

Now the next time 12:15 p.m. rolls around, *cron* invokes this entry from your *crontab* file and runs *vscanx* in the background, hopefully while you're out eating lunch. When you come back, you should see the *vscanxreport.txt* file on your Desktop, which you can read through at your leisure.

To learn more about *cron* and the *crontab* file, see their respective manpages (*man cron* and *man crontab*).

CHAPTER 6
Using Backup

One thing that many long-time Mac users have learned the hard way is that you need to back up your data. Whether you're archiving files that you plan to delete from your Mac to free up space, or backing up important files for a project you're working on, the last thing you want to have happen is for your data to suddenly not be there when you need it.

The Backup application that comes with your .Mac membership is a powerful little program that takes on the task of backing up files to your iDisk, to removable media such as CDs, DVDs, and also to external USB, FireWire, or networked drives, including your iPod. This chapter provides you with a thorough overview of the Backup application, including information on what you should back up.

This is the longest chapter you'll find in this book, and it is not without reason. Backups are very important, and you're encouraged to take them seriously. This chapter provides you with the information you need to conduct proper backups of your system, and to restore data when the need arises.

What to Back Up?

If you've never done a backup before, figuring out what you should back up is the first hurdle you'll need to overcome. There are two types of backups you can perform:

- A *complete backup*, which means that you backup *everything* on your hard drive, including the system software.
- A *partial* or *incremental backup*, which means that you will only backup certain files.

For example, long-time Mac users know the importance of keeping a backup floppy of your *Preferences* folder (*/System Folder/Preferences*). With earlier versions of the Mac OS, the greatest source of startup problems had to do with extension errors, which often traced their way back to a corrupt preference file. If you had a recent copy of your preferences, you could simply pop in your backup floppy, drag the *Preferences* folder onto your System Folder, and restart. Sure, you'd lose any preferences that were set since the last backup was made, but at least you could get into your system. If you backed up your *Preferences* folder once a week, the risk of you being locked out of your system reduced greatly. In that case, the act of dragging the *Preferences* folder onto a floppy disk would be considered a *partial backup*.

What you back up depends very much on how you use your system, and how important you determine its data to be. For me, my Mac is my life. If my hard drive were to crash and burn, or if my house were broken into and my Mac were stolen, my only recourse of getting my information back is having a complete backup. But I also do partial backups as well.

Confused? Don't be. This is a fairly standard practice.

Backing up your entire system can be time consuming, but it's worth it. For me, I typically do a complete backup once a week on Sunday, and partial backups nightly. The weekly backup saves everything on my hard drive to a set of CDs, while the nightlies save specific folders to an external FireWire drive connected to my Power-Book.* That way, if my system crashes midday on Wednesday, I can restore my system to the complete backup performed on the previous Sunday, and then restore files from Monday and Tuesday's nightly partial backup. Without the combination of complete and partial backups, who knows how much work I would have lost, and trying to remember what I've edited or written in a week is impossible, let alone the emails.

Backups—both complete and partial—are a way for you to protect yourself from partial or permanent loss of data. Take the time to consider what's important to you, and back it up accordingly.

At a minimum, some things you should consider backing up include:

Email

> Depending on how much mail you receive in a day, you may only need to back up your email on a weekly basis. However, if you receive a lot of email and it's a critical part of your daily communications, you should consider backing it up every day. If you are using Mac OS X's Mail application, your mail is stored in *~/Library/Mail*.

Preferences

> Old habits never die. Backing up your Preferences (*~/Library/Preferences*) can save you a lot of time from having to reset your application and system preferences if something goes amiss.

---

* I also back up files to my iDisk daily, but the backup to my iDisk is limited to just a few things, mainly for redundancy.

Home directory

Backing up your *Home* directory can simplify the task of selecting which files to back up. By selecting your *Home* directory to back up, you will catch everything in all of the directories you see in the Finder when you click on the Home icon. This includes the contents of the following folders:

- Desktop (only the files on your Desktop will be backed up, not the contents of any mounted drives)
- Documents
- Library
- Movies
- Music
- Pictures
- Public
- Sites

Mind you, if you have a lot of files, a complete backup of your *Home* folder can take a long time, and you probably won't be able to back up all of this onto your iDisk. However, if your Mac is equipped with a Combo or SuperDrive, you will be able to back up to CD or DVD instead, or to a networked or external drive that's mounted on your system.

These are just a few ideas of things you should consider backing up. One thing you don't need to back up, at least according to Apple, is all of the information on your iDisk. Apple makes nightly backups of all .Mac members' iDisks.

Where to Back Up?

Now that you have an idea of what you should back up and how often, the next question is to what location should you back up that data?

If you are using the Backup application, there are two options as to where you can back up your data:

- Your iDisk
- CDs or DVDs (depending on whether your Mac has a Combo or SuperDrive, respectively)
- USB and FireWire drives, including your iPod (which connects to your Mac via FireWire)
- Networked file shares such as a remote server or even to another Mac that has File Sharing enabled

Ah, decisions, decisions...but let's look at this in terms of data storage capacity, frequency of backups, and the cost factor involved.

Backup may not play well with some third-party CD/DVD burners. To see whether your device is supported, go to *http://www.apple.com/macosx/upgrade/storage.html*.

The Price of Backing Up

With a basic .Mac membership, you get 100 MB of storage space. This can be used for anything you desire—including for backups—but keep in mind that the files you use for your Mac.com HomePage (see Chapter 7) are stored on your iDisk in the *Sites* folder, QuickTime movies are stored in the *Movies* folder, and the photos you use to create slideshows with iPhoto are stored in the *Pictures* directory.

If your Mac has a Combo or SuperDrive, you can back up your data on CDs or DVDs, respectively. Depending on which you have, you can back up anywhere from 750 MB to 4.5 GB. CD-R's are fairly inexpensive these days, and they make a cheap solution for quick, throwaway backups. CD-RWs cost a bit more, but you can reuse the CDs a few hundred times before having to toss them. If you plan to use CD-RW discs for doing backups, you should probably pick up 20 or 30 of them so you can have one set of discs for each week. DVD-R's are probably twice the cost of CD-RWs, but they hold far much more data—up to 4.5 GB.

If you look at the cost per megabyte (CPM) for storage media and compare that with the cost of purchasing additional space for your iDisk (Table 6-1), you'll quickly see the cost savings.

Table 6-1. Cost per megabyte (CPM) for storage media

Media type	Maximum storage capacity	Retail cost	CPM
iDisk	100 MB	$100/year	$1.00
	200 MB	$160/year	$1.25
	300 MB	$200/year	$1.50
	500 MB	$280/year	$1.79
	1 GB	$450/year	$2.22
CD-R	700 MB	$0.40/disc	$0.00057
CD-RW	700 MB	$0.80/disc	$0.0011
DVD-R	4.5 GB	$2.00/disc	$0.00044

As you can see from Table 6-1, unless your Mac has a SuperDrive for burning DVDs, CD-R's are probably the most inexpensive way to go, particularly if you can find the discs on sale somewhere. You can typically find a 50-disc spindle of CD-R's for around $20 (or $0.40 each), while a 50-disc spindle of CD-RW's will run around $60 (or $0.80 each).* Since CD-RWs can be erased and written again many times, they're more cost-effective in the long run (and you'll have less waste going to the landfill every month, too).

So to What Location Do I Back Up?

Chances are that you will overshoot the 100 MB limit if you try to back up everything in your *Home* directory to your iDisk. Even if you upgrade your iDisk's capacity to 1 GB, you could be pushing it. So what should you do?

I actually use a three-step backup method:

- I backup the bare bones to my iDisk daily. By "bare bones," I mean that I'm mostly backing up my preferences, my Keychain file, and some of the default backup packages.
- Every night, I back up my *Documents* folder and my email from Mail.app to an external FireWire drive.
- Once a week, I back up my entire system to a set of CDs (if my PowerBook G4 had a SuperDrive, I would back up to DVDs).

While this might sound like overkill, you should never take your data for granted. Give some thought to your backups, and find the time to work them into your daily or weekly routines. The only backup that takes any amount of time from me is my weekly backup of the entire system; the others are scheduled to run in the middle of the night when I should be sleeping. While it might seem like you're wasting time that you could spend watching the latest reality TV show, you'll actually be doing yourself a favor. You never know when your system is going to crash hard, and when it does, you'll be thankful that you have a backup you can restore from.

Backup works best if the drive you are backing up to is formatted as HFS+ (Mac OS Extended). While I haven't had any problems backing up to my USB key fob or to my LaCie FireWire drive, you should check to see that the filesystem you're going to back up to is formatted properly.

To do this, launch Disk Utility (*/Applications/Utilities*), click on the name of the drive in question, and then click on the Info button. The third item down should be labeled "File System"; if it says either Mac OS Extended or Mac OS Extended (Journaled) next to it, you're good to go.

Now that we've discussed the why's and where's of backing up, it's time to get rolling with it.

---

* Disc spindles don't include jewel cases or sleeves for the CDs. If you want to store your CDs in jewel cases, you can purchase the writeable CDs with the jewel cases, but they might cost a little more.

Backup's Cans and Can'ts

Just when you thought you were getting somewhere, there are some things that you need to know about using Backup before you get too far:

- Backup 2 (the non-beta form) runs only on Mac OS X Panther. If you are still running Jaguar, you can download an older version of Backup from your iDisk; just look in */Software/Apple Software/Backup for OS X 10.2* and grab the highest 1.2.*x* version.

- If you just have a trial .Mac membership, you can only back up to your iDisk. As odd as it may seem, you won't be able to use Backup to back up *your* data to CDs, DVDs, or other types of external drives.

- If you are backing up to an external drive (including USB or FireWire drives, an iPod, or a networked file share), these items must be connected to or mounted on your system. Otherwise the backup won't perform as planned.

- If you are backing up to your iDisk, your Mac must be connected to the Internet, although your iDisk doesn't have to be mounted on your Mac.

- If you connect to the Internet with a dial-up modem (i.e., not with DSL or a cable modem), your Mac must be dialed in to your ISP to back up to your iDisk. To ensure that your Mac will be connected or that you don't lose your connection to your ISP, you should:

  1. Launch System Preferences and click on the Network preference panel

  2. Select Internal Modem from the Show pop-up menu

  3. Click on the PPP pane

  4. Click on the PPP Options button

  5. Check the box next to "Connect automatically when needed". This will ensure that your Mac will connect to your ISP to perform scheduled backups to your iDisk.

  6. Check the box next to "Prompt every 30 minutes to maintain connection". You'll notice that you can alter the number of minutes in this line as well; change this from 30 to 10 minutes. This option sends a signal to your ISP's server to let them know that you're still there and are prepared to do something.

  7. Leave the "Disconnect if idle for 10 minutes" line checked, but change the idle time to something like 20 or 30 minutes. That way, if Backup completes and you're still connected to the Internet, the modem will disconnect after a short while.

- Backup hasn't been localized to support languages other than English and Japanese. It is unclear whether future versions of Backup will support other languages. If you need another language, go to Backup → Provide Backup Feedback to send a message to Apple's developers with your language request. While it may not remedy your immediate situation, it lets Backup's development team know of your need.

- If you prefer to back up your applications, you probably won't be able to fit all of the *Applications* folder's contents on your iDisk. Instead, you should back them up to CD, DVD, or to a connected drive that has enough space. Remember, when you back up your *Applications* folder, you're also going to back up everything in the *Utilities* folder as well because it is a subfolder within the *Applications* folder.

- Backup only lets you schedule backups to your iDisk or to a connected drive, but not to CDs or DVDs. Part of the reason for this is that you (or someone else) would have to be sitting in front of your Mac to insert and remove discs as needed during the backup process.

- You cannot add the hard drive or partition (named "Macintosh HD" by default) that contains Mac OS X's System folder to the list of Backup Items. If you do try to do this, Backup just emits an alert sound to let you know that the action you requested isn't possible. This is very much unlike what would happen with Backup 1.2.1, which would freeze if you tried to add your hard drive to a backup list. The result was that you would have to force quit Backup. Instead, you will need to select all of the folders at the root level of the drive. Another option is to create an alias of your hard drive and add that to your backup list.

- If you're manually running a backup when a scheduled backup is set to run, the scheduled backup will fail to run as planned. The currently running backup continues without fail, and the scheduled backup will run the next time it is scheduled. For example, if you decide that you need to back something up to a Drive and the backup you've scheduled to run daily to your iDisk is triggered, the backup to your iDisk won't happen until the next day at the scheduled time. If you need to run the scheduled iDisk backup, you should manually run that as soon as the backup to the Drive completes.

For most users, Backup should be fine for taking care of your everyday backup needs. However, if you feel limited by Backup, there are other backup utilities you could explore, including:

- Carbon Copy Cloner (Bombich Software, *http://www.bombich.com/software/ccc.html*; freeware)

- PsyncX (Acorn Software, *http://psyncx.sourceforge.net*; freeware)

- Retrospect Desktop (Dantz Software, *http://www.dantz.com*; $129)

There are also Unix utilities that you can run from the Terminal's command line, or shell scripts you could write to batch up files and store them on a remote drive, but that is way beyond the scope of this book.

Finding and Installing Backup

As with many of the .Mac applications, how you install Backup depends greatly on how you purchased your .Mac membership. If you purchased the boxed set from a retail outlet, Backup should be on the CD. And if you purchased and registered your .Mac membership through the online Apple Store, Backup can be found on your iDisk in */Software/Apple Software/Backup for OS X 10.2*. You can also download Backup from the Mac.com site by clicking on the link for Backup and logging in.

To install Backup, follow these steps:

1. From either the CD or your iDisk, double-click on the *Backup_2.0.dmg* file. This mounts a disk image that contains the install package for Backup.

2. In the window that pops up, double-click on the *Backup.pkg* file; this is the package file that's used to install Backup.

> In addition to the *Backup.pkg* file, you will also see a file named "Read Before You Install Backup" in the disk image. You should take the time to read this file (double-clicking its icon opens the file in TextEdit) because it contains information you should know about before installing or upgrading your current version of Backup.

3. The first screen of the installer prompts you to enter an administrator's password before the installation can proceed. In most cases, providing the password you use to log in to your Mac should work. Enter your password in the space provided and click on the OK button.

4. Read through the next two screens of the installer, clicking the Continue button to proceed after you've read the information.

5. Read through the Software License Agreement. If you agree to its terms and conditions, click on the Continue button. When you do this, a sheet will slide down from the Install Backup Software window's titlebar. If you agree to the terms of the license, click on the Agree button to proceed with the installation process.

> If you don't agree with the terms of the license, click on the Disagree button. You cannot proceed with installing Backup on your system if you don't agree to the license. However, the Installer application won't quit by itself. Instead, you will need to quit the Installer manually by issuing the universal quit command, ⌘-Q.

6. Select the destination (drive or partition) where you would like Backup installed, and then click on the Install button. By default, Backup is installed in the *Applications* directory.

7. Backup will install and your system will be optimized. When complete, you will see a message above the progress meter that says: "The software was successfully installed". To quit the Installer and return to using your Mac, click on the Close button.

8. Close the window that contains the *Backup.pkg* file.

9. Unmount the Backup 2.0 disk image by dragging it to the Trash, or by clicking on the Unmount icon next to the image in the Finder's Sidebar.

10. Delete the *Backup_2.0.dmg* file (if you downloaded it to your Mac) by dragging the file to the Trash or selecting File → Move to Trash (⌘-Delete) from the Finder's menu.

Now that Backup is installed on your Mac, you're about ready to start using it. But first, you should consider what you need to back up and how often you should perform the process.

Using Backup

Backup is installed on your Mac in the *Applications* folder (*/Applications*), and can be launched by double-clicking its icon in the Finder. Since you will be using Backup frequently, you should consider adding its icon to the Dock. To do so while Backup is running, Control-click on Backup's Dock icon and select Keep In Dock from the contextual menu that appears.

As Backup starts, it performs a check of your iDisk to look for a Backup that might be stored there. If no previous backups are found, a *Backup* directory is created on your iDisk to where backup data can be stored. In addition to the *Backup* directory, a dot file (*._Backup*) is also created at the root level of your iDisk.

 One common problem I've encountered with backing up my Preferences (*~/Library/Preferences*) is that most items with Installer in their names cause the backup to fail. Fortunately, you can choose which items to back up using the QuickPicks. My solution is to simply uncheck the troublesome Installer files, and then the Backup goes smoothly.

Backup's interface (shown in Figure 6-1) is defined as follows (the items in the following list refers to the callouts in Figure 6-1):

1. This area, known as the Backup List, lists the default "packages" to be backed up, as well as any items you add to the list. Items in this list have a checkbox next to them to denote whether they will be backed up. The checkbox can have one of three states: checked, unchecked, or, with some packages and folders, a minus sign. If the checkbox has a minus sign in it, that means the selected package or folder has items within that you can opt not to back up in the QuickPicks drawer.

2. The Backup/Restore pull-down menu lets you select to which location the items in the Backup List will be backed to or from where they will be restored. The options in this menu include:

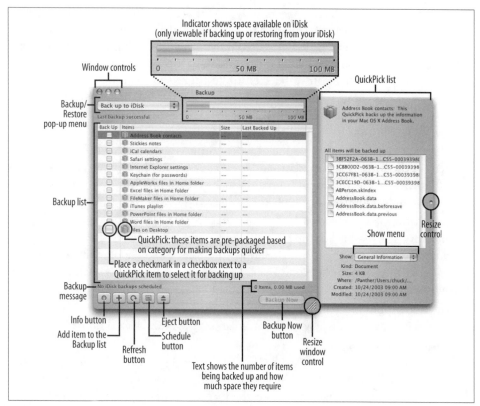

Figure 6-1. An overview of Backup's interface.

Back up to iDisk

When you select this item, the iDisk Storage Meter (discussed next) appears next to the pop-up menu.

Backup to CD

When you select this item, you won't see anything like the iDisk Storage Meter, but you will see a text message appear above the row of buttons at the bottom left of Backup's window. This message will tell you how many CDs or DVDs are required to perform your backup.

Back up to Drive

With this item selected, a Set button appears next to the menu. Clicking on this button opens a sheet from which you can select a drive (USB, FireWire, networked file share, iPod, etc.) that's connected to your Mac. This is the drive to where your backup will be made.

Restore from iDisk
Restore from CD/DVD
Restore from Drive

Depending on where the backup data is that you need to restore or recover, select the appropriate menu item and pick the item(s) you need to restore.

3. The iDisk Storage Meter appears only if you are backing up to your iDisk; it won't appear if you are backing up to disc media. The meter is there to help you gauge how much data is already stored on your iDisk (dark green), and provides indicators to let you know how much additional space a backup will take (light green) or when what you've selected to be backed up will push you over your iDisk's storage limit (red). If you see red in the iDisk Storage Meter, you will need to either purchase additional iDisk space to perform the backup or use the QuickPicks drawer to trim down your selection.

4. The QuickPicks drawer is hidden by default; it is only revealed if you select an item in the list of backup items and then click on the Info button at the lower-left corner of the window. You can also use the Show Info keyboard shortcut (⌘-I) to hide and reveal the QuickPicks drawer.

5. The list in the QuickPicks drawer tells you which files in a selected package or directory will be backed up. Some items in the QuickPicks drawer may have checkboxes next to them, which allows you to pick and choose which items will be backed up. See the section "Using QuickPicks" later in this chapter for more information about selecting items from the list.

6. The Show pull-down menu has two options: General Information and Backup Information, which display information about the files selected for backup.

   General Information
   With this menu item selected, the QuickPicks drawer will tell you some basic information about the files that will be backed up, including its kind, size, where the file is saved on the local filesystem, and when the file was created and when it was last modified.

   Backup Information
   With this menu item selected, you will see when the file was last backed up (if ever), where it will be backed up to on your iDisk, and it's status, which will either read as "Unchanged since last backup" or "Will be backed up". If an item is "Unchanged since last backup", that file will not be backed up the next time around, which saves time during the backup process.

7. The Backup Now button should only be pressed when you are ready to start the backup process.

8. This text tells you how many items have been selected for backup and how much space they require.

9. The Eject button is used for ejecting disc media from your Mac.

10. The Schedule button is used for automating backups. See the section "Scheduling Backups" later in this chapter for details on how you can use Backup's scheduling feature to automate your backups.

11. When clicked, the Refresh button updates the items in the backup list and the status bar.

12. The Add items button is used for adding files and folders to your backup list.

13. With an item selected in the backup list, clicking the Info button will open the QuickPicks drawer to reveal additional information about the file, or list the items in the package or folder.

   If you are backing up to your iDisk, this text lets you know when regular backups are scheduled. If you are backing up to disc media, this text lets you know how many CDs or DVDs are required to perform the backup.

Now that you have a basic understanding of Backup's interface and how to use its controls, let's dive in and learn how to use the QuickPicks drawer and perform some backups.

Backup's Keyboard Shortcuts

As with most Mac applications, Backup is not without it's own set of keyboard shortcuts. A menu-by-menu overview of the commands and keyboard shortcuts available for Backup are listed in Appendix A.

Backup is unlike most traditional Mac applications, in that its menu names don't seem to fit their purpose, and some of the options (like Cut, Copy, and Paste) don't even have a purpose. Some other oddities of Backup, in regard to keyboard shortcuts and menus, include:

- You can only have one Backup window open; there is no File → New Backup Window (⌘-N) option, and thus, no other windows to bring to the front via Window → Bring All to Front.

- If you select the Close Window option or use its keyboard shortcut (⌘-W), Backup quits.

- The standard Mac Find keyboard shortcut, ⌘-F, does not work. Instead, you have to use File → Find to open a Find dialog.

- Although the menu item for Backup Help shows that you can use ⌘-? to open Backup's Help window, the keyboard shortcut doesn't work. If you need Backup's Help system, you will have to select the menu item itself.

- If you select Edit → Special Characters, the Character Palette will open. If you want to close the Character Palette, you *must* to click on its close window button; if you think you can use ⌘-W to close the Character Palette, think again. Instead of closing the Character Palette, it closes and quits Backup and the palette's still there.

- There is no keyboard shortcut for adding items to the backup list.

 It's obvious that Backup 2 still needs some work; in many cases, Backup 1's interface was much more usable. In fact, with the earlier version of Backup, you didn't need to use any of the menus because the toolbar (which is missing from Backup 2) had everything you needed to get the job done.

Working with the Backup List

In looking at the list of possible items to back up, you'll notice that there's a little package icon next to the list in the Items column. The package icon, which resembles a box wrapped in brown paper, means that Apple has conveniently gathered all of the files for that particular item and packaged them together so they can be quickly backed up. This ensures that, when you select the checkbox next to that item, you won't miss something important. If a critical file is missing, you may not be able to restore the data from a previous backup.

Depending on where your backups will be saved to (iDisk, CDs, or DVDs), the list of packages can vary. Table 6-2 lists the default QuickPick packages for backing up to your iDisk, and Table 6-3 lists the default QuickPick packages for backing up to CD, DVD, or to a drive. While you can always view a package's contents in the Quick-Pick list, not all of them let you select and deselect individual items. The right-hand column of Tables 6-2 and 6-3 indicate whether you can select or deselect items in a package.

Table 6-2. Packages available for backing up to an iDisk

Package name	Select/deselect items in the QuickPick list?
Address Book contacts	No
Stickies notes	No
iCal calendars	No
Safari settings	No
Internet Explorer settings	No
Keychain (for passwords)	No
AppleWorks files in *Home* folder	Yes
Excel files in *Home* folder	Yes
FileMaker files in *Home* folder	Yes
iTunes playlist	Yes
PowerPoint files in *Home* folder	Yes
Word files in *Home* folder	Yes
Files on Desktop	Yes

Table 6-3. Packages available for backing up to CD, DVD, or to a Drive

Package name	Select/deselect items in the QuickPick list?
Address Book contacts	No
Stickies notes	No
iCal calendars	No
Safari settings	No
Internet Explorer settings	No

Table 6-3. Packages available for backing up to CD, DVD, or to a Drive (continued)

Package name	Select/deselect items in the QuickPick list?
Keychain (for passwords)	No
Preference files for applications	No
AppleWorks files in *Home* folder	Yes
Excel files in *Home* folder	Yes
FileMaker files in *Home* folder	Yes
iPhoto library	No
iTunes library	Yes
iTunes purchased music	Yes
Mail messages and settings	No
PowerPoint files in *Home* folder	Yes
Word files in *Home* folder	Yes
Files on Desktop	Yes

In looking at Tables 6-2 and 6-3, you'll notice a difference in the two iTunes packages. When backing up to your iDisk, the package contains only information found in your iTunes playlists (song titles, etc.), while the package for backing up to CD, DVD, or a Drive lets you backup the actual audio files. Also, there is no option for backing up the preference files for your applications to your iDisk. However, that doesn't mean you can't add it to the list of items; for that, see the next section. As with selecting the iTunes library, if you select the iPhoto library package when backing up to CD, DVD, or a Drive, this option backs up all of the image and data files stored in your iPhoto library.

One thing to keep in mind is that if you delete any of the QuickPick packages from the backup Items list, you can get them back by selecting Edit → Restore All QuickPicks.

Adding and removing items to the backup list

The default list of packages provided by Backup are nice, but what can you do if there's something else you'd like to back up? Are you locked out from backing up anything else? Fortunately, the answer to that question is no, you're not restricted to backing up just the QuickPick packages. You can add additional files or folders to your backup list by either:

- Clicking on the button with the plus sign (+) on it at the bottom of the window and selecting items from a Finder-like interface.
- Dragging-and-dropping items, including files, folders, and mounted drives (either from the Finder or the Desktop), to Backup's window.

For example, if you want to back up the preference files for the applications on your system to your iDisk, there isn't a package available by default. However, if you want to add it to the list, follow these steps:

1. Click on the Add Items button (the one with the plus sign), located at the bottom of Backup's window. A sheet will slide out Backup's titlebar, as shown in Figure 6-2.

Figure 6-2. The selector sheet, which looks similar to an Open dialog, lets you choose files, folders, and even mounted hard disks to add to the Backup Items list.

2. In the dialog that opens, select Library from the right column as shown in Figure 6-3.

3. After the dialog expands to the right, scroll down in the right column and select Preferences, as shown in Figure 6-4.

4. With the *Preferences* folder selected in the left column, you can see all of its contents to the right. Click on the Choose button to add the *Preferences* folder to your list of Backup Items, shown in Figure 6-5.

Figure 6-3. Select the Library folder in the panel.

When you add something to the Backup Items list, its checkbox is automatically checked. After adding the item to the list, Backup calculates the size of item and places that information in the Size column.

If you look at the green indicator bar, just above the list of items, you can see how much space is already taken up on your iDisk (indicated in dark green), how much space is needed for the item you've just added (indicated in light green), and how much space is available (indicated in white). If the item you've added takes up more space than what is available on your iDisk, the remainder of the bar will turn red. If you still want to back up that item to your iDisk, you will either need to purchase additional iDisk space or use the QuickPick list to deselect a few items until you're back in the green.

Once you've added a folder or drive to the backup list, you can use the QuickPick list to pick and choose which items within you'd like to back up. Figure 6-6 shows the QuickPick list for the *Preferences* folder I added to the backup list earlier. If there was something in that list that I didn't want to back up, all I have to do is click on the checkmark next to the items, which deselects them from the backup.

Figure 6-4. Now select the Preferences folder in the left column; all of the preference files show up in the right column.

If you have trouble backing up your *Preferences* folder (*~/Library/Preferences*), look for items that have "install" in the name and deselect them. These items are preferences for the installer that was used when you installed an application. Sometimes, these preference files will cause your backups to fail. Deselect these items and try the backup again. If it goes okay, then you know where the problem lies. Also, since the preference files for the installers are only used when you installed that application, they aren't needed anymore. If you want (and you should), you can delete these files from your system by going to the *~/Library/Preferences* folder in the Finder and dragging any files with "install" in their name to the Trash.

Finding and adding items to the backup list

Say you want to back up all of the files you've created or edited today. Backup really doesn't provide an easy way for you to do something like this, but it can be done. If you select File → Find, a Finder search window (shown in Figure 6-7) pops open.

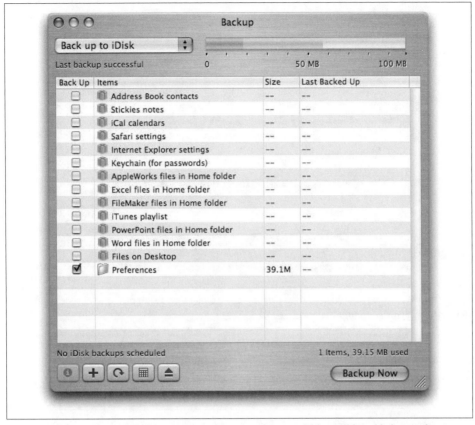

Figure 6-5. After clicking the Choose button, your Preferences folder will be added to Backup's Items list.

 At the time of this writing, you cannot use the standard keyboard shortcut ⌘-F to open the Find dialog. For some reason, Apple forgot to set this shortcut before they released Backup 2.

Using this window, you can select where the Finder will search by selecting an item in the "Search in" pop-up menu. The options you have to choose from are:

Everywhere

With this option selected, the Finder searches on any disk that's mounted on your Mac, including your iDisk and other networked drives.

Local disks

With this option selected, the Finder searches disks mounted on your Mac, including your Mac's hard drive and any external FireWire or USB drives.

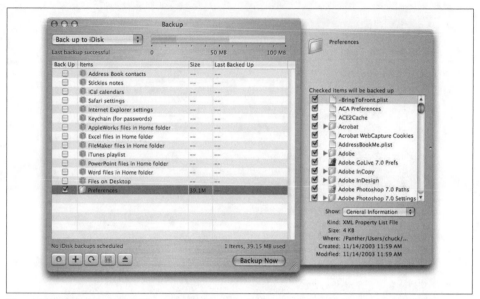

Figure 6-6. After adding a folder or hard drive, use the QuickPick list to pick and choose the items you want or need to back up.

Figure 6-7. When you need to search for files to back up, select Find from the File menu to open a Find window in the Finder.

Home

   With this option selected, the Finder searches only for items in your *Home* folder.

Specific places

   If you select this option, the Find window changes slightly, allowing you to select specific folders or drives mounted on your Mac.

Once you've selected where the Finder will search, you need to specify what the Finder will search for in the lower portion of the window, which is labeled "Search for items whose:". At first, you'll see just one line, as shown earlier in Figure 6-7. To refine your search, start out by selecting what you want the Finder to search for by clicking on the first pop-up menu. This menu has the following options:

Name

   This option includes a pop-up menu that lets you select up to three of four possible options to search upon, including *contains*, *starts with*, *ends with*, and *is*. Next to the pop-up menu is a text field in which you can enter information about the filename.

   Clicking on the plus button (+) to the right of the text field expands the search so you can select other options from the pop-up menu. For example, Figure 6-8 shows a search that would look for filenames that contain and/or start with *dotmac* and have a file extension of *.doc*.

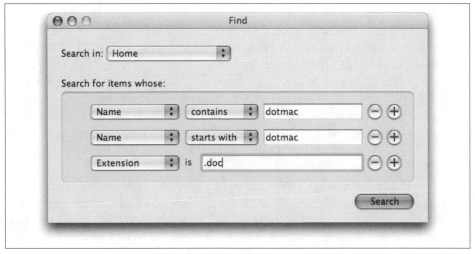

Figure 6-8. Searching for files based on information contained in their filename.

Content

   Searching by content allows you to do context-based searches for files to add to your backup. For example, if you want to back up all of the files that have the word "hydrocephalus" in them, just enter that word in the text field and click on the Search button. Any files that contain that word in its contents will be listed in the Search Results window.

Date Modified

   This allows you to search for files that were modified within a specific day or date range.

Date Created

   This option lets you search for files that were created on a specific day or date range.

Kind

> This option lets you search for specific file types, including *alias*, *application*, *folder*, *document*, *audio*, *image*, or *movie*.

Label

> Labels are new to Mac OS X's Panther release, but many Mac OS 9 users are familiar with them. You can use labels to flag files, folders, etc., with a colored label, so by searching for a specific label color, you can quickly find, for example, anything you've labeled as "Red."

Size

> This option lets you search for files that are less than or greater than a specific file size. The file size you specify must be in kilobytes (KB). So, if you want to search for files that are less than 1 MB in size, you should enter 1000 in the search field.

Extension

> This lets you search on a specific file extension. When entering an extension in the search field, you do not need to enter a period before the extension; for example, to search for Word files, use *doc* instead of *.doc*. To search for multiple file types, place a comma between the extensions. For example, to search for all HTML files, you might want to search for files with an extension of *html* and *htm*. In this case, you need only to search on *htm*, because that will pick up all HTML files with an *html* and *htm* extension. Unlike the other options, there is only one text field provided when conducting searches based on a file's extension.

Visibility

> When this option is selected, you can opt to have your searches look for files and folders whose names begin with a period (otherwise known as *dot files*). Typically, dot files are hidden from view in the Finder, however, this is the one time that an extension of the Finder will let you search for a hidden file.

Type

> Every file on your Mac has a specific file type. The Type code is a four-character code that gets assigned to a file when it is created, which is used by the filesystem to denote what type of file it is. Type codes are exactly four characters in length, and are case sensitive. Table 6-4 lists some common Type codes. In this table, an underscore (_) means that you should insert a space where a character should be (remember, Type codes have to be exactly four characters).

Table 6-4. Common Type codes to be used when searching for files

File extension	Type of file	Type code
.pdf	PDF file	PDF_
.doc	Word document	W8BN
.xls	Excel document	XLS8
.psd	Photoshop file	8BPS

Table 6-4. Common Type codes to be used when searching for files (continued)

File extension	Type of file	Type code
.dmg	Disk image	devi
.txt, .html, .htm, .rtf, .rtfd	Raw text, HTML, and Rich Text files	TEXT
.tiff	TIFF image file	TIFF
.jpeg, .jpg	JPEG image file	JPEG
.gif	GIF image file	GIFf
.avi	Video file	VfW_
.mov	QuickTime movie	MooV
.mp4	MPEG 4 movie	mpg4
.aif	AIFF audio	AIFF
.m4p	Audio files purchased through iTunes Music Store	M4P_

Creator

Creator codes are similar to Type codes, except that they denote the application that was used to create a particular type of file. Type codes and Creator codes are different. Their only similarity is that Creator codes are exactly four characters in length and they are case sensitive. Table 6-5 lists some common Creator codes you can use when searching for files to add to your backup list.

Table 6-5. Common file Creator codes

Application or file type	Creator code
Preview	prvw
Adobe Acrobat	CARO
Microsoft Word	MSWD
Microsoft Excel	XCEL
Adobe Photoshop	8BIM
Disk Image	ddsk
Text files (including files saved as RTF)	R*ch
QuickTime movies and .avi files	TVOD
.mp4 files	TVOD
.aif audio files	stlu
.m4p audio files purchased through iTunes Music Store	hook

If you're not sure what a file's Type or Creator code is, you can use the *GetFileInfo* command-line utility that gets installed with the Xcode Tools. If you have installed the Xcode Tools, *GetFileInfo* can be found in */Developer/Tools*. For example, to use *GetFileInfo* on a TIFF file in your *Pictures* folder, follow the steps shown next.

1. Launch the Terminal application (found in */Applications/Utilities*).

2. Change directories to */Developer/Tools* with the following command:

   ```
   $ cd /Developer/Tools
   ```

3. Now issue the command as follows:

   ```
   $ ./GetFileInfo ~/Pictures/poweron.tif
   file: "/Users/chuck/Pictures/poweron.tif"
   type: "TIFF"
   creator: "8BIM"
   attributes: avbstClinmed
   created: 11/03/2003 15:11:16
   modified: 11/03/2003 15:23:43
   ```

 If you haven't installed the Xcode Tools, you can do so by inserting the Xcode Tools CD that came with Panther (or your system) and double-click on the *developer.mpkg* file within.

While you might think of the Xcode Tools as being something that only programmers and geeks might need, some of the utilities are actually quite useful for everyday Mac users.

If you look at the command issued, *./GetFileInfo ~/Pictures/poweron.tif*, you'll see that it contains two parts, separated by a space. The first part, *./GetFileInfo*, tells the Terminal that you want to issue the *GetFileInfo* command. The *./* (or dot-slash, in Unix terms) tells the shell to issue the command that follows (in this case, *GetFileInfo*). The second part, *~/Pictures/poweron.tif*, tells *GetFileInfo* to look for the *poweron.tif* file in your *Pictures* folder. If the file is found, which it was in this case, the command's results are returned to the Terminal window.

In looking at the results for the command, you can see that the file Type has been saved in the Tagged Image File Format (better-known as a TIFF). On the next line, you can see that it's Creator code is 8BIM, which, in looking back at Table 6-5, is the Creator code for Adobe Photoshop.

Using QuickPicks

If you select a QuickPick package in the Items column and click on the Info button (the one with the little "i" at the lower-left corner of Backup's window), a drawer slides out of the side of Backup's window, showing you all of the files that will be backed up as part of that package. For example, click on the Address Book contacts item, click on the Info button, and you'll see something similar to Figure 6-9.

 You can also reveal and hide the QuickPick list by selecting an item and using the keyboard shortcut ⌘-I (or File → Show/Hide Info).

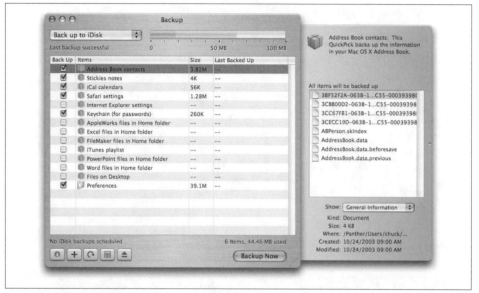

Figure 6-9. The QuickPick drawer, shown for the Address Book contacts item.

When the QuickPick drawer is open, the area around the "i" in the Info button turns blue.

Relocating and resizing the QuickPick drawer

Depending on where the main Backup window is located, the QuickPick drawer will pop out of the right side of the window when you click on the Info button, as shown in Figure 6-9. However, if the right edge of Backup's window is too close to the right edge of your display, the QuickPick drawer opens on the left side, as shown in Figure 6-10.

To make the QuickPick drawer open on the righthand side again, drag the Backup window so that the drawer is off the display, and then click twice on the Info button to close the drawer and reopen it on the other side.

By default, the QuickPick drawer opens only so far, but what if that isn't wide enough? What if you can't read an entire filename or the details about a file displayed at the bottom of the drawer? If you move the mouse to the far-right (or left) edge of the drawer, click and drag the mouse further in that direction. Doing so will extend the width of the drawer, but as with most things in life, there are limitations. An example of a fully extended QuickPick drawer is shown in Figure 6-11.

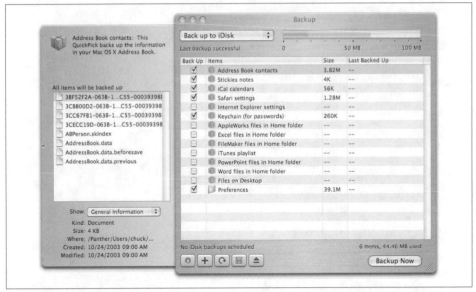

Figure 6-10. Backup for lefties...you can force the QuickPick drawer to open on the left side by moving the window to the far right edge of your display, and then clicking on the Info button.

 The mouse pointer will not change from an arrow symbol to a resize symbol when you go to resize the QuickPick drawer. As Obi-Wan Kenobi said to Luke: "Trust your feelings..."—just click and drag to the right.

To resize the QuickPick drawer, do the same, just in reverse. Click on the right edge of the drawer and drag it toward Backup's main window. If you drag the edge of the drawer too close to Backup's window, the QuickPicks drawer springs back to its default (minimum) width. The sproingy action only goes so far, though. If you drag the far edge of the drawer to about two-thirds its default size, the QuickPicks drawer closes all the way.

Selecting items in a QuickPick package or folder

Some packages, like the one named "Address Book contacts", list only the files that will be backed up as part of that package. However, certain packages give you the option of selecting specific items for backup. Out of the default list of packages, the following packages in the Items column allow you to pick and choose which items will be backed up from the QuickPick drawer:

- AppleWorks files in *Home* folder
- Excel files in *Home* folder
- FileMaker files in *Home* folder

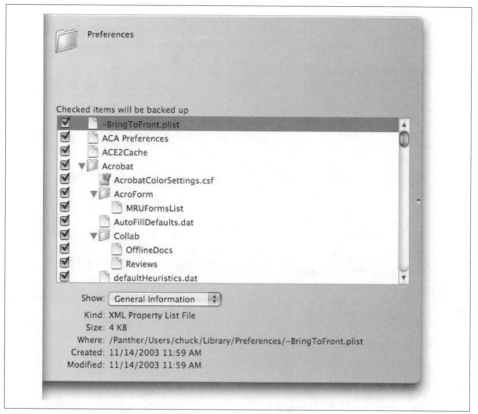

Figure 6-11. A fully extended QuickPick drawer can let you see more information about selected files at the bottom of the window.

- iTunes playlist
- PowerPoint files in *Home* folder
- Word files in *Home* folder
- Files on Desktop

If you want to back up all of the files in a package, simply click on its checkbox in the main Backup window. This places a checkmark next to that item in the Back Up column, and all of the files for that package will be selected for backup in the Quick-Pick drawer, as shown in Figure 6-12.

You can see whether an item in the backup list gives you the option of selecting its items by just selecting its name in the Items column—not by selecting its checkbox, as shown in Figure 6-13. In this case, I just clicked on the name of the package, "Excel files in Home folder," to see the list of possible files to backup in the Quick-Pick drawer.

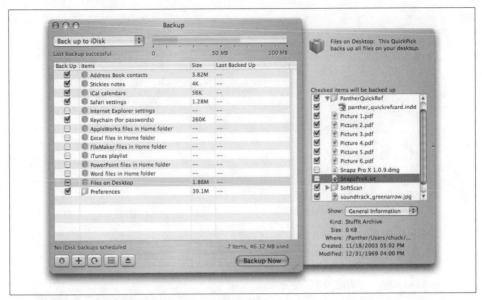

Figure 6-12. The QuickPick list for Files on Desktop.

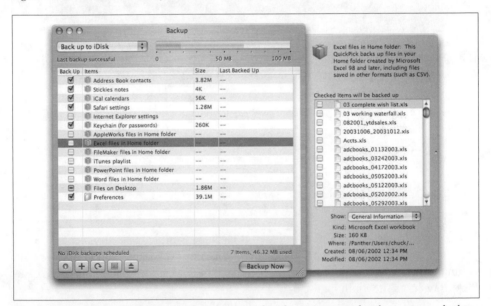

Figure 6-13. Selecting package in the Items column of Backup's main window lets you see whether all of the items for that package will be backed up, or if you can select/deselect items in that package.

All of the Excel files in the QuickPick drawer are grayed out, and all of their checkboxes aren't selected. If you click on any of the files in the list, information about the selected file will appear at the bottom of the drawer. However, if you click on a checkbox for one of the files, that file will be included as part of the next backup. Also notice that the checkbox next to "Excel files in Home folder" in the main window will change, but it won't have a checkmark in the box. The checkbox will turn Aqua blue, but there will be a minus sign in the box instead of a checkmark, as shown in Figure 6-14. This is a visual queue to indicate to you that not all of the items in that package are selected for backup.

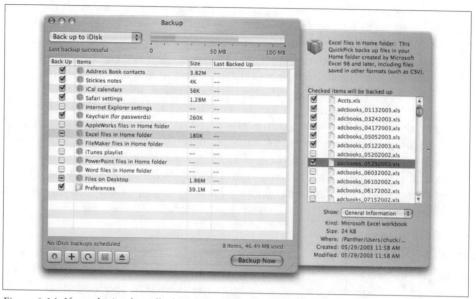

Figure 6-14. If you don't select all of a package's files for backup in the QuickPick list, a minus sign will appear in the checkbox in the Back Up column next to the package name.

Save Time with Home-Style Backups

When an item in the Backup list says "...files in Home folder" next to it, that means that Backup will search through all of the folders in your *Home* directory (*/Users/your_username*) to look for files of that particular type. This means that Backup will root through the *Desktop*, *Documents*, *Library*, *Movies*, *Music*, *Pictures*, *Public*, and *Sites* folders—and any folders within—on the quest for any files that fit the bill. Backup places the files it finds into the QuickPick drawer, where you can pick and choose the files you really want to back up. This can save you a great amount of time.

Showing a file's information in the QuickPick list

Not only does the QuickPick list give you a way to pick and choose which files will be backed up, you can also use it to display information about a file.

The Show pop-up menu, located just below the list of files in the QuickPick drawer, has two options for revealing information about a selected file or folder. By default, the Show menu is set to General Information. With this option selected, you can see five pieces of information about a file, including the file's type and size, where it is located in the filesystem, and when the file was created and last modified. If you select a folder in the QuickPick list, its Kind will be displayed as Folder.

The other option in Show's pop-up menu is Backup Information. With the Show pop-up menu set to Backup Information, you will be able to see the date and time the file was last backed up, a destination where the file will be backed up to, and a status report, stating whether the file is unchanged since the last backup or if the file or folder will be backed up the next time around. If you are backing up files to your iDisk, the location will be */Backup/Users/username*, followed by the original path for the file. For example, if I'm backing up a file located in my *Documents* directory that's named *booksignatures.xls*, that file's path on my Mac is */Users/chuck/Documents/booksignatures.xls*. So, when that file gets backed up, it will show up on my iDisk (in backed-up form) in */Backup/Users/chuck/Documents/booksigna-tures.xls*. If you are making your backup to CDs or DVDs, the path will be similar, except that it won't have an initial *Backup* directory (e.g., just */Users/username*, not */Backup/Users/username*).

Scheduling Backups

Backups, like brushing your teeth, are useless if you don't do them regularly. Of course you won't need to back up your Mac after every meal, but you should work backups into a daily and weekly routine. Fortunately, Backup just happens to be equipped with a scheduling feature so you'll never forget when to perform a backup.

Backup Scheduling Caveats

Before you start scheduling backups, there are some things you need to remember:
- You cannot schedule a backup to CDs or DVDs.
- If you are backing up to a Drive (networked or otherwise), it must be mounted on your system.
- Also, in order for you to back up to your iDisk, your Mac must be connected to—or configured to automatically connect when needed—the Internet.
- Your iDisk does not need to be mounted on your Mac.
- If your Mac is in Sleep mode, Backup won't run as scheduled.

Keep these things in mind as you plan your Backup schedule.

By default, Backup isn't configured to perform backups according to any sort of schedule. If you look at the row of buttons at the lower-left corner of Backup's window, you'll also see a note that says "No backups scheduled"; this adds confirmation that Backup won't act on its own. Since you're the keeper of your Mac, you'll have to set this up yourself.

To change Backup's scheduling options, click on the fourth button from the left at the lower-left corner of Backup's main window. This button, shown earlier in Figure 6-1, looks like a calendar, except without the dates and all your appointments written into the little squares. When you click on that button, the sheet shown in Figure 6-15 slides out of the top of the window, giving you options for scheduling your backups.

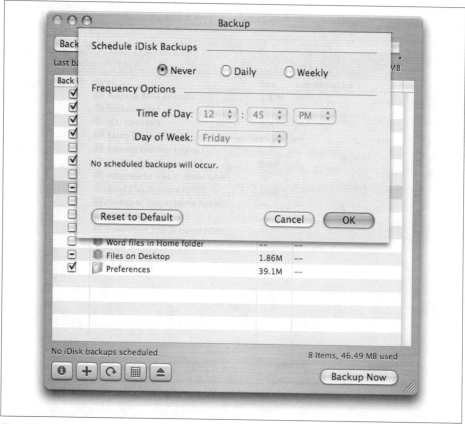

Figure 6-15. Backup's scheduling sheet.

Scheduling a backup is as simple as clicking on one of the radio buttons next to either Daily or Weekly, depending on how frequently you'd like your backups to be. If you select Daily, the pop-up menus next to Time of Day become available. Here, you can select the time that you would like for your backup to be performed. If you select Weekly, both the Time of Day and Day of Week pop-up menus are available. In addition to picking a time slot to do the backup, you can also select which day of the week the backup will be performed.

 The backup actually occurs within a two-hour window of that time setting. For example, if you set your backup to run at 12:00 p.m. (Noon), the backup will take place sometime between Noon and 2:00 p.m. The reason for this delayed reaction is that Backup checks the system to see whether it's busy. If there are a lot of applications or processes running, Backup will hold off until the next available opportunity to squeeze in the backup.

With Backups, Timing Is Everything

As with most things in life, timing is everything—and that includes backups. When scheduling a backup, you should pick a time when you're least likely to be using your Mac. Why? Well, the simple answer is because backing up can take a lot of time, and it can eat up lots of your CPU. If you're working on a deadline, crunching away in some multilayered Photoshop file and Backup kicks in, you'll find that your Mac will slow down significantly.

Another reason why you should schedule your backups when you have some down time is because one of the files you want (and need) to back up might be in use. Rather than backing up the file in its finished form, you'll instead get a snapshot of the file where it was at the time the backup was performed.

So, rather than schedule your backup for sometime during the day when you're likely to be working away on your Mac, schedule your backups for lunchtime or later in the evening when you're away from your desk or sound asleep.

After you click the OK button to accept your newly scheduled backup time (and day, if you opt to only perform weekly backups), the "No backups scheduled" note at the bottom of the window will change to something like "iDisk backups scheduled daily at 12:00PM".

It's worth noting that you cannot schedule a time to backup your Mac to CDs or DVDs; the scheduling feature is only available for backing up data to your iDisk or to a Drive. The reason for this is because someone needs to physically be sitting at your Mac to back up to CDs or DVDs to insert and remove discs as needed. When backing up to your iDisk, however, the only requirement is that your Mac have a live Internet connection. (Your iDisk doesn't need to be mounted on your Mac, either.) As long as your Mac is connected to the Internet, or a specified Drive is mounted on your Mac, the backup will be performed. At the scheduled time, Backup launches to see that your Mac is online or searches for a mounted Drive. If the scheduled device is available, the backup will be performed. If not, you will see the alert message shown in Figure 6-16, telling you that you're not online or that the Drive isn't connected.

Figure 6-16. If you're not online when a backup is scheduled, you will see this alert message, asking you to verify your Internet connection.

When you see this alert message, you can do one of two things: click the OK button to dismiss the window and do nothing, or click on the Open Network Prefs button to check your Internet connection. If you click on the Open Network Prefs button, System Preferences will launch and take you directly to the Network preferences panel. If all of the connection lights are red, that means you're not connected to the Internet, and you should connect if you want to back up to your iDisk.

Backing Up to an iDisk

The first thing to keep in mind about backing up to your iDisk is that the amount of data you can back up is limited by the amount of space on your iDisk. With the basic .Mac membership, this means that your base amount is 100 MB of space, which is hardly enough room for a complete backup of your system. However, it is enough room for backing up basic things like your Address Book contacts, iCal calendars, Safari bookmarks, application preferences, and a few other things.

 Remember, too, that you'll need to reserve some space on your iDisk if you plan to put up a .Mac HomePage.

By default, Backup assumes that you want to back up files from your Mac to your iDisk. When you launch Backup, it checks to see whether you're connected to the Internet; if so, the pop-up menu at the top of Backup's window will be set to "Back up to iDisk". If Backup cannot detect an Internet connection, the menu switches to "Back up to CD". If your Mac doesn't have a Combo or Super Drive for backing up to CDs or DVDs, Backup looks for any drives (networked or external) that might be mounted on your Mac. If it detects one, the menu will be set to "Back up to Drive".

While you can schedule a backup to run automatically, you can back up your data at any time by clicking on the Backup Now button. So, regardless of the fact that my backup has been scheduled to run at Noon, let's go ahead and back up now.

The first step is to select the QuickPick packages you want to back up to your iDisk. The items I will be backing up to my iDisk are:

- Address Book contacts
- Stickies notes
- iCal calendars
- Safari settings
- Keychain (for passwords)
- My Preferences folder (*~/Library/Preferences*), which I added to the list back in Figure 6-6

As you click on each item, Backup calculates how much space is required and places that information in the Size column. Also, keep an eye on the iDisk storage indicator bar near the top of the window. If there is room to back up the item you've selected, a light green area is added on the bar. If the bar turns red, that means you don't have enough space on your iDisk to back up that item, so you should consider backing that item onto CD or DVD or to a Drive.

After selecting these items, Backup displays a message just above the Backup Now button that says how many items I've selected, and how much space is required on my iDisk for the backup. In this case, Backup displays the message "6 Items, 44.46 MB used", as shown in Figure 6-17.

As the backup starts, Backup's window collapses. In the window that remains, you'll see a progress bar along with a series of messages throughout the backup process. These messages, shown in Figure 6-18 at different stages of the backup process, tells you that Backup is creating a series of folders on your iDisk to contain the backup, followed by messages for each file being backed up.

When the backup is complete, Backup's window pops back open to its full size. Backup's window gives you various cues to let you know that the backup was completed, as highlighted in Figure 6-19.

The first backup to your iDisk will take a little longer than subsequent backups. This is because Backup must first create the directories to place your backup in. However, when Backup runs in the future, if it doesn't need to create or remove any directories, it compares the files being backed up with the files that were previously backed up to the iDisk and looks for changes. If a file hasn't changed, it won't be backed up again. Likewise, if a file has changed since its previous backup, the latest version of the file (the one on your Mac) will be backed up to your iDisk. This ensures that your backup always contains the latest set of your data, making it easy for you to restore something if necessary.

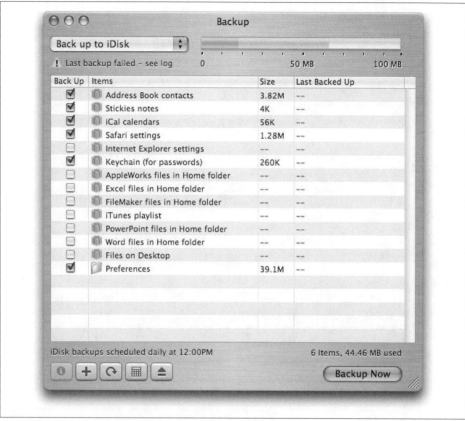

Figure 6-17. After selecting the QuickPick packages and other items to be backed up, look above the Backup Now button to find out how much space the backup requires.

Backing Up to CD or DVD

With your iDisk, backups are limited by the amount of space your .Mac membership provides, and how much other data you have stored on your iDisk, such as your .Mac HomePage. However, when backing up to disc media (CD or DVD), you have a lot more freedom, mainly because your backups can span multiple discs, making the size of your backup virtually limitless.

One of the first things you'll notice when you select "Back up to CD" (or DVD) from the pull-down menu is that Backup's interface changes slightly. As Figure 6-20 shows, there are more backup items to select from in the main window, and the iDisk storage meter has disappeared. Instead, when you select an item in the backup list, a message appears above the row of buttons at the lower left of Backup's window, telling you how many discs are required for the backup.

For this example, I'll walk you through the process of backing up your email.

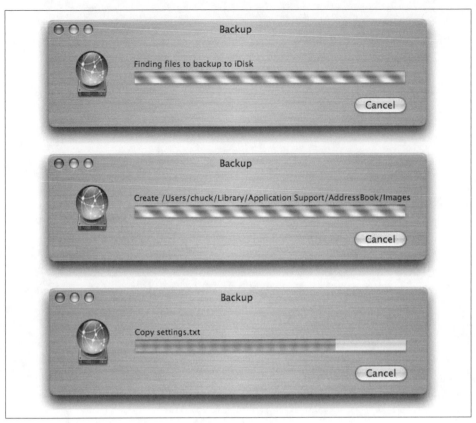

Figure 6-18. Progress bars at different stages of the backup process.

1. Select "Back up to CD" from the pull-down menu, located just below the toolbar at the top of the window. As mentioned earlier, Backup's interface changes slightly, giving you more packaged items from which to select.

2. Click on the checkbox next to "Mail messages and settings". Backup computes the size of your email archive and places that amount in the Size column. In looking at Figure 6-20, my mail archive is a little over 2.3 GB, which is more than a single CD can handle. However, Backup displays a message (located above the row of buttons at the lower-left corner of the window), telling you how many CDs are required for the backup. In this case, I'll need four CDs to back up all of my email.

   If you open up the QuickPicks drawer by clicking on the Info button (or by hitting ⌘-I), you'll see a listing of all the files that will be included as part of this backup. Notice that you can't pick and choose which items will be backed up in the QuickPicks drawer; this ensures that all of your mail settings, email messages, and attachments are backed up in one fell swoop.

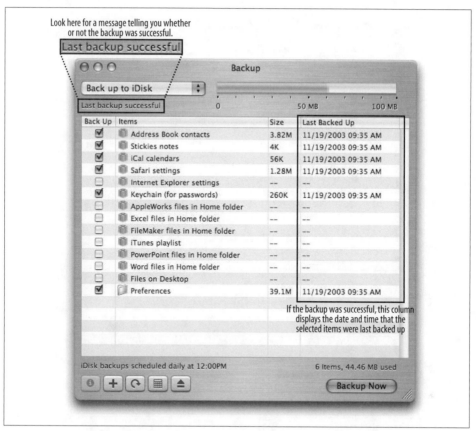

Figure 6-19. Look below the pop-up menu for a message telling whether the backup was successful or not, and in the Last Backed Up column for the date and time of the backup.

3. Click on the Backup Now button to begin the backup process. A window pops up, asking you to assign a name to the backup. The default name for the backup is My Backup followed by a date and timestamp, as shown at the top of Figure 6-21; the bottom image shows that I renamed the backup to Mail Backup, leaving the date and timestamp in place to keep track of my backup sets.

4. After naming your backup set, click on the Begin Backup button.

5. Next, you will be prompted to insert a blank CD, as shown at the top of Figure 6-22. After inserting a blank CD, the Burn button is enabled (as shown at the bottom of Figure 6-22). Just click on the Burn button to start burning your backup to the first disc.

After clicking on the Burn button, Backup's window changes size, displaying messages and a progress meter throughout the backup. The first thing Backup does is prepare the files for backing up, and then you'll see messages about the disc being burned and verified, as shown in Figure 6-23.

Figure 6-20. Backup's interface changes slightly when you opt to backup to disc media, such as CDs or DVDs.

In the case of this backup, where I have over 2.4 GB of data being backed up, the disc will eventually run out of space. When the first CD has been burned, the disc will eject from your Mac. You should label the disc using the name supplied in the alert window, as shown in Figure 6-24. In this case, the first CD of my email backup will be labeled *Mail Backup 11-19-2003-10-21 Disc 1*.

This process of preparing, copying, burning, finalizing, and verifying the backup continues until all of the data you've selected in the backup list is burned onto CDs. When a disc is full, you'll be prompted to label the disc that was just burned and to insert another blank. Continue this process until you see the final message, shown in Figure 6-25, telling you that your backup has been completed.

Once the backup is complete, make sure you have labeled the CDs using the names provided by the alert messages. In particular, make sure that you label the last disc of your backup set as Master, not a disc number as with the previous discs. The reason for this is because if and when you need to restore data from a backup CD/DVD set, you will be asked to insert the Master disc first. The Master disc contains detailed

Figure 6-21. Giving your backup a name.

Figure 6-22. Of course, before you can actually back something up, you'll need to insert a blank CD.

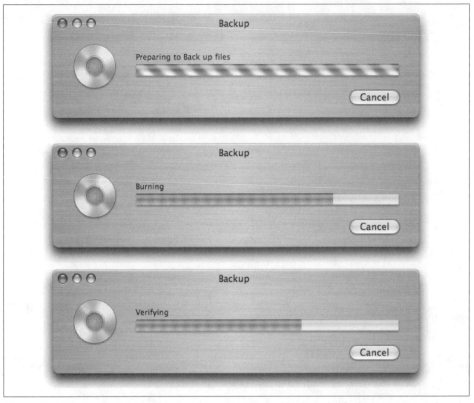

Figure 6-23. Backup lets you know when it's preparing the files to be backed up, copying and burning them to disc, and verifying the burn.

information about your backup and what's stored on each disc in the set. If you need a specific file, the Master disc helps Backup locate the file quickly, and you will be directed as to which disc to insert to restore the file from.

The final step is to store the discs in a safe place. If you have access to a fireproof safe or have a safety deposit box at your bank, you couldn't get any safer than that.

 If you're like me, you'll make a copy of your backup, keeping one at work and taking one home. That way, if my PowerBook crashes while I'm at work or home, I'll have a backup set wherever I am.

As Robin Williams (the comedian) once said: "Redundant, redundant, redundant, redundant, redundant."

Backing Up to a Drive

New to the 2.0 version of Backup is the ability to back up to a Drive. This "Drive" can be any of the following:

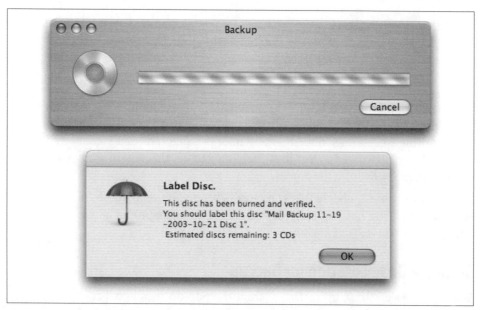

Figure 6-24. After burning each disc, Backup lets you know that the burn went okay and gives you instructions on what you should name each disc.

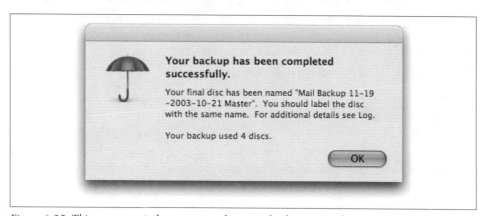

Figure 6-25. This message window appears when your backup is complete.

- An external FireWire or USB drive
- A USB flash memory key fob
- Your iPod (which is essentially a medium-sized FireWire drive that stores and lets you play music files)
- A networked drive, including AFP, NFS, and WebDAV shares

The word "Drive" is used throughout this chapter in a generic form to mean any type of "Drive" to which Backup can back up data.

The main rule that applies to backing up to a Drive is that it must be mounted on your Mac in order for the backup to take place; otherwise, to what location would the data be backed up? This means that USB and FireWire devices must be connected to the Mac, either directly or to an applicable hub that's connected to the Mac, and any networked drives must be mounted on the system using Go → Connect to Server (⌘-K) from the Finder.

The other rule that applies is that you must have read/write privileges on the drive or share to which you're backing up. If you do not have the proper access privileges to write data to a drive, your backup will fail (without fail).

Setting a Drive Location for Backup

When you select "Back up to Drive" from the pop-up menu on Backup's window, you'll notice that a Set button appears next to it, as shown in Figure 6-26.

In order to back up to a Drive, you must first Set (or specify) a Drive and a location on that drive where the backup will be saved. If you haven't backed up to a Drive yet, you'll see the message "Location not set" immediately to the right of the Set button. This is the case with Figure 6-26, so let's set a Drive.

1. Select Back up to Drive from the pop-up menu.

2. Click on the Set button.

3. If you haven't Set a Drive location before, an alert sheet (shown in Figure 6-27) flops out of Backup's titlebar.

4. Click on the Create button to set a new backup Drive location. The alert sheet is replaced by another sheet (shown in Figure 6-28), which resembles an Open dialog and is used to select a Drive to be used by Backup.

5. For this example, I will be backing up my *Home* folder (named *chuck*, after my user account name) to an external FireWire drive on my home network, which is named Vesuvius. I've named my backup "Chucks Home Folder Backup," and I've selected the drive Vesuvius in the sheet's sidebar, as shown in Figure 6-29.

6. Click the Create button to create the location for the backup set. The top part of Backup's window will look like Figure 6-30.

Since I plan to back up my *Home* folder, the backup won't contain any of the default QuickPick packages. So now I need to add my *Home* folder to the backup list:

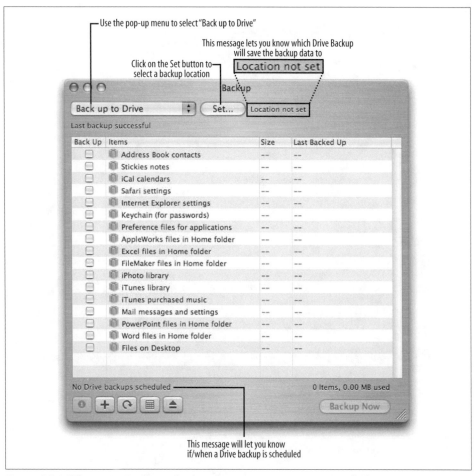

Use the pop-up menu to select "Back up to Drive"

This message lets you know which Drive Backup
will save the backup data to

Click on the Set button to—
select a backup location

Location not set

Backup

| Back up to Drive ▲▼ | (Set...) | Location not set |

Last backup successful

Back Up	Items	Size	Last Backed Up
☐	Address Book contacts	--	--
☐	Stickies notes	--	--
☐	iCal calendars	--	--
☐	Safari settings	--	--
☐	Internet Explorer settings	--	--
☐	Keychain (for passwords)	--	--
☐	Preference files for applications	--	--
☐	AppleWorks files in Home folder	--	--
☐	Excel files in Home folder	--	--
☐	FileMaker files in Home folder	--	--
☐	iPhoto library	--	--
☐	iTunes library	--	--
☐	iTunes purchased music	--	--
☐	Mail messages and settings	--	--
☐	PowerPoint files in Home folder	--	--
☐	Word files in Home folder	--	--
☐	Files on Desktop	--	--

No Drive backups scheduled —   0 Items, 0.00 MB used

ⓘ ＋ ↻ ▦ ⏏   (Backup Now)

This message will let you know
if/when a Drive backup is scheduled

Figure 6-26. When using Backup to backup data to a Drive, note its specific features.

1. At the lower-left of Backup's window, click on the button with the plus sign (+). This opens another sheet, shown in Figure 6-31, from which I can select my *Home* folder.

2. To do this, click on the icon for your *Home* folder in the sheet's sidebar, and then click on the Choose button to close the sheet and add the *Home* folder to Backup's list of Items, shown in Figure 6-32.

With my *Home* folder added to Backup's Items list, I can go to the QuickPicks drawer and deselect any items that I don't want to include in the backup. But since I want this to be a backup of everything that's in my *Home* folder, I won't deselect anything. The only step remaining is to click on the Backup Now button to kick off the process.

When the backup is finished, Backup places a file named *Chucks Home Folder Backup.backup* onto the drive Vesuvius. Now if I ever need to restore my *Home*

Figure 6-27. This alert sheet lets you Create a new Drive location, or open a previously saved location for conducting another backup.

folder after reinstalling Mac OS X, I have a safe backup waiting in the wings on my external FireWire drive. To ensure that the backup of my *Home* folder is always current, I have it scheduled Backup to back up my *Home* folder to my external FireWire drive every night at 2:00 a.m.

Restoring Files from a Backup

Okay, you're swimming along and everything's going fine with your Mac. You've gotten into the routine of backing up basic files to your iDisk every day, and you're backing up more important stuff to CDs or to an external drive. Great, you've bought into the backup religion.

Then one day, your hard disk starts making this odd clicking noise and the next thing you know, your system crashes, you can't reboot, and you're in the middle of a project. Not so great. What are you going to do?

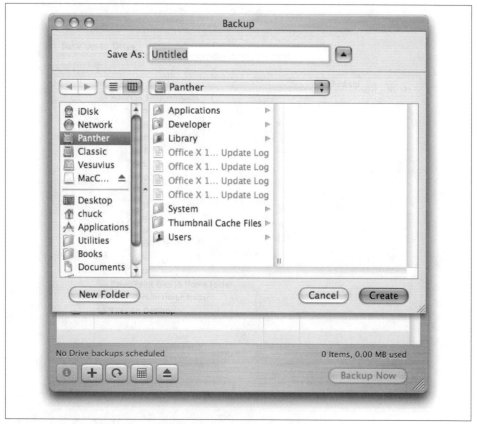

Figure 6-28. Backup's sheet for naming and selecting a Drive location.

Well, first, if you've purchased an AppleCare Protection Plan (*http://www.apple.com/support/products/proplan.html*) for your Mac, call AppleCare and tell them what happened. Their response is to tell you that your hard drive just crashed and that you need to send your Mac in to replace the hard drive. The next day, you get a package from AppleCare so you can send your Mac in for repair, and a couple days later you get a call, saying that the data on your drive was unrecoverable but a new drive was inserted and you'd be getting your cherished Mac back the next day.

Great. You're getting a new drive and all of your data has been lost. Ah, but you have those backups waiting in the wings you can restore from, so all hope is not lost, right? You have been backing up, right? Good.

When you get your Mac back, one of the very first things you should do if you've been using iSync (see Chapter 9) is to synchronize your Mac with the iSync server. The reason you're going to do this first is because iSync will pull down your Address Book contacts, iCal calendars, and to-do items, as well as all of your bookmarks for Safari. Okay, that's step one; now on to the bigger task at hand: restoring data from your backups.

Figure 6-29. Assign a name to your backup and select the Drive in the sheet's sidebar.

Figure 6-30. Notice that the name of the backup set, "Chucks Home Folder Backup" is placed next to the Set button at the top of Backup's window.

Restoring from an iDisk

Earlier, we backed up the following items to our iDisk:

- Address Book contacts
- Stickies notes
- iCal calendars
- Safari settings
- Keychain (for passwords)

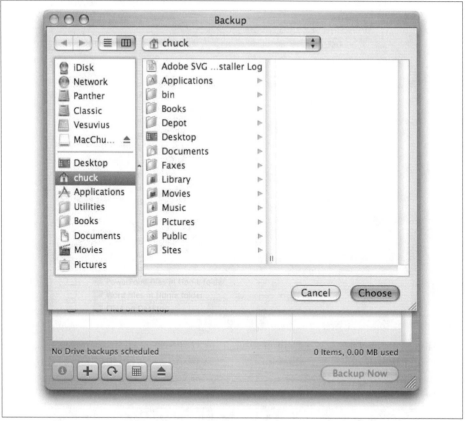

Figure 6-31. Select your Home folder in the dialog's sidebar and then click the Choose button to add your Home folder to the Backup Items list.

- My *Preferences* folder (*~/Library/Preferences*), which contains the settings not only for applications, but also for how I've set up my Mac

Of these, the two most important items that I've backed up to my iDisk are the Keychain data and my *Preferences* folder. Since I've already used iSync to get my Address Book, iCal, and Safari data back, the only other thing I need to restore is the Stickies notes. To restore these three items, launch Backup and follow these steps.

 Before you restore from any backup, you should quit all other running applications, particularly if you're restoring Preferences.

1. Select Restore from iDisk in the pop-up menu. You'll notice that Backup's interface changes to show you just the Items you've previously backed up.

2. Click on the checkboxes next to Stickies notes, Keychain (for passwords), and the *Preferences* folder to select these Items to be restored.

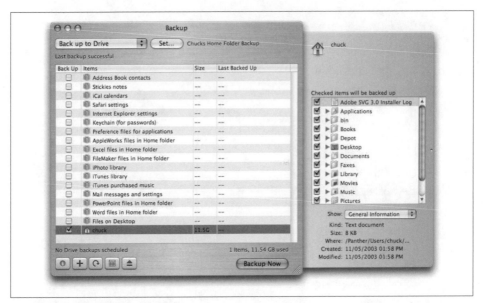

Figure 6-32. With my Home folder added to the Backup Items list, it's time to get cracking.

3. Click on the Restore Now button.

4. Alert windows appear, asking you whether you're sure that you want to replace the data that's on your Mac with the data from your backup. Since you know that this is what you want to do, click on the checkbox next to Apply to All, and then click on the Replace button to start restoring files.

Backup's window collapses as it restores the data on your Mac, and it expands to its normal size afterward. If the restore operation was successful, you'll see a message that says "Last restore successful" beneath the pop-up menu at the top of Backup's window.

Restoring from CD/DVD

Restoring from a CD or DVD backup set is actually quite painless; just follow these steps:

1. Select Restore from CD/DVD in the pop-up menu.

2. Backup immediately prompts you to insert the Master disc from the backup set from which you want to restore. If your CD or DVD backup spanned over multiple discs, the last disc of the backup should be labeled as Master.

 This refers back to the earlier section, "Backing Up to CD or DVD," where I mentioned it was important for you to label the discs exactly how Backup instructs you. Sure, you can always label the fourth disc of a four-disc backup set as "Disc 4" instead of "Master," but if someone else needs to restore from that backup, how are they to know that "Disc 4" is the "Master"?

3. Insert the Master disc from the backup you want to restore.

4. Backup's window displays the Items that were backed up to disc.

5. Click on the checkboxes for the Items you want to restore.

6. Click on the Restore Now button to start restoring files.

When you click on the Restore Now button, you'll hear your CD or DVD drive kick into high gear as it restores the data from the disc onto your Mac. If the data you need isn't on the Master disc and the backup spanned multiple discs, you will be prompted to insert the appropriate CD or DVD.

After the Items you've checked have been restored, Backup's window opens back up, and you'll see the message "Last restore successful" beneath the pop-up menu.

Restoring from a Drive

If you have only one backup set going to a Drive, restoring data from that backup is pretty simple. However, if you have multiple backup Sets, you'll first need to select which set you want to restore from before proceeding with the restoration.

Restoring when you only have one backup set

Depending on how you have your backups configured to run, you may only have one backup going to an external drive, such as with the earlier example where I backed up my *Home* folder to an external FireWire drive. Follow these steps to restore from that backup set:

1. Launch Backup and select Restore from Drive in the pop-up menu.

2. Make sure that the Drive you want to restore from is mounted on your Mac. To do so, open a Finder window and look for the drive in the Sidebar. If you see the drive there, you're set. However, if you don't, you'll need to connect the drive to your Mac; otherwise, you'll see the alert message shown in Figure 6-33.

Figure 6-33. If a Drive is not connected to your Mac when you select either "Back up to Drive" or "Restore from Drive," you will see this alert message, reminding you to connect the drive.

3. Make sure that the backup set you want to restore from is checked in the Backup Items list.

4. If you want to restore everything from that set, just click on the Restore Now button. However, if you want to restore a particular file or folder from that backup set, select the set by clicking on its checkbox and then click on the Info button (or use the keyboard shortcut ⌘-I) to open the QuickPicks drawer. For this example, I'll just restore my *Pictures* folder, as shown in Figure 6-34.

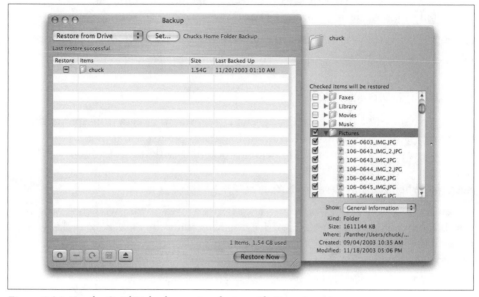

Figure 6-34. Use the QuickPicks drawer to select specific items to restore.

5. After selecting the *Pictures* folder in the QuickPicks drawer, if you click on the black disclosure triangle next to the folder's name, you can see the items contained within that will be restored. If you want to, you could select the specific file you need and just restore that; however, for this example, we'll restore all of the contents of the *Pictures* folder by clicking on the Restore Now button.

6. Backup's window will collapse, but as it starts to restore files, it will first query you about whether the restoration should overwrite any files that already exist, as shown in Figure 6-35.

To restore all of the items in the *Pictures* folder, click on the checkbox next to Apply to All and then click on the Replace button to continue with the restoration process.

After you click on the Replace button, Backup restores the file to your Mac from the *.backup* file on the Drive. When the restoration is complete, Backup's window opens up and reveals the message "Last restore successful" below the pop-up menu.

Figure 6-35. If an item you're restoring might overwrite something on your hard drive, Backup queries you first (at top). To restore everything, click on the Apply to All checkbox and hit the Replace button (bottom).

Restoring when you have multiple backup sets

If you have multiple backup sets going to a Drive, whether the backup is going to the same drive or not, you will need to select the proper set to restore from. To do this, follow these steps:

1. Select Restore from Drive from the pop-up menu.

2. Click on the Set button.

3. In the selection sheet, locate the appropriate *.backup* file from the Drives shown in the sheet's Sidebar (any disks mounted on your Mac should show up in the Sidebar).

4. After selecting the *.backup* file you want to restore from, click on the sheet's Choose button.

5. As with conducting a restoration from a single backup, if there are any particular files you want to restore, click on the backup Item's checkbox and then hit ⌘-I to open the QuickPick drawer, from which you can pick and choose the files to restore.

6. Click on the Restore Now button to start the restoration process; if you are overwriting any files, you will see similar alert windows as what appears in Figure 6-35.

When Backup completes the restoration process, its window opens up to its normal size, and the message "Last restore successful" should appear below the pop-up menu.

When a Backup Fails

Some time, some day, one of your backups will fail. Maybe the planets are out of alignment, maybe your network or AirPort connection dropped out in the middle of the backup process, or maybe there's some funky file that's throwing things off kilter. Whatever the case may be, you'll need to know how to deal with a failed backup.

If a backup fails because of a lost Net connection or a Drive not being connected, you'll see an alert message similar to the ones shown earlier in Figures 6-16 or 6-33, respectively. The alert window shown in Figure 6-16 provides an Open Network Prefs button, which opens the Network preferences panel (System Preferences → Network) when clicked. If you click on that button and see a row of red dots to the left of the various network connection types, (shown in Figure 6-36), you should double-check your Internet connection by double-clicking on the appropriate connection type (such as Built-In Ethernet or AirPort, etc.).

Figure 6-36. A row of red dots to the left of the network connection types signifies a missing connection somewhere.

It's possible that your dial-up or broadband connection to your ISP or your network connection went down. Attempt to reconnect to the network and try launching Backup again.

Clearing a Corrupt or Old Backup

If Backup is able to connect to your iDisk but detects a problem with a previous backup, you will see the alert message shown in Figure 6-37.

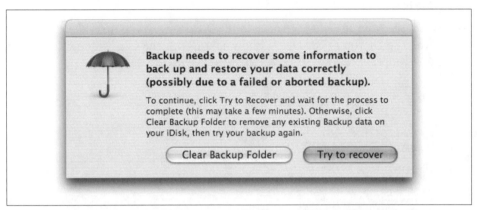

Figure 6-37. Backup's alert message is cryptic, but it offers some solutions to get your backups back on track.

If you see a message like this, the first thing you should do is go with the default button choice and "Try to recover" the previous backup. If Backup can recover, or resolve, the problem, it finishes launching and you'll be able to try backing up again. However, if the recovery fails for some reason, this alert message reappears again. You can try to recover again, but chances are that second attempt will also fail. At this point, your only option is to cross your fingers (and maybe your toes), and click on the Clear Backup Folder button.

Clicking on the Clear Backup Folder should be used as a last resort. When you click on that button, any and all backup data that's on your iDisk (in the *Backup* folder) will be deleted.

If you've only backed up to your iDisk before, and you have a Combo or Super Drive, you might (nudge) want to consider doing a backup to disc first. That way, you'll have some backup on file just in case something goes missing after you've cleared out your iDisk's *Backup* folder.

Backup also displays a message in its interface (shown in Figure 6-38), preceded by a little yellow Yield sign, as a way of letting you know that the previous backup failed.

Figure 6-38. Backup lets you know that a previous backup has failed by displaying a message in its interface.

Backup log files

As you can see from the message next to the Yield sign in Figure 6-38, it says "see log" at the end. If you select File → Show Log (⌘-L), the Log window (shown in Figure 6-39) appears.

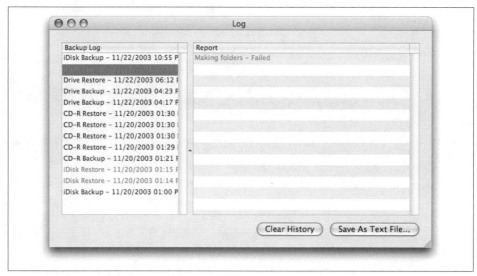

Figure 6-39. Backup keeps track of all your backups, even the ones that fail, by recording that info in a log file.

The Log window has two sides:

Backup Log
> This side of the window lists, in chronological order, all of the backups that have been performed for each particular backup type (i.e., to iDisk, to CD or DVD, or to a Drive). Successful backups are displayed in black, and unsuccessful (failed) backups are displayed in red.

Report
> This side of the Log window will list all of the files included as part of the backup. If a backup has failed, the item that caused the problem will be highlighted in red, followed by more red text saying, "Backup failed".

To see the details of what happened with the backup, click on the backup that's highlighted in red in the Backup Log window on the left, and then scroll down to the bottom of the display on the Report to the right.

If a backup failed because your Mac lost its Internet connection, there probably isn't a problem with the last file listed in red on the Report side. The reason why it is listed in red is because that's when the failure occurred, and probably means that the file is not corrupt.

However, if you've reconnected to the Internet and the backup fails when it hits that file a second time, you might want to consider deselecting that file in the QuickPick list and trying the backup again. If your backup is successful on the third time around, you know where your problem was.

The Log window has two buttons on its bottom edge; one is for clearing Backup's history log, and the other lets you save the log file for all of the backups to a text file, as shown in Figure 6-40.

Figure 6-40. Saving a Backup log file gives you a permanent record (in the way of a text file) of the latest backup.

When saving Backup's log file, you should save it in a location that you're likely to remember (such as your *Documents* folder), and give it a name that reflects the state of the log, such as *backuplog_date.txt*, where *date* would be a numbered date such as *11222003*, which denotes the date, November 22, 2003.

You can review the log file in any text editor (such as TextEdit or BBEdit) to see what the log report has to say. When reviewing the log file, each file that is backed up will end with one of three labels:

Success
> This means that the file was successfully backed up.

Unchanged
> This means that the file wasn't backed up. Don't fret, though. The selected file was verified against a version of the file that was previously backed up and was determined that it hasn't changed since the last backup. Backup won't backup a file that doesn't need backing up, thus shaving some time off the process.

Failed
> This means that the backup failed when it hit this file. Again, this label doesn't necessarily mean that this file is corrupt, so you should try doing the backup again to be safe.

The Backup.log file

Backup builds the Log file from data that's stored in *~/Library/Preferences/Backup/Backup.log*. If you open that file with TextEdit or BBEdit (my favorite text editor, available at *http://www.barebones.com*), you'll see roughly the same data as the log file you can save from the Log window, except that it's a bit cryptic in form, as shown in Figure 6-41.

> Do not double-click on the *Backup.log* file when attempting to open the file. If you do, your Mac won't know how to interpret a file with a *.log* extension, and a crash will occur.
>
> Instead, open your text editor of choice and open the *Backup.log* file from the File menu (File → Open), or by dragging the *Backup.log* file's icon from the Finder and dropping it on TextEdit's icon in the Dock.

When trying to read the *Backup.log* file, you'll start to notice a pattern in how the backup information is logged. Each line of the *Backup.log* file begins with a T, B, or an R. Lines that begin with a T indicate the start of a backup along with its date, time, and the type of backup (to an iDisk, CD, DVD, or Drive). Lines that begin with a B are the individual files included in that backup. And lines that begin with an R indicate files that were restored. For example, the date/timestamp for a backup might look like:

```
T::Backup::2003-11-20 13:00:11 -0800::iDisk
```

If you break that line apart, you can see that the backup was performed on November 20, 2003 at 1:00 p.m., as indicated by 2003-11-20 13:00:11. The -0800 part of that line indicates the location of your Mac in relation to Greenwich Mean Time (GMT); in this case, my Mac is located eight hours behind GMT. The last part, iDisk, indicates that the backup was made to an iDisk.

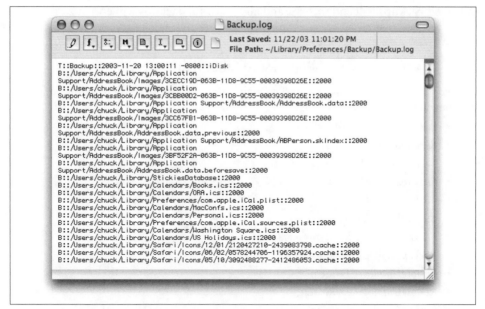

Figure 6-41. The Backup.log file...can you say "gibberish"?

 If you haven't noticed, double colons (::) are used as delimiters to separate the key pieces of information in each line of the *Backup.log* file. Just read the information between the sets of double colons, and things will start to make sense.

Files included in the backup will look similar to the following:

```
B::/Users/chuck/Library/Application Support/AddressBook/ AddressBook.data::2000
```

Breaking this line apart, you can see the name of the file that was backed up (*AddressBook.data*) and its path in the filesystem (*/Users/chuck/Library/Application Support/AddressBook*). The last part of this line is a four-digit number preceded by two colons. This number indicates whether the file backed up successfully (2000), was unchanged (2001), or if it caused the backup to fail (usually a number ranging from 2010 to 2019). If a backup fails, the following message can be found in the log:

```
B::Making folders::2017
```

This notation tells you that the backup failed as it was trying to create the folders to store the backup in. When a backup has reached its end successfully, the following message is displayed in the log:

```
B::Backup completed successfully.::2072
```

When restoring files, all files that have been successfully restored will begin with an R and end with 2009, as follows:

```
R::/Users/chuck/Library/Keychains/chuck::2009
```

All failed backups will end in 2085, and all successful backups will end in 2070.

Want More Gibberish?

If you took a look in the *~/Library/Preferences/Backup* directory, you probably noticed a bunch of other files, including:

- *BackupSet-CD-R.cat*
- *BackupSet-CD-R.cat.gz*
- *BackupSet-DVD-R.cat*
- *BackupSet-DVD-R.cat.gz*
- *BackupSet-Folder.cat*
- *BackupSet-Folder.cat.gz*
- *BackupSet-iDisk-R.cat*
- *BackupSet-iDisk-R.cat.gz*
- *RestoreCatalog-CD-R.cat*
- *RestoreCatalog-CD-R.cat.gz*
- *RestoreCatalog-Folder.cat*
- *RestoreCatalog-Folder.cat.gz*
- *RestoreCatalog-DVD-R.cat*
- *RestoreCatalog-DVD-R.cat.gz*
- *RestoreCatalog-iDisk.cat*
- *RestoreCatalog-iDisk.cat.gz*

These are catalog files that contain information about the backups you've performed, the packages you've selected, folders you've added to the backup list, etc. If you try to open one of the *.cat* files in a text editor, you'll see lots of encoded text used by Backup as a way of remembering how you last used the interface. (The *.cat.gz* files are gzip'd archives that contain the like-named *.cat* file.)

The *RestoreCatalog* files are used by Backup whenever you restore data on your Mac from a previous backup.

PART III

.Mac and Your Digital Life

Not long ago, Apple introduced their Digital Hub strategy where Mac OS X (and the Mac hardware itself) were to become the centerpiece for how you interact with the outside world. And no doubt, .Mac was meant to be an integral part of this strategy.

With your .Mac membership, you have access to powerful tools for building web pages on the fly, for synchronizing data from your Mac to other devices, and, with the help of some third-party tools, creating your own web log (or *blog*).

This part of the book shows you how to pull together all of your vital information and package it up in digital form so you can share it with your friends and family, and more.

The chapters in this part include:

- Chapter 7, *Building a HomePage*
- Chapter 8, *Blogging with iBlog*
- Chapter 9, *Using iSync with .Mac*
- Chapter 10, *Slide Shows and iCards*

CHAPTER 7

Building a .Mac HomePage

Aside from the Mac.com email account and the iDisk, one of the best services a .Mac membership offers is the ability to create your own web site using .Mac's HomePage tools. The HomePage tools use Apple's own technology, WebObjects, which offers a set of page templates and styles that you can select to quickly and easily create a web site.

When you build a .Mac HomePage, your web site can be accessed by going to *http://homepage.mac.com/membername*. All of the information for your HomePage is stored in the *Sites* directory on your iDisk, but the HomePage tools require some files to exist in other directories as well. In such instances, those items will be discussed in this chapter.

Rather than showing you how to build each possible page and/or combination of pages, this chapter shows you how to build a simple, four-page web site containing a main page, a photo album, a movie page, and a file-sharing page. You'll also learn how to use the HomePage tools with other applications such as iPhoto and iMovie, as well as learn how to manage your .Mac HomePage. As with the other chapters in this book, you'll also learn about what goes on behind the scenes of your .Mac Home-Page, and how to personalize it with a favicon.

Planning Your HomePage

Before you set out to start building your HomePage, one of the first things you should do is come up with a game plan of what you'd like to have on your site, and who it's intended for. Since the .Mac services is for personal use, Apple has given you plenty of options for building a HomePage that allows you to extend your digital life and share it with your friends and family.

 This doesn't mean that schools, nonprofit organizations, and businesses can't put up a .Mac HomePage—you can and many people do—it's just Apple's perception on who uses .Mac and how.

Some things you can use your .Mac HomePage for include:

- A place to show off your digital images (photos or otherwise), or maybe the movies you create with iMovie.
- A way to let your friends and family keep on top of what you're up to
- Provide easy access to files you want to share with the world
- Create and post your résumé on the Web

For an example of what you can do with your .Mac HomePage, you can either examine mine (*http://homepage.mac.com/chuckdude*), or go to Steve Jobs' HomePage (*http://homepage.mac.com/steve*). Of course, my résumé isn't as flattering as Steve's, but it gets the job done.

Building a .Mac HomePage from Windows

While some may think that the HomePage tools are for Mac users only, think again. If you're using a Windows XP system, you can use the iDisk Utility for Windows XP (see Appendix C) along with Internet Explorer 6 (*http://www.microsoft.com/windows/ie/default.asp*) to build and manage your .Mac HomePage.

This makes it even easier for people who use a Windows machine by day and a Mac by night to have full access to the .Mac services. All you need to do is point IE to the main .Mac HomePage site (*http://www.mac.com/homepage*), log in using your .Mac member name and password, and then start building!

What You Can't Do with a .Mac HomePage

While the Web is a wonderful thing, there are a few things you cannot do with your .Mac HomePage, some of which are restricted, either legally or technologically.

The following technologies are not supported by .Mac's HomePage service:

- Perl and other programming languages used for CGI; you cannot run executables on the .Mac server
- PHP
- MySQL and other web databases
- You cannot host your own domain name from your iDisk; instead, your site is served from your iDisk's *Sites* folder from *http://homepage.mac.com/membername*
- Server-side includes

Basically, anything that requires server-side processing cannot be done within the realm of your .Mac HomePage. You can, however, use client-side technologies such as JavaScript, Java, and Flash, since web browsers (the clients) can handle these.

To make sure you stay within bounds, you should read (and re-read) the .Mac Terms and Conditions, found at *http://www.mac.com/1/membership_terms.html.* This page includes details that specifically apply to what you can and cannot do with your .Mac HomePage. If you violate any of the acceptable use terms, Apple can terminate your .Mac membership without notice or issuing a warning first.

What Goes Where on Your iDisk

Whether you're building your own web site with the web-based HomePage tool, there are some things you need to know about where the files are placed on your iDisk.

If you plan to use the HomePage tools to build your site, you need to place the files for your site in specific folders on your iDisk. If you recall from Chapter 3, there are nine folders on your iDisk, of which the following five play an important role in how your HomePage comes together:

Movies

Place the movies you create with iMovie or any other digital movie application in this directory. iMovie 4, which is included with iLife '04, makes it incredibly easy for you to publish the iMovies you create directly to your .Mac HomePage. iMovie 4 automatically compresses your movies down to size and takes you to the HomePage tools so you can customize the web page and publish it to your .Mac HomePage. For details on how to use iMovie 4 to publish a movie, see "Creating a Movie Page with iMovie 4," later in this chapter.

Music

This directory can be used to hold audio files for use with your HomePage.

Pictures

This folder is provided for storing image files you want to use with your HomePage. This folder is also home to any Photo Albums you create with the HomePage tools or iPhoto, as well as any Slide Shows (more commonly known as screensavers) you create with the .Mac Slides Publisher or from iPhoto.

Public

You can create a File Sharing page (described later) to make it easier for people to download files stored in your iDisk's *Public* folder. Rather than telling a friend to mount your *Public* folder, you can direct them to the File Sharing page on your .Mac HomePage.

 If your iDisk's *Public* folder is password-protected, anyone who goes to your File Sharing page will not be challenged for a password before they can download or upload files from your *Public* folder. Keep this in mind if there is something in your iDisk's Public folder that you don't want the rest of the world to have access to.

Sites

> The *Sites* folder is the primary directory for your .Mac HomePage. When someone points a web browser at your .Mac HomePage (*http://homepage.mac.com/ membername*), the web browser is really grabbing the page found at *http://homepage. mac.com/membername/Sites/index.html*.

To upload files to your iDisk, simply drag and drop them from one Finder window to another. Just remember to drop the files in their appropriate folder on your iDisk. Otherwise, you might not be able to add a picture or movie to your site if you've copied them to the incorrect folder.

> If you have a local copy of your iDisk, and you're not using the Home-Page tools to build your .Mac site, you can conveniently work offline and store any files for your site in their appropriate folder. Then, when you connect to the Internet again, you can sync your local iDisk with the .Mac servers to update your site.
>
> For more information about keeping a local copy of your iDisk, see Chapter 3.

HomePage Styles and Themes

The HomePage site (*http://www.mac.com/homepage*), shown in Figure 7-1, is divided into two parts. The top portion of the page is devoted to managing your .Mac Home-Page, while the bottom half lets you select different page styles and themes to use for creating your .Mac HomePage.

If you've used iPhoto, iMovie, or iDVD, you'll instantly recognize some of the page themes, since some are part of the theme set you can use from those applications. Once again, it's this level of integration between the iApps and .Mac that make it easy for you to build up your HomePage in a familiar environment.

While web site management is important, we'll skip over that for right now and take a look at the different styles and themes offered in the Create a Page section.

To help jump-start your .Mac HomePage, Apple provides 10 different page styles, each of which has a few different themes you can choose from, as described in the following sections.

Photo Album

Photo Album pages can be created with either the HomePage tools or directly from iPhoto. The HomePage tools offer 23 different page themes, as shown in Figure 7-2. However, if you create a Photo Album with iPhoto, you can change its theme to one of the themes offered online. For information on how to create a Photo Album using iPhoto and changing its theme, see the section "Creating a Photo Album Page with iPhoto."

Figure 7-1. The .Mac HomePage site.

When you create a Photo Album, the images are stored on your iDisk (in */Pictures/ Photo Album Pictures*) in folders whose name corresponds to the date and time the Photo Album was created. For example, the images used for one of my Photo Album's are stored in a folder named *2003-12-29 02.53.53 –0800*. While this may look cryptic, it tells us that the Photo Album was created at 2:53:53 a.m. on December 29, 2003. The *–0800* part of the folder name is a timestamp that relates to Greenwich Mean Time (or GMT).

The actual page that gets served is stored in the *Sites* folder and is named something like *PhotoAlbum1.html*. If you have more than one Photo Album, the others

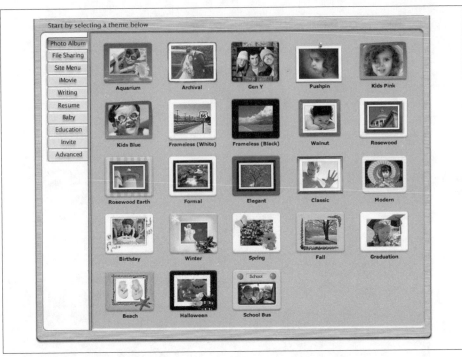

Figure 7-2. The Photo Album themes.

will follow along in the numbered sequence; for example, *PhotoAlbum2.html*, *PhotoAlbum3.html*, and so on. So, to direct someone to one of your Photo Albums, you would pass along a link similar to the following:

http://homepage.mac.com/chuckdude/PhotoAlbum8.html

If the page exists, they will be able to view your pictures or view a slide show of them in larger form. If the page doesn't exist, they will see an error page that tells them the page isn't there.

If you look at the page source for a Photo Album (in Safari, use View → View Source, or Option-⌘-V), you will see that page uses a mixture of HTML and JavaScript to layout the page and to control what happens when you click on an image. For example, one link for an image in the Photo Album page mentioned earlier looks like this:

```
<A HREF="javascript:openSlideShow(0)" onClick="openSlideShow(0)"↵
onFocus="this.blur();"><IMG BORDER=0 SRC=↵
/chuckdude/.cv/chuckdude/Sites/.Pictures/Photo%20Album%20Pictures/↵
2003-08-26%2006.11.49%20-0700/Image-D0FB4936D7C411D7.jpg-thumb_140_105.jpg↵
WIDTH=140 HEIGHT=105></A>
```

The first part of the link (the `<A HREF="...">` part) uses JavaScript to control what happens when somebody clicks on one of the images in the Photo Album. This tag uses the JavaScript method `onClick` to open the image in a Slide Show window so you can see a larger version of the picture. The next part of the link, what's inside the image (`<IMG/>`) tag, is what the web browser uses to display the image on the web page. However, if you look at this a little closer, you can see the *.cv* script (mentioned in Chapter 2), which is used to convert the image file (named *Image-D0FB4936D7C411D7.jpg*) and displays it as a 140 × 105 pixel thumbnail (as noted by the *–thumb 140 105.jpg* extension to the original image's filename).

The width and height of the thumbnails are determined by the layout you choose for the Photo Album. Photo Album pages can have either two or three images on each row. Thumbnails on a two-column page are sized 269 × 202 pixels (horizontal), and 140 × 105 pixels (horizontal) on a three-column page.

If you try to load the *–thumb* extension into a web browser, you'll see a page error. But if you load the direct link to the image:

```
http://homepage.mac.com/chuckdude/.Pictures/Photo%20Album%20Pictures/↵
2003-08-26%2006.11.49%20-0700/Image-D0FB4936D7C411D7.jpg
```

the picture is displayed in the web browser, as expected.

If you're paying close attention to the image links, you'll see that the link to the *Photo Album Pictures* folder is shown as `Photo%20Album%20Pictures`. The %20's are what the HTTP protocol uses to replace spaces found in folder/directory and file names. You'll also see some %20's in the file names of the folders that contain the images for your Photo Albums.

File Sharing

If you want to add a web interface to your iDisk's *Public* folder, you can use the File Sharing page style. As Figure 7-3 shows, there are two themes for the File Sharing page: graphite (gray) or magenta (hot pink). And with the latest revision of the .Mac services, a new theme has been added, called My Downloads.

See the section, "Sharing Files on your HomePage," later in this chapter for details on how to build pages for File Sharing and My Downloads.

When you create a File Sharing page, the contents of your iDisk's *Public* folder instantly become available to the world, regardless of whether your *Public* folder is password-protected. That's right: the File Sharing page will not challenge anyone to enter a password to download a file from your site, even if you've set a password in the iDisk preference pane (System Preferences → .Mac → iDisk → Your Public Folder).

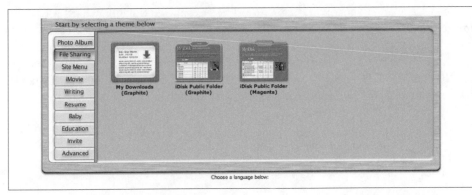

Figure 7-3. The File Sharing HomePage themes.

Site Menu

The Site Menu page style (shown in Figure 7-4) is used to create the main page for your .Mac HomePage that people will see when they go to *http://homepage.mac.com/membername* (where *membername* is your .Mac member name).

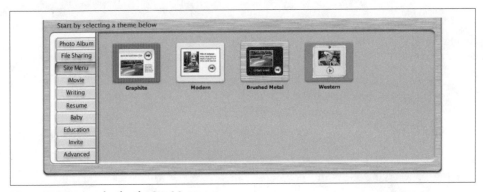

Figure 7-4. Page styles for the Site Menu page.

Until you create the Site Menu page, the lowest numbered page in your *Sites* folder will be used as the main page for your .Mac HomePage. For example, if you have created two Photo Album pages and a File Sharing page, they could be named as follows:

- *PhotoAlbum2.html*
- *FileSharing3.html*
- *PhotoAlbum4.html*

In this case, the person who's trying to find your main page would end up being redirected to *http://homepage.mac.com/membername/PhotoAlbum2.html*, since there's no main page to see.

When you create the Site Menu page, however, that page will be named *Menu#.html* and placed in the *Sites* folder. For example, if the tenth page you create for your .Mac site is the Site Menu, the name of that file will be *Menu10.html*. After the *Menu#.html* page has been saved to your *Sites* folder, the *index.html* file (also in the *Sites* folder) will be updated to redirect people who come to your web site so that the first page they see is the Site Menu page. Actually, the entire *index.html* file is nothing more than a few simple HTML tags and the redirect itself, as shown in Example 7-1.

Example 7-1. A .Mac HomePage's index.html file

```
<HTML><HEAD><meta http-equiv="refresh" content="0;url= http://homepage.mac.com/↵
chuckdude/Menu10.html"></HEAD><BODY></BODY></HTML>
```

Here you can see that the `<meta/>` tag is used to supply the redirect using `http-equiv="refresh"`. The rest of the information in the `<meta/>` tag, `content="0;url=http://homepage.mac.com/chuckdude/Menu10.html"` tells the browser to instantly take the viewer to the Site Menu page (*Menu10.html*).

See the later section "Creating Your Main Page" for details on how to use the Home-Page tools to build the Site Menu page for your site.

iMovie

Regardless of whether you've just dabbled with iMovie or if you consider yourself the next Alfred Hitchcock, you might want to consider adding a special page to show off that iMovie of yours. When you do, you'll have plenty of themes to select from, as shown in Figure 7-5.

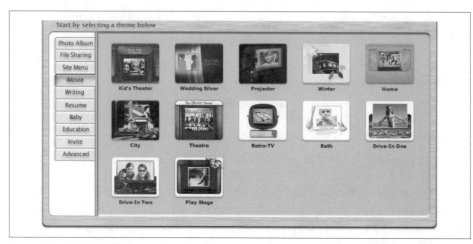

Figure 7-5. iMovie Themes.

If you're using iMovie 4 to create your movies, you can quickly create a movie page by selecting File → Share from iMovie's menu bar. iMovie 4 compresses your movie down to size (240 × 180 pixels), saves it as a QuickTime movie, uploads it to the

Movies folder on your iDisk, and then opens the HomePage Movie site in your default web browser. This makes is really easy for you to quickly show off your iMovies and share them with your friends over the Web.

---

iMovie 2 Users

If you're still creating movies with iMovie 2, you'll have a few extra steps to take to get your iMovie published to your .Mac HomePage. Before you create that iMovie page, keep these three things in mind:

- Export your iMovie by using File → Export → Export (menu) to QuickTime → Formats (menu) Web, and then click on the Export button
- Save the iMovie file so that it is no larger than 240 × 180 pixels
- Once you've exported your iMovie in web format, drag a copy of the Quick-Time movie file (with a *.mov* file extension) and place it in the *Movies* folder on your iDisk

If you export your iMovie following the menu options in the first bullet item, you won't have to worry about the second item; iMovie exports all movies for web viewing at 240 × 180 pixels. If you're like me and don't want to think about exporting the file and making sure that it's sized properly, I'd highly recommend upgrading to iLife '04 (*http://www.apple.com/ilife*) so you can work with iMovie 4. Not only does it make it super easy for you to publish your movies to your .Mac HomePage, it's also a significant improvement over iMovie 2, with lots of new features, better titles, etc.

See the section "Creating an iMovie Page" later in this chapter for details on how to create this page.

Writing

This page style can be used as a place to write and publish your random thoughts, or to produce an online newsletter to keep your friends and family informed on what you're up to. The themes included in the Writing style are shown in Figure 7-6.

As you can see from looking at the different themes, there are quite a few here for use by teachers or people who work with schools or sports teams. These include the Events, Classroom, Homework, School, and Teacher themes. Students can also use the Paper theme for writing stories, book reports, etc., before submitting them to their teachers. There is also a separate Education style (described later) that includes the themes mentioned here.

 You can use the Writing themes to create a blog of sorts, but if that's what you're interested in creating, don't miss Chapter 8.

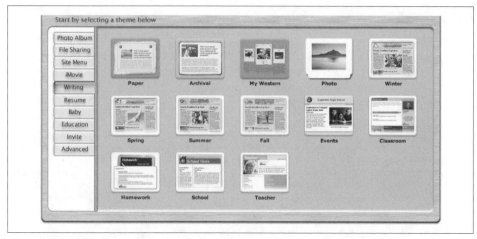

Figure 7-6. Themes for the Writing style pages.

Resume

It's always a good idea to keep your résumé up to date, and the Resume style is a great way to do that. This style, shown in Figure 7-7, has four different themes to choose from.

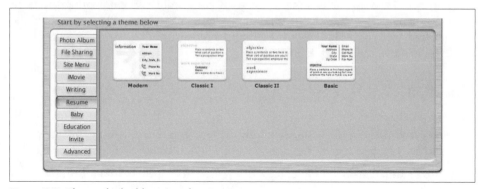

Figure 7-7. Themes for building an online Resume.

If you create your résumé using the .Mac HomePage tools, you can direct prospective employers to your web page, and also use this page to print a copy of your resume to submit with your cover letter.

For an example résumé created with the Resume style's Modern theme, go to *http://homepage.mac.com/steve/Resume.html*.

Baby

One of the proudest moments for most adults is when they get to introduce their newborn child to their friends and family. More often than not, it takes a while to circulate the pictures or get the word out. But with your .Mac HomePage and iPhoto, you can quickly create a photo page to announce the new addition to your family using the Baby styles, shown in Figure 7-8.

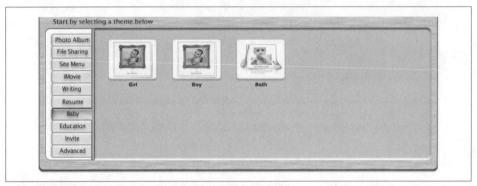

Figure 7-8. Themes for the Baby page style.

There are three themes available: Girl and Boy are for creating birth announcements, and Bath can be used for hosting a movie of your child. When creating the birth announcement pages, make sure that the picture of your child is stored in the *Pictures* folder of your iDisk. With the Bath page, ensure that your movie has been saved in the *Movies* folder of your iDisk.

Education

As mentioned earlier, the Writing page styles offer some themes for students, teachers, and administrators of schools. Those themes have been combined with a few more and are grouped together in the Education styles, shown in Figure 7-9.

There are 11 different themes to choose from, including special ones for promoting a school play, sporting events, and a special résumé-building theme for teachers.

Invite

If you're planning to have an event—be it a birthday party, New Year's bash, or just a chance to gather some friends around the tube to watch *Survivor*—you can use one of the themes from the Invite styles (shown in Figure 7-10) to extend your invitation.

Keep in mind that any Invite pages you create will be added to the listing of Pages for your site, which means that anyone who comes to your .Mac site will see the invite as well. If you don't want certain people to attend a private affair, you might consider hiding this page from view. To see how to do that, see the section "Sharing Files on your HomePage," later in this chapter.

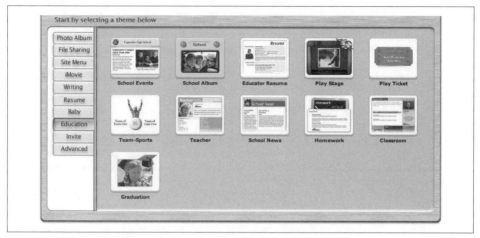

Figure 7-9. Themes for Education-related pages.

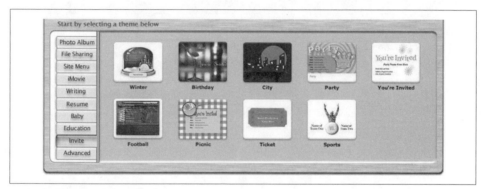

Figure 7-10. Themes for creating custom Invites.

Advanced

This new option, shown in Figure 7-11, allows you to integrate the HTML-based web pages you create with tools such as BBEdit, Macromedia Dreamweaver or Contribute, or Adobe GoLive into your .Mac HomePage. When you add an External HTML page to your HomePage, you can create a link to the page that gets added to your HomePage's navigation area at the top, as seen later in Figure 7-13.

To add an External HTML page to your .Mac HomePage, just save your HTML files (and any associated graphics) to the *Sites* folder on your iDisk. When you select the External HTML theme, you will be taken to the page shown in Figure 7-12, which displays any HTML files it sees in your *Sites* folder. Just select the file you want to use and click on the Choose button to add the page to your .Mac HomePage site.

This is a great new feature since it allows you to mix how you create your HomePage, letting you build custom pages to suit your style and needs while at the same time

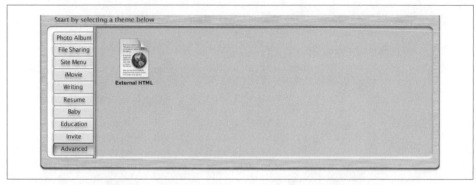

Figure 7-11. Use the External HTML theme to integrate the web pages you build with your .Mac HomePage.

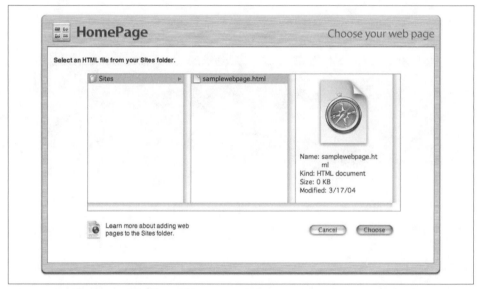

Figure 7-12. Select an HTML file to add to your .Mac HomePage.

adding those to your HomePage site. In addition, when you add an External HTML page, you also have the option of announcing that new page (by sending an iCard), just as you can with any of the other .Mac HomePages you build.

Creating Your Main Page

Every web site needs a main page, and your .Mac HomePage is no exception. As mentioned earlier, until you create a Site Menu page, anyone who goes to your .Mac HomePage will be redirected to the lowest-numbered web page in your *Sites* directory.

To create a main page for your .Mac HomePage, follow these steps:

1. Go to the .Mac HomePage site (*http://www.mac.com/homepage*) and log in with your .Mac member name and password

2. Click on the Site Menu tab in the Create a Page section, and then select one of the four themes to the right; for this example, I've used the Brushed Metal theme. When you select a theme, you will be taken to a page similar to the one shown in Figure 7-13. If you have created any other pages, they will show up in the content area for your site's main page.

At the upper right of Figure 7-13, you can see three icons: Themes, Preview, and Publish. When clicked, these icons let you change the theme, edit, or publish the current page, respectively. Since this will be the main page, we have some work to do on it before we actually publish the page.

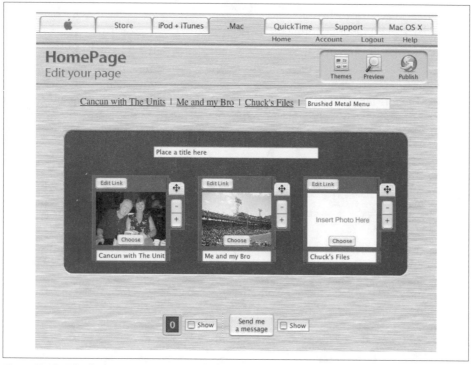

Figure 7-13. Edit the Site Menu page to welcome your visitors.

3. In looking at Figure 7-13, you can see that there are a lot of different text fields that you can edit, and different controls for moving any existing page links around. We'll start by changing a couple of the text fields. At the top, you will see a text field that contains the name of the theme you've chosen (in this case, it says "Brushed Metal Menu"). Change the text in this field to "Home" (no quotes), and then tab down to the next field. The reason you want to name (or consider) this item "Home" is because the top row is a set of links to the various

pages of your .Mac HomePage. This row of links will appear on every page of your site. By naming this page "Home," you guarantee that the people who visit your site can quickly find their way back to your Site Menu page.

 The name you assign to your Site Menu page in the link row will also be used in the `<title/>` tag for the *Menu#.html* page. Since this will just say "Home," you can go back later and edit the `<title/>` tag in the HTML file to display the title as something that identifies the site with you; for example, "Chuck's .Mac HomePage." Changing the text in the `<title/>` tag won't change the text of the link at the top of your site.

4. In the field that says "Place a title here", type in something that will help people identify this page with you.

5. Now let's look closely at the contents portion of what could appear on your Site Menu page. In looking at Figure 7-13, you'll see that I have two Photo Album pages and a File Sharing page already waiting for my site. Since I want to change the pictures that will be seen when someone comes to my site, I will click on the Choose buttons on each of these images. When I do, I'm taken to a page (shown in Figure 7-14) that lets me select a different image from that Photo Album's set.

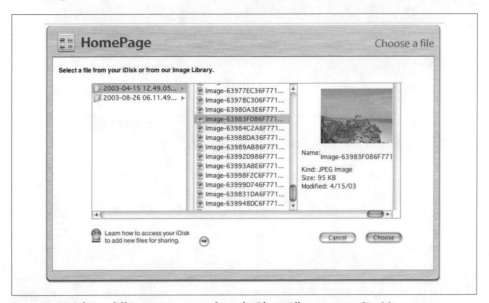

Figure 7-14. Select a different image to use from the Photo Album on your Site Menu page.

To select a different image, simply click on a filename in the middle column, and a thumbnail of the image will appear to the right. When you've found the picture you want to use, click on the Choose button. Repeat this process for each of the images you want to use.

If you don't want to use an image from one of your Photo Albums, but want something else, just make sure that you've selected a JPEG or GIF image that's saved to your iDisk's *Pictures* folder. This means that you can create custom icons for any of the pages in your site, upload them to your iDisk's *Pictures* folder, and then go back and edit your Site Menu page, if you so choose.

6. Below the content area for your site, you will see two options for adding a counter and an email link to your .Mac site's main page. If you want to keep track of how many people have visited your site, or if you'd like people to be able to email you from it, select the checkboxes next to these items, respectively.

When you've edited all of the fields, changed pictures, etc., the Site Menu page will look similar to Figure 7-15.

Figure 7-15. Almost there...

7. If you're sure this is how you want your site's main page to look, click on the Preview button to see what the page will look like (shown in Figure 7-16). If you like what you see, click on the Publish button; if not, click on the Edit button and go back and tweak the things you want to change.

Figure 7-16. Previewing your .Mac HomePage's Site Menu page.

8. After you have clicked on the Publish icon, the *Menu#.html* page will be created and saved to the *Sites* folder on your iDisk, and you will be greeted with the message shown in Figure 7-17.

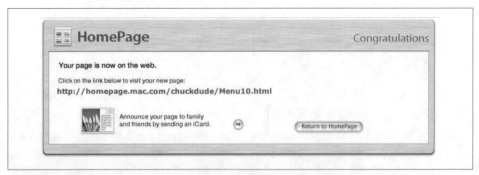

Figure 7-17. With your main page created, there's little work left to be done (or is there?).

From here, you can opt to send an iCard to your friends and family to let them know how to access your .Mac HomePage, or you can click on the Return to

HomePage link to go back and build more pages for your site. As mentioned earlier, though, you don't have to direct your friends to the URL shown on this page. Instead, you can just direct them to *http://homepage.mac.com/membername* (where *membername* is your .Mac member name).

Rather than sending off a message, click on the Return to HomePage button. When you do, you will see all of the Pages for your .Mac site listed at the left of the page, as shown in Figure 7-18.

Figure 7-18. Pay close attention to the listing of your HomePages (on the left).

As you can see, the listing of Pages shows the "Home" page as last in the list; this is because the Site Menu page was the last one created. Unfortunately, this also means that the Home link will be the last one to appear in the list of links at the top of my .Mac site. Worse yet, any other pages that get added after this page has been created will appear after the Home link. If you have only a few pages, this probably won't matter much, but if you have 20 pages, you're forcing your friends and family to find your Home page by reading through all of the links.

Fortunately, this page is interactive, which means you can drag and drop the names of Pages within that listing. Simply click on the name of your Site Menu page (in this case, mine is Home), and drag it to the top of the list and let go of the mouse button. When you do, the Site Menu page will appear at the top of the list, as shown in Figure 7-19.

Now when people go to visit your .Mac HomePage, the Home link appears first in the list, as shown in Figure 7-20.

If you decide later that you want to change the theme for your Site Menu page, simply go back to the .Mac HomePage site (*http://www.mac.com/homepage*), select the file in the Pages listing, and then click on the Edit button.

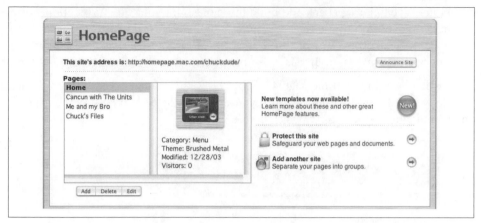

Figure 7-19. Now the Site Menu page (named Home) is listed on top.

Figure 7-20. Check out the list of links on the page; Home is listed first on every page for the site.

Whenever you add a page to your .Mac site, you should consider going back and editing the Site Menu page. That way, you can get the right image you want on your main page.

Creating a Photo Album Page with iPhoto

When it comes right down to it, the easiest way to build a Photo Album page is directly from iPhoto. You can simply select the photos you want to publish from an iPhoto library and click one button to start the process. You can, of course, use the Photo Album style from the .Mac HomePage styles, but you'll first need to upload all of the photos to your iDisk's *Pictures* folder. However, when you create your Photo Albums with iPhoto, iPhoto does all the work for you, so why go through all the extra trouble?

One thing to keep in mind when uploading a Photo Album from iPhoto is that the maximum number of photos you can load on a page is 48. If there are too many photos in the iPhoto Library you want to post, you should look for a way to split them up into separate pages and then group those pages together from the .Mac HomePage page.

To create a Photo Album page from iPhoto, follow these steps:

1. Launch iPhoto by clicking on its icon in the Dock, or by double-clicking its icon in the Finder (*/Applications*).

2. If you want to use all of the images in one of the Photo Albums you've created in iPhoto, simply select the name of the Photo Album in the left column and proceed to the next step. However, if you want only to use a few of the photos in the Photo Album, select the name of the Photo Album and then ⌘-click on the images you want to use. You'll know that a photo has been selected when it has a light blue border around it. In the left column, select the iPhoto Library that contains the photos you want to publish on your .Mac HomePage, as shown in Figure 7-21.

3. When you've selected the photos you want to use in your Photo Album, click on the HomePage button at the bottom of iPhoto's window. After clicking the HomePage button, iPhoto connects to your iDisk to prepare for storing the Photo Album page there, and then opens the window, shown in Figure 7-22.

4. As you can see from Figure 7-22, you can click and edit any of the text fields that will appear on the page, select a theme from the drawer on the right of the window, select layout options (two or three columns), and opt to include an email link and page counter. By default, the captions beneath the photos use the text from the image's filename; just double-click on the filename to select all of its text, and then type in something new. When you're done editing everything, your page should look similar to that shown in Figure 7-23.

5. Click on the Publish button to publish your photos to your iDisk's *Pictures* folder and to create the Photo Album page. When iPhoto is finished building the Photo Album page, it displays the message shown in Figure 7-24, which conveniently includes a link to take you to the page you just created.

   If you click on either the View Page Now or OK buttons (shown in Figure 7-24), the page-building window shown in Figure 7-23 closes.

Figure 7-21. Select the iPhoto library that contains the photos you want to use for your Photo Album page.

Figure 7-22. Building the Photo Album page in iPhoto.

Figure 7-23. Your near-finished Photo Album page.

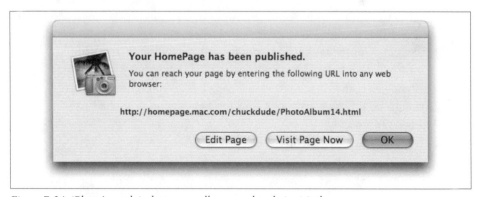

Figure 7-24. iPhoto's work is done; now all you need to do is visit the page.

At the basic level, you're done, but there's more you can do with your Photo Album page, if you so choose. For example, you can go to the .Mac HomePage site and edit the Site Menu page to rearrange the placement of the Photo Album, or you can edit the page itself to change its theme or to add or remove photos. First let's add the new Photo Album to the Site Menu:

1. Go to the .Mac HomePage site (*http://www.mac.com/homepage*).

2. In the Pages column, select the name of your Site Menu page (with me, it's named Home).

3. Click on the Edit button beneath the Pages column.

4. Review the page, and if everything looks as it should, click on the Preview icon.

5. Click on the Publish button to republish your .Mac site's Site Menu page.

Now let's run through the process of changing the theme for your Photo Album. You don't have to if you don't want to, but keep in mind that the HomePage tool offers a few more themes, so you have lots more options to choose from. Just follow these steps to change the theme for a Photo Album page:

1. Go to the .Mac HomePage site (*http://www.mac.com/homepage*).

2. In the Pages column, select the name of the Photo Album page that you want to change the theme of (in this case, it's Pictures of Max).

3. Click on the Edit button beneath the Pages column.

4. When the Photo Album page opens, you'll notice some changes in the toolbar near the top of the window (shown in Figure 7-25).

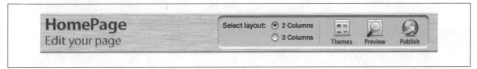

Figure 7-25. When editing a Photo Album, you have more options to choose from in the toolbar.

As you can see from Figure 7-25, you can opt to change the layout from two- to three-columns, in addition to changing themes. For now, though, just click on the Themes icon; when you do, you'll be presented with the complete list of Photo Album themes that the HomePage tools offer, as shown in Figure 7-26.

5. When you select the theme you'd like to use (I've chosen Frameless (Black) for this example), the page refreshes, and the new theme is applied to your Photo Album, as shown in Figure 7-27.

6. Now click on the Publish icon to make the circle complete.

You'll be greeted with another screen, similar to the one shown in Figure 7-17, with a link to the Photo Album page, and options to either announce the page or return to the HomePage tools page. For now, click on the link to the page and bask in the glory of your newly themed Photo Album.

Sharing Files on your HomePage

If you plan to share files from your iDisk's *Public* folder, why not add a web interface to the files within for the people who visit your .Mac HomePage? As mentioned earlier, the latest revision to the .Mac services includes a new option for creating a

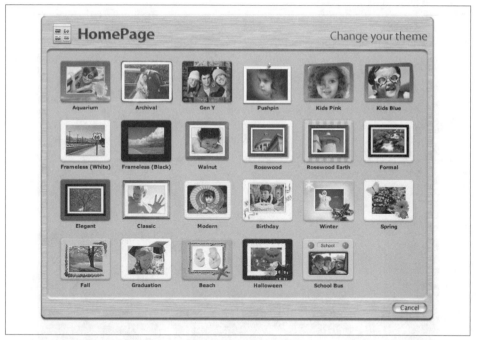

Figure 7-26. Now you can select from one of 23 different themes.

My Downloads sharing page as well. This section shows you how to create both a File Sharing page and a My Downloads page.

Creating a File Sharing Page

To create this page, just follow these steps:

1. Go to the .Mac HomePage site (*http://www.mac.com/homepage*) and log in with your .Mac member name and password.

2. Scroll down to the Create a Page section and click on the File Sharing tab, and then select either the Graphite or Magenta theme (we'll get to the My Downloads theme shortly). When you select the theme, you will be taken to a page that looks similar to Figure 7-28.

   As you can see from Figure 7-28, the name of your File Sharing page shows up in the page navigation at the top, and the page itself looks similar to a folder icon. The tab on the folder has your .Mac member name on it, and next to the heading My iDisk is a space for putting a message for the people who visit this page. These three items (the link at the top of the page, the name on the folder's tab, and the message) can be customized to suit your needs.

3. Now go through the page and change the name of the link at the top of the page, the text in the tab of the folder, and the message next to My iDisk, as shown in Figure 7-29. Use the Tab key to move from one text field to another.

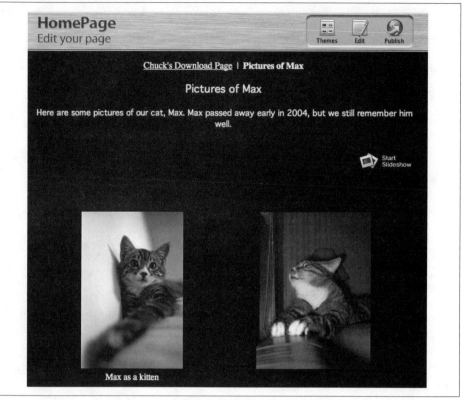

Figure 7-27. Max's page, with the Black theme applied.

4. After you have edited the text fields, click on the Preview button in the toolbar to see the changes you've made to the File Sharing page, as shown in Figure 7-30.

5. If you are satisfied with the changes you've made, click on the Publish icon in the toolbar; if not, click on the Edit icon and re-edit the text fields. After clicking on the Publish icon, you will be taken to a page similar to the one shown in Figure 7-31. This page gives you the URL to your HomePage's File Sharing page, as well as options to announce your File Sharing page or to return to your HomePage.

The actual web page that gets created for your File Sharing page is stored in the Sites folder of your iDisk. As Figure 7-31 shows, the file is named *FireSharing#.html*, where the # is an actual number that's assigned, based on which number the page is for your .Mac HomePage. (In the case of the example shown in Figure 7-31, the File Sharing page created for my site is *FileSharing9.html*, so it's the ninth page I've added to my .Mac HomePage.)

Your iDisk's Public folder now has a web frontend to it, as shown in Figure 7-32.

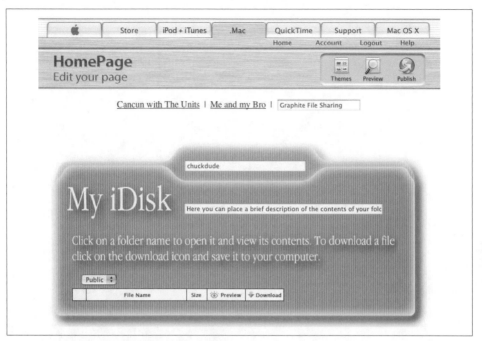

Figure 7-28. Customizing the File Sharing page.

Figure 7-29. Editing the text fields of the File Sharing page.

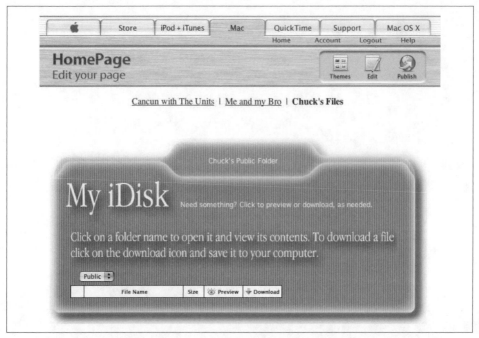

Figure 7-30. My File Sharing page.

Figure 7-31. Out in the Public, my iDisk's Public folder as seen through the File Sharing page.

The files and folders stored in your iDisk's *Public* folder are displayed in the file listing. This area displays the filename and its size, and includes two links: Preview and Download. If you click on the Preview link for an image file, a smaller version of the image will be displayed to the right, as shown in Figure 7-33. If you click on the Download icon, the file will download to your Mac.

If you have added any folders to your iDisk's *Public* folder, they too will be displayed in the file listing, as shown in Figure 7-33. If you click on a folder, the actual folder won't download to your computer; instead, you will be taken to another page,

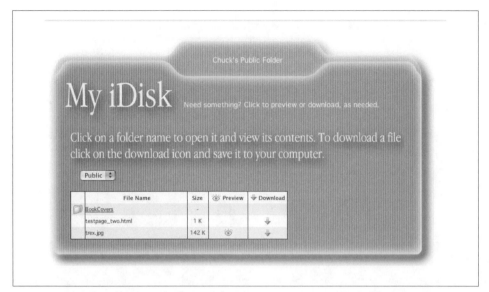

Figure 7-32. My HomePage's File Sharing page.

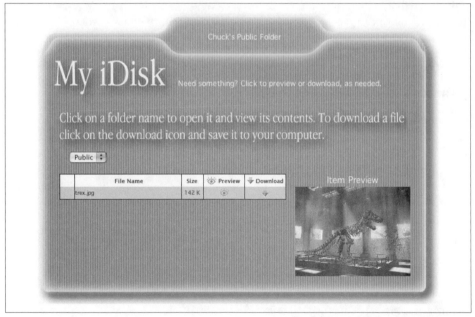

Figure 7-33. See pictures before you download them from someone's Public folder.

showing you the contents of that folder. Also, the folder within your iDisk's *Public* folder appears in the pop-up menu above the file listing, as shown in Figure 7-34.

As mentioned earlier, if you have opted to password-protect your iDisk's *Public* folder, that won't apply to people who come to your File Sharing page through your .Mac

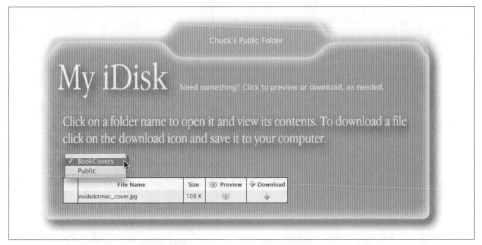

Figure 7-34. Switch between folders in your iDisk's Public folder from the pop-up menu.

HomePage. (However, it does stay in effect for people who opt to connect to your *Public* folder through the Finder or by using the iDisk Utility.)

Unfortunately, you cannot password-protect a single page for your .Mac HomePage. Instead, if you opt to password-protect your HomePage, the password applies across the board to any page of your site that people try to enter (but once in, they're free to roam about and view and download whatever they'd like).

Creating a My Downloads Page

There are times when all you want to do is point someone to your .Mac HomePage for a file they can download. While this is possible by just dropping a file in the *Sites* folder on your iDisk and sending them a link in an email (such as *http://homepage.mac.com/chuckdude/randomfile.zip*), wouldn't it be nice if you could add a graphical interface for the download? Well now you can with the new My Downloads theme. When you select this theme from the File Sharing tab, you'll be taken to the Edit page for setting up your My Downloads page. To customize the My Downloads page, follow these steps:

1. Change the default text in the text fields to something that fits the item being downloaded, as shown in Figure 7-35. Don't forget to change the text in the field at the top of the page, since this will be the name of the link that appears in your .Mac HomePage's navigation area.

2. Click on the "Choose file" button to select the file on your iDisk that you want people to be able to download. After clicking on the "Choose file" button, you'll be taken to the page shown in Figure 7-36. Select a file from one of the available iDisk folders, and then click on the "Choose" button.

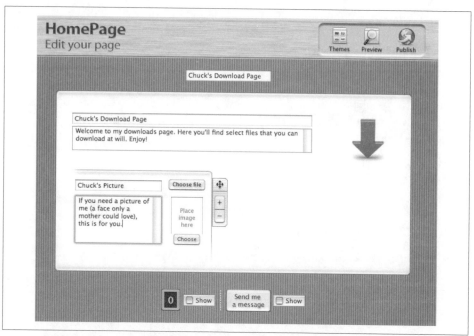

Figure 7-35. Customize the My Downloads page with your own text.

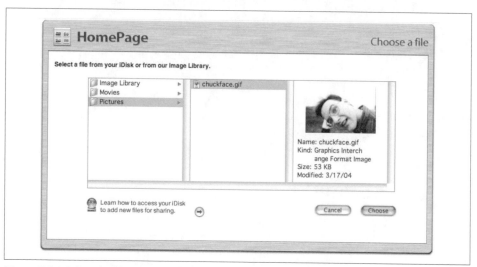

Figure 7-36. Select the file you want people to download.

3. After you've selected the file, you will be returned to the Edit page shown in Figure 7-35. If you want to attach an icon (or image) for the file you've chosen, click on the Choose button beneath the box that says "Place image here". You can choose from one of the images in the Pictures folder on your iDisk, or you can go to the Image Library folder to select one of the image icons Apple has

provided. Also, Apple has added a folder named Application Icons to the Image Library so you can choose an image of a Word or Excel icon, if that's what your document is.

If you're okay with the changes you've made, you can click on the button with the plus sign (+) in it to add another item to the My Downloads page, or click on the Preview button at the top of the page to view your My Downloads page. Click on the Publish button to publish the My Downloads page to your .Mac HomePage. After publishing the My Downloads page, you will be greeted with the message shown in Figure 7-37, which gives you a link to the page.

Figure 7-37. Here's the link for your My Downloads page.

 To copy this link so you can paste it in an email, Control-click on the link and select Copy Link to Clipboard from the menu that appears. To paste the link into an email message, use the standard keyboard shortcut, ⌘-V.

When all is said and done, your My Downloads page should look similar to the one shown in Figure 7-38. When someone goes to your My Downloads page, all they need to do is click on the icon for the file.

Creating an iMovie Page

After you've tried your hand at digital video editing with iMovie, you'll probably want to show it off to your friends and family. Sure, you're not a member of the Coppola family, but who knows, you could be the next Hitchcock, and publishing your iMovie on your .Mac HomePage could get you some exposure.

Earlier in this chapter, in the "HomePage Styles and Themes" section, we mentioned what you needed to do to export your iMovies for use on your .Mac HomePage. Rather than rehash that here, let's just move ahead and create an iMovie page; simply follow these steps:

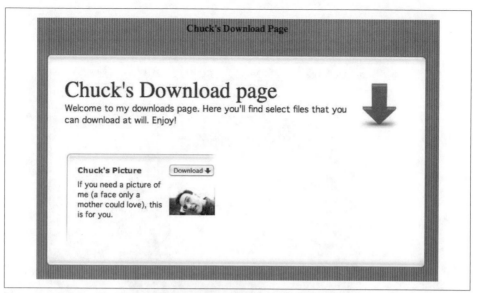

Figure 7-38. The My Downloads page, as published on your .Mac HomePage.

1. Go to the .Mac HomePage site (*http://www.mac.com/homepage*) and click on the iMovie tab.

2. Select a theme to use; try to choose something that matches the style of your iMovie. For this example, I've chosen the Retro-TV theme, as shown in Figure 7-39.

3. Click on the Choose button to select the iMovie you want to use. When you click on this button, you are taken to the *Movies* folder on your iDisk (shown in Figure 7-40), from which you can select the Movie you want to put on display. After you've selected the movie, click on the Choose button to apply the movie to the theme.

4. Click on the Preview icon in the toolbar and take a look at the page and your movie to make sure that everything appears as it should.

5. If you're satisfied with how the page looks, click on the Publish icon in the toolbar.

When the page is published, you will see a message similar to the one shown in Figure 7-17. If you've already created the Site Menu page (described earlier), you will need to click on the Return to HomePage button to add the iMovie to your .Mac site's main page. Once there, follow these steps:

1. Go to the .Mac HomePage site (*http://www.mac.com/homepage*).

2. In the Pages column, select the name of your Site Menu page (with me, it's named Home).

3. Click on the Edit button beneath the Pages column.

Figure 7-39. Edit the iMovie theme page.

4. Review the page, and if your iMovie page is now showing up, click on the Preview icon to see how the finished page will look.

5. Click on the Publish button to republish your .Mac site's Site Menu page.

The page for the iMovie is named *iMovieTheater#.html*, which is stored in the *Sites* directory of your iDisk.

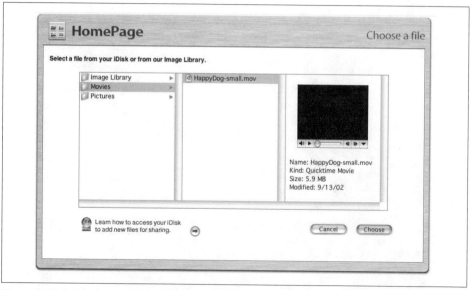

Figure 7-40. Select the movie you want to use.

Creating a Movie Page with iMovie 4

One of the most well-known iApps in Apple's arsenal is iMovie, which first saw its debut back in the Mac OS 9 days. Over the last few years, Apple has continued to improve iMovie, adding new features like the Ken Burns effect, more titling schemes, and integration with your iTunes music library. With iLife '04, iMovie 4 takes another leap forward in all sorts of ways, but one that's of interest to .Mac members is that you can quickly publish your iMovies direct to your .Mac HomePage with just a few simple clicks.

To create a new movie page from iMovie 4, follow these steps:

1. Create your movie in iMovie.

2. Once you've finished your masterpiece, select File → Share (Shift-⌘-E) from the menu bar; a sheet slides out of iMovie's titlebar, presenting you with some options for sharing your movie.

3. Click on the HomePage button at the top of the sheet (shown in Figure 7-41) to see the options iMovie offers for creating your movie page.

4. When you click on the Share button in the sheet, iMovie 4 compresses your movie to 12 frames per second, squeezes it down in size to 240 × 180 pixels, and then uploads a QuickTime movie file to the *Movies* folder on your iDisk. After the movie has successfully loaded on your iDisk, iMovie 4 launches your default web browser to the page shown in Figure 7-41.

5. Click on one of the nine themes to apply the theme to your movie, as shown in Figure 7-42.

Figure 7-41. Click on the HomePage button in the sheet to start the process of creating a movie page.

6. Click on the Edit button in the toolbar at the top of the page to change the link for your HomePage's navigation area, and to add a title and description for your movie, as shown in Figure 7-43.

7. Once you've edited the text fields (see Figure 7-44), click on the Preview button to view the page.

8. If you're happy with how the page looks (and you've checked the spelling), click on the Publish button to add the movie page to your .Mac HomePage.

As you can see, iMovie 4 really makes it incredibly easy for you to publish movies on your .Mac HomePage. You don't have to worry about resizing the movie; just click a few buttons, change some text, click another button or two, and your masterpiece is published to the Web.

Password-Protecting Your HomePage

Say you've got a bunch of stuff on your HomePage that you don't want anyone else to see, or that you only want a select few to have the privilege of viewing. For this, you can password-protect your .Mac HomePage. Keep in mind that password-protection does two things:

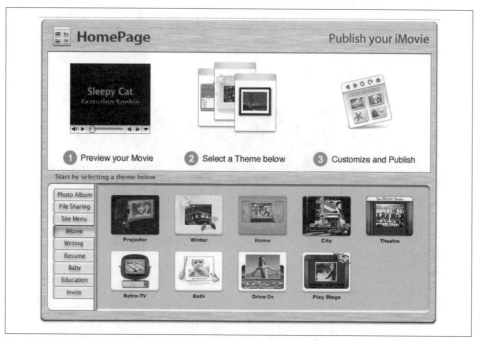

Figure 7-42. Once on your iDisk, it's time to select a theme to wrap around your iMovie.

- It gives you the option of selecting who can view your HomePage.
- It lets you keep others out.

But most importantly, if you created the File Sharing interface to your iDisk's *Public* folder, password-protection makes it so only those who have a password for your site—people you've trusted—can access the files in your *Public* folder. This point is really important because adding the web interface to your *Public* folder instantly makes the contents of your *Public* folder available to anyone, even if you've set up password-protection in the iDisk preference pane (System Preferences → .Mac → iDisk).

To enable password-protection for your .Mac HomePage, follow these steps:

1. Go to the .Mac HomePage site (*http://www.mac.com/homepage*).
2. Click on the arrow to the right of the Pages column for the "Protect this site" link.
3. After clicking on the arrow, you will be taken to the page shown in Figure 7-45.
4. If you want to password-protect your .Mac HomePage, click on the checkbox next to On and then type in a password in the text field provided. Passwords must be 3–8 characters in length, and as the page notes, they are also case-sensitive. You can use the letters a–z and A–Z, the numbers 0–9, and any of the following characters: –, _, ~, !, *, and '; passwords cannot contain spaces.

Figure 7-43. Now your movie has been "themed"; time to edit the page.

5. After you have entered the password for your site, click on the Apply Changes button.

Now when someone tries to view your .Mac HomePage, they will first be challenged for a password, as shown in Figure 7-46.

Announcing Your HomePage

Every time you create a new page for your .Mac HomePage, you are given the opportunity to send out a notice, announcing the new page. If you are creating a new HomePage from scratch (including the Site Menu, Photo Albums, a File Sharing page, and more), you might want to hold off on sending out notices for each page and just send an announcement when your site is complete. Wait to send individual page announcements until later when you add something new to your site.

To send an announcement about the existence of your .Mac HomePage, follow these steps:

1. Go to the .Mac HomePage site (*http://www.mac.com/homepage*).

2. Click on the Announce Site button in the upper-right corner of the web page.

Figure 7-44. Edit the text fields for your movie page.

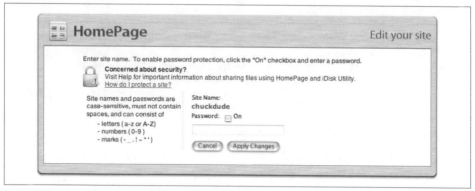

Figure 7-45. Password-protecting your .Mac HomePage.

3. The page shown in Figure 7-47 appears, which lets you select an iCard to send out as the notification for your site.

4. Select an iCard to send.

Figure 7-46. Enter the correct password, enter the site; enter the wrong password, and you will be denied access.

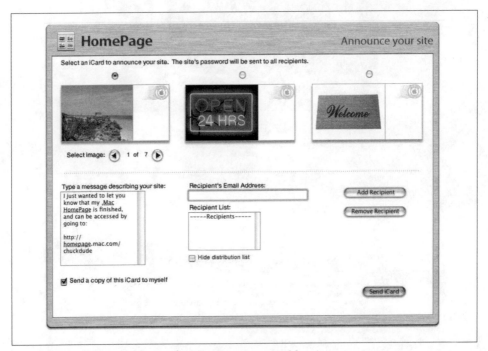

Figure 7-47. Select an iCard to send out to announce your .Mac site.

5. Type in a message to let people know about your site (you don't need to add the URL for your HomePage in the message).

6. Enter an email address in the "Enter emails" field. If you want to send the iCard to more than one person, place a comma between the email addresses (e.g., *chuckdude@mac.com, insidedotmac@mac.com*).

7. After you have entered all of the email addresses, click on the Send iCard button in the lower-right corner of the page.

The people who receive your iCard will also get a brief message saying that you are pleased to announce your new .Mac HomePage, followed by a link they can click on to take them to your site.

Adding a Favicon to Your HomePage

One of the latest trends of corporate web sites is the addition of a *favicon* that gets dropped in before the URL on the location line in most modern web browsers. For example, Figure 7-48 shows O'Reilly's favicon in Safari.

Figure 7-48. O'Reilly's favicon.

As you can see, O'Reilly's favicon is a smaller image of our company mascot, the tarsier (otherwise known as "The vi Guy"). While favicons aren't necessary, they are something cool that you can add to your web site to help people identify the site with you.

 Unfortunately, there's no easy way to add the favicon to all of the pages in your .Mac web site if you are using the HomePage building tools. It would have been great if Apple let you automatically use the image you associate with your .Mac email account (in the Account preference settings, described in Chapter 4) as your favicon, but you can't. Instead, if you want to use a personalized favicon for your HomePage, you will need to roll up your sleeves a bit to get the job done.

Favicon Gotchas

Before you run off and start creating your favicon, there are a couple things that you need to know:

- The size of the favicon is limited to 16 × 16 pixels square (and not a pixel larger).
- The favicon must either be saved as an ICO or PNG file. ICO files are generally Windows icon files, while PNG files (portable network graphics) are also acceptable by most browsers.

- Favicons should be reduced to 4-bit color to not only help keep their file size small, but to also make them viewable on a wider variety of web browsers and platforms (primarily Windows, though).

 My preference is to use PNG as the format for favicons and other web graphics because it's a web standard and PNG files offer things like alpha channel transparency that you can't get with a GIF or JPEG.

For more information about the PNG image format, see the World Wide Web Consortium's (W3C) page at *http://www.w3.org/Graphics/PNG/*.

Choosing and Resizing Your Image

So what makes a good favicon? Something that doesn't have a lot of color and is pretty clear in its original size is always a good choice. Because the image will be reduced to a mere 16 × 16 pixels, the image shouldn't have a lot going on in it, otherwise, it will just look muddy once you've reduced it in size.

For example, I decided to use a picture of my friend's dog, Rowan, as my favicon image. The original image (a grayscale version of which is shown in Figure 7-49), was originally 475 pixels square. When reduced to 16 pixels square, you could still tell that it was a dog's head with a yellow background.

How you resize the image depends on the tools you have at your disposal. You can use anything from high-end applications such as Adobe Photoshop (*http://www. adobe.com*), to web-graphics apps such as Macromedia's Fireworks (*http://www. macromedia.com*) or GraphicConverter from Lemke Software (*http://www.lemkesoft. com*). But you can also use iPhoto to resize and save an image in PNG format; you just have to get a little creative with how you use it.

To take the image shown in Figure 7-49 and convert it into a favicon, follow these steps:

1. Launch iPhoto by either clicking on its icon in the Dock or double-clicking its icon in the Finder (*/Applications*).
2. Locate the image you want to use as your favicon in the Organize section, select the image, and then click on the Edit button.
3. In the lower-left corner of iPhoto's window, click on the Constrain pop-up menu and select the very last option in this pop-up menu: Square.
4. Move the mouse pointer over the image; you'll see that the arrow changes to a set of crosshairs. Click-and-drag a selection of the image; you'll notice that the selected area is constrained to the dimensions of a perfect square, as shown in Figure 7-50.

Figure 7-49. The original image for your favicon shouldn't be busy; something simple works best.

Figure 7-50. Constrain your selection to a square, as shown here.

5. Select the area of the image you want to use. If you need to move the selection square around to adjust the selection, you'll notice that the mouse pointer changes to a hand with its index finger extended. Just click and drag the square around to how you want it to be.

6. To make the image a perfect square, click on the Crop icon (located to the right of the Constrain pop-up menu).

7. Select File → Export (Shift-⌘-E) from the menu bar; this opens the Export Photo window, shown in Figure 7-51.

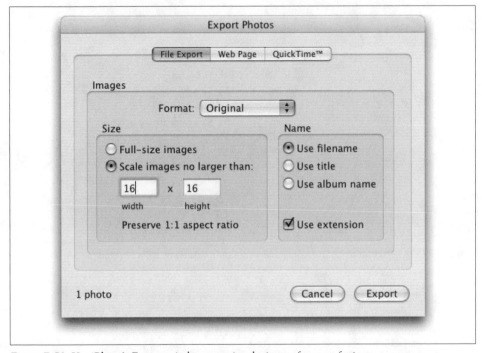

Figure 7-51. Use iPhoto's Export window to resize the image for your favicon.

On the left side of the window (in the Size section), select the radio button next to "Scale images no larger than" and then tab down to the width field below. Type in 16; since the image is a perfect square, the height will be constrained to 16 pixels as well. Leave the Format menu set to Original, and in the Name section, leave "Use filename" as the selection.

8. Click on the Export button; when you do, a sheet slides out of the window's titlebar, giving you the option of changing the image's filename and selecting a place to save it. As shown in Figure 7-52, we've opted to save the file in the *Pictures* folder, since that's the logical place to save an image.

If you look closely, you'll notice that the file was named *rowan_16x16*. I named the file this way to remind me that it is only 16 pixels square. As for the file

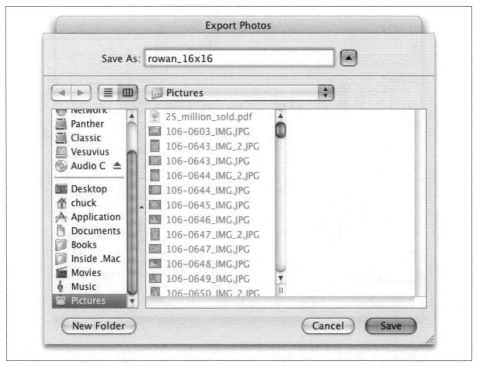

Figure 7-52. Save the resized image in your Pictures folder.

extension, iPhoto will save the image in its original format, since that's the option we selected in the Format menu. In this case, the file will be saved as a JPEG image.

9. Select File → Import (Shift-⌘-I) from iPhoto's menu bar, navigate to the *Pictures* folder, and select the image you've just exported, as shown in Figure 7-53, and then click on the Import button.

10. In iPhoto, click on the Last Import icon to the left, and then select the image. Because its size is so small, you'll notice that the image is fairly distorted; don't worry about that right now.

11. Go back to the menu bar and select File → Export (Shift-⌘-E).

12. In the Format pop-up menu, select PNG as the format. Now you may be wondering why we just didn't do this earlier and save all these steps. Well, the answer is because you can't; iPhoto won't let you export a PNG image and resize it at the same time.

13. Click on the Export button to bring up a dialog similar to that shown earlier in Figure 7-51. Instead of leaving the file named as *rowan_16x16*, I've renamed it as *favicon*. After clicking on the Export button, iPhoto converts the image to a PNG graphic and saves it as *favicon.png* in my *Pictures* folder.

14. Quit iPhoto (⌘-Q).

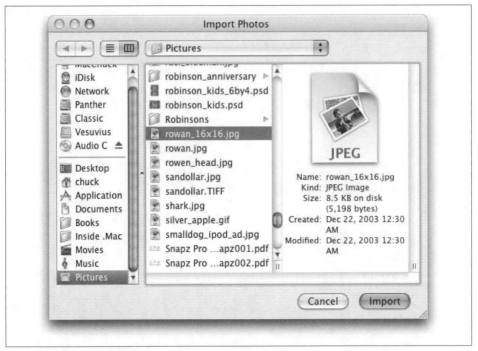

Figure 7-53. Select the image and import it into iPhoto.

That's it; you've created and saved your favicon using nothing more than some random image and iPhoto. Best of all, you didn't have to run out and spend $500 on Photoshop just to resize and convert an image. Now let's put that little graphic to work as a favicon for your web pages.

Uploading the Favicon to Your iDisk

Now that you've created a PNG graphic to use for your favicon, you need to upload the image file to your iDisk. Just follow along:

1. If your iDisk isn't already mounted, open a Finder window and click on the iDisk icon in the Sidebar.

2. After the iDisk mounts, switch the Finder window to Column View (View → as Columns, or ⌘-3), and then click on the *Sites* folder.

3. Open another Finder window by selecting File → New Finder Window (⌘-N), and select the *Pictures* folder in the Sidebar

4. Place the two Finder windows side by side, as shown in Figure 7-54.

5. Locate and select the *favicon.png* file in the *Pictures* folder, and then drag it into the iDisk's *Sites* folder in the other Finder window. When you let go of the mouse button, the *favicon.png* file will be copied to your iDisk.

6. Close the two Finder windows.

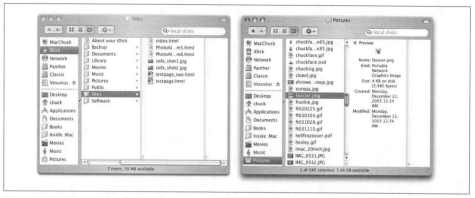

Figure 7-54. Use two Finder windows to upload the favicon to your iDisk's Sites folder.

Now you're ready to start deploying the favicon throughout your .Mac HomePage.

Creating the HTML Tags for a Favicon

Example 7-2 shows the basic HTML code used for creating a test page to see whether favicons can actually be used on .Mac HomePages. The two lines that you'll want to pay attention to are the `<link/>` tags, which are highlighted in bold.

Example 7-2. Basic HTML source code for a page that uses favicons

```
<html>
<head>
<title>Chuck's .Mac HomePage</title>

<link rel="shortcut icon" href="favicon.png"></link>
<link rel="icon" href="favicon.png" type="image/png"></link>

</title>
</head>

<body bgcolor="#FFFFFF">

<h2>Just Testing my Favicon</h2>

<p>
This page is simply here to test whether or not <i>favicons</i>
work on .Mac HomePages.
</p>

</body>
</html>
```

As you can see, there are two `<link/>` tags that get added to the header section (the area between the `<head>` and `</head>` tags) of the HTML file. The first line:

```
<link rel="shortcut icon" href="favicon.png"></link>
```

tells the web browser that the icon, which is linked in with href="favicon.png" is to be used as a shortcut icon for the web page. If somebody bookmarks your .Mac page, the favicon will show up along with the bookmark in their list of favorite sites. Meanwhile, the second line:

```
<link rel="icon" href="favicon.png" type="image/png"></link>
```

is the link to the image (href="favicon.png") that gets pulled into the location line of the web browser.

To see whether this works, I saved the HTML code shown in Example 7-2 and named it as *testpage_two.html* in my *Sites* folder. When you load the URL *http://homepage.mac.com/chuckdude/testpage_two.html*, you will see the page shown in Figure 7-55.

Figure 7-55. The favicon worked!

It worked! As you can see, the very tiny image the dog shows up as the favicon for this page. As mentioned earlier, there's no way to automatically add the tags for the favicon with the HomePage building tools. Unfortunately, you'll have to copy and paste the two <link/> tag lines into the headers of every HTML page of your .Mac HomePage.

Rolling Your Own

Just because Apple provides the tools for building your HomePage doesn't necessarily mean that you have to use them. If you want, you can design and build your web site and still host it online from your iDisk.

The advantage to building your web site this way is that you have more control over the style, graphics, and layout of the web site, and you can use any tool you want from vi or BBEdit as a plain text editor for hacking your own HTML, or other WYSIWYG design tools like Macromedia's Dreamweaver MX or Adobe's GoLive.

If you take on the task of building your own web site, follow these simple rules:

- The main page for your site (named *index.html*) should be placed in the *Sites* folder of your iDisk. Do not use *default.html* as the filename for your main page as the .Mac servers won't serve that page if people try to load its directory. For example, if you place a *default.html* page in your *Sites* directory and point someone to *http://homepage.mac.com/membername*, they will see an error message saying that the page could not be found. However, if you give them the link of *http://homepage.mac.com/membername/default.html*, the page would be viewable in their web browser.

- You can either place all of the graphics files within a folder in the *Sites* folder, or you can store them in the *Pictures* folder. If you store your graphics in the *Sites* folder, just remember to use relative links when referring to other pages of your site. For example, if the HTML files for your web pages are in the *Sites* folder and the graphics are in the *Pictures* folder, you would refer to them with either of the following tags:

```
<!-- Absolute Link -->
<img src="http://homepage.mac.com/chuckdude/.Pictures/
psychomax.gif" alt="Picture of Max" height="100" width="500">

<!-- Relative Link -->
<img src=".Pictures/psychomax.gif" alt="Picture of Max"
height="100" width="500">
```

- If you try mixing .Mac HomePages with your own pages, be warned that you could run into problems, particularly if there's a conflict in filenames found in any of the directories. You should devise your own file-naming scheme and stick to that, but make sure that you're not using something that exactly matches the filenames used by the HomePage building tools.

- To add your own web pages to an existing .Mac HomePage, click on the Advanced tab and select the External HTML theme (see "Advanced," earlier in this chapter).

Learning More About Web Design

If you've caught the bug and want to learn more about how to build a web page and maybe stray away from using the HomePage tools, there lots of resources available to you.

Some books that are worth picking up include:

- *Learning Web Design*, by Jennifer Neiderst (O'Reilly, 2003)
- *Web Design in a Nutshell*, by Jennifer Neiderst (O'Reilly, 2001)
- *HTML & XHTML: The Definitive Guide*, by Chuck Musicano and Bill Kennedy (O'Reilly, 2002)
- *Cascading Style Sheets: The Definitive Guide*, by Eric A. Meyer (O'Reilly, 2004)
- *Designing with Web Standards*, Jeffrey Zeldman (New Riders, 2003)

Additional web-related books from O'Reilly can be found at *http://web.oreilly.com*. Here you'll find a complete listing of books they have available for web designers, and sample chapters from their books as well. In addition to these books on web design, you might also be interested in the following:

- *iPhoto2: The Missing Manual*, by David Pogue and Derrick Story (O'Reilly/Pogue Press; 2003)
- *iMovie 3 & iDVD: The Missing Manual*, by David Pogue (O'Reilly/Pogue Press; 2003)

The following web sites can come in handy as well, especially if you're looking for tutorials to help you learn more:

Web Monkey
  http://www.webmonkey.com

WebReference
  http://www.webreference.com

CHAPTER 8

Blogging with iBlog

iWhat? iBlog (*http://www.lifli.com/Products/iBlog/main.htm*), produced by Lifli Software, is a web-logging application for Mac OS X. It's a third-party application, which means that it doesn't come from Apple, nor is it supported by them. At the time of this writing, iBlog is still a beta application, meaning it's still under development.

What Is a Blog?

A blog is the hip, short term for "web log." A blog is basically a way for you to publish information on the Web. Your blog can be anything: a diary or journal, your views on current events, recent activities of your cat, whatever.

Most blogs are also interactive, which means that people who read your blog can post responses.

Blogging goes way back, and can be traced down to Frontier, but has really become popular in the last two or three years. If you search on Google for "blog" and any other keyword (e.g., blog + Macintosh), you will find quite a few Mac-centric blogs to read.

Why iBlog?

Yes, there are other blogging tools available, but they often require more set up and work to get them going. With iBlog, all you need to do is download the software, register it (if you want to continue posting a blog to your .Mac HomePage for more than 15 days), and install iBlog in your *Applications* folder. The registration fee for iBlog is $19.95, and is payable via PayPal.

 A trial version of iBlog can also be downloaded from your iDisk, located in */Software/Members Only/iBlog*.

iBlog is also one of the few all-in-one blogging tools. iBlog offers both an authoring and publishing environment, which enables you to write the content for your blog and post it up to your .Mac HomePage.

For .Mac Members who want to have a blog but don't want to deal with the hassles of running your own web server, iBlog is the perfect answer. While it might not have all the bells and whistles as the other blogging tools, you'll find that iBlog serves its purpose and is well worth the shareware fee to keep it going.

The only downside to using iBlog is that you have to be using your Mac (or another Mac with iBlog installed) to connect to your iDisk to post your blog entries. This is unlike other blogging tools, such as Movable Type (*http://www.movabletype.org*), which lets you blog from pretty much anywhere.

 For a complete overview of blogging software options, see Scott Hacker's article, *Put Weblogs to Work*, in *Macworld* magazine's July 2003 issue.

Installing iBlog

The latest version of iBlog can be downloaded from Lifli Software's web site (*http://www.lifli.com/Products/iBlog/download.htm*). iBlog downloads to your Mac as a disk image (a *.dmg* file), and should automatically mount on your Desktop. After the disk image mounts, a Finder window will pop open, revealing its contents, as shown in Figure 8-1.

Once the disk image has mounted, next you'll need to install iBlog on your Mac. To do this, follow these steps:

1. Open a new Finder window (File → New, or ⌘-N). This opens another Finder window, placing it on top of the Finder window that contains the contents of iBlog's disk image.

2. In the new Finder window, click on the Applications icon in the Finder's Sidebar, or use its keyboard shortcut, Shift-⌘-A.

3. Create a new folder called iBlog in the *Applications* folder. To do this, go to File → New Folder (Shift-⌘-N). An "untitled" folder appears in the *Applications* directory.

4. Change the name of the folder from "untitled" to "iBlog"; this is where you're going to move the contents of iBlog's disk image.

5. Scroll up in the Finder view and click on the *iBlog* folder. If your Finder isn't in Column View, you should switch to that view by selecting View → as Columns (or ⌘-3). You'll notice that iBlog's folder is empty.

6. Now bring iBlog's disk image window to the front by selecting Window → iBlog from the Finder's menu bar. Now a window similar to the one shown in Figure 8-1 will be on top.

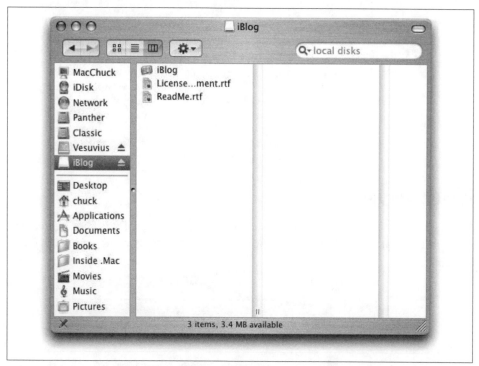

Figure 8-1. After iBlog's disk image mounts, a Finder window pops open, revealing its contents.

7. Next, select and drag the contents of iBlog's disk image window into the *iBlog* folder you've created in the *Applications* folder. To do this, you can either drag-select all of the icons in iBlog's window or use Edit → Select All (⌘-A). All of the icons in window will be selected.

8. Drag the icons from iBlog's disk image window and place them in the *iBlog* folder you've created in the *Applications* folder. A window will appear, informing you that the files are being copied to the *Applications* folder on your hard drive.

9. Once the files have been copied into the *iBlog* folder, you can close the iBlog window and unmount the iBlog disk image from your Desktop by selecting File → Eject (⌘-E). This automatically closes the iBlog window and unmounts the disk image all at the same time.

Now you're ready to start learning how to use iBlog. If you're planning to write to your blog frequently, you should consider placing iBlog's icon in your Dock. To do this, simply select iBlog's icon in the Finder and drag it to someplace on the Dock. You could also just launch iBlog and then right-click on its Dock icon and select Keep In Dock from its contextual menu.

It's worth noting that you don't have to copy all of the files from iBlog's disk image onto your Mac; you can just drag iBlog's icon into the *Applications* directory where it will live and function normally.

It's always good practice to keep any associated files with an application, though. For example, iBlog comes with RTF versions of its license agreement and a README file. While you might not need these immediately, there may come a time when you might want to refer back to them for some reason. If you find that you never use these, you can always delete them, and then drag iBlog out of the folder and just drop it into the *Applications* folder.

iBlog Overview

When you first launch iBlog, and after you've read through its license agreement, you'll notice that its window (shown in Figure 8-2) has a fairly complex interface.

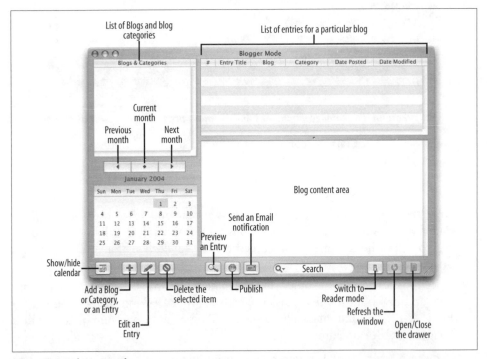

Figure 8-2. iBlog's interface.

Most of iBlog's basic functions can be accessed from the row of buttons along the bottom of the window. The window itself has four main areas for creating and managing your blog entries.

For a complete rundown of iBlog's menu items and keyboard shortcuts, see Appendix A.

Registering iBlog

Like most third-party software (i.e., software not provided or sold by Apple), iBlog is shareware. That means that you can use iBlog for up to 15 days before you will need to pay for a license to use the software all of the time.

When you register your copy of iBlog, you're agreeing to the license terms, and most importantly, agreeing to fork over the $19.95 registration fee for two seats (which means you can legally install iBlog on no more than two Macs). But once you have registered iBlog and have that license key in-hand, you can use iBlog beyond the 15-day limit and publish a blog to your .Mac HomePage.

After your payment has been received, Lifli Software will send you an email containing the license key. To register your copy of iBlog, go to the iBlog menu (the Application menu) and select Register. A window similar to the one shown in Figure 8-3 appears.

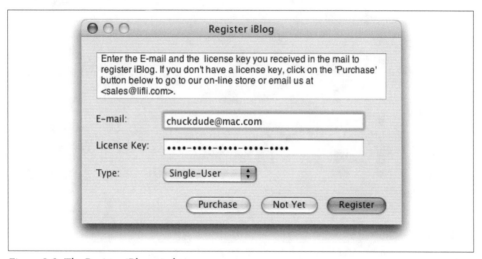

Figure 8-3. The Register iBlog window.

To register your copy, enter the email address that Lifli sent the email to, and then enter the License Key from the email in the appropriate field. With both of those fields complete, click on the Register button.

 You must be connected to the Internet to register your copy of iBlog. The reason is because iBlog sends the information you enter in those fields to Lifli's servers. If everything checks out just fine, you're free to use iBlog to your heart's content. (Get it? Content?)

Once you've registered your copy of iBlog, the next thing you'll need to do is configure its preferences.

iBlog's Preferences

iBlog works in mysterious ways. Well, not really, but you will need to tweak iBlog's preferences before you can start your life as a blogger.

To open iBlog's Preferences window, select iBlog → Preferences (⌘-;). As you can see from Figure 8-4, there are four different "panes" to iBlog's preferences, each of which can be accessed by clicking on its icon in the toolbar. iBlog's preference panes are described in the following sections.

General

The General pane, shown in Figure 8-4, is where most of the action happens for iBlog.

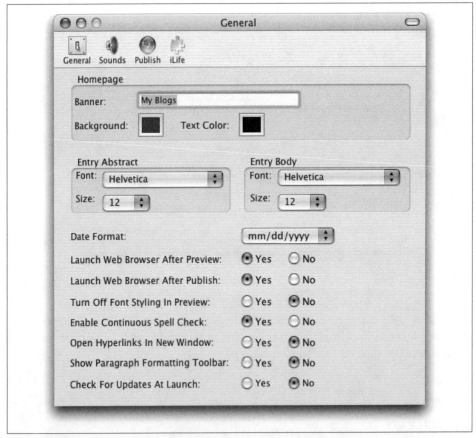

Figure 8-4. iBlog's General preferences pane controls most of iBlog's settings.

The General preferences pane is split into the following three sections that let you specify some of the basic elements of your blog:

Homepage

The Homepage section lets you specify a name for the name that will appear as the Banner for your blog. By default, this is set to My Blog, but you can change that to anything you'd like, such as Chuck's Blog.

Also in this section are color selectors, which let you specify the Background and Text Color for your blog's homepage. By default, the Background color is set to a burgundy color, and the Text Color is set to black. To change the colors, simply click on the colored box to open the Color palette, shown in Figure 8-5.

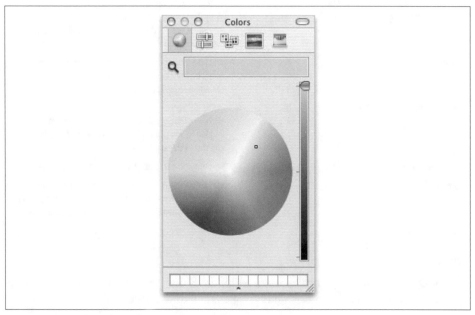

Figure 8-5. Use the color palette to select a different color for either the Background or the Text Color.

When you've selected the color you want, simply close the Colors window, and the color you've chosen appears in the appropriate box in the Homepage section.

Entry Abstract
Entry Body

These two sections allow you to specify the fonts and font sizes for the blog entries. By default, the Font is set to Helvetica and the Size is set to 12 (points) for both. Remember, this is your blog, so get creative and change things up a bit. Pick fonts and sizes that reflect your style, but keep in mind that they need to be readable.

Date Format

This menu lets you select the date format that gets added to your blog entries. Your options are mm/dd/yyyy (the default) or dd/mm/yyyy.

Following these sections are a series of items with Yes/No radio buttons, which are described in Table 8-1.

Table 8-1. iBlog's General preferences radio buttons

Item	Default	Action
Launch Web Browser After Preview	Yes	This launches the default web browser when you preview a blog entry.
Launch Web Browser After Publish	Yes	This launches the default web browser after you publish a blog entry.
Turn Off Font Styling in Preview	No	With "No" specified as the default, this means that the styles specified for the fonts will be viewable when you preview a blog entry.
Enable Continuous Spell Check	Yes	All of the blog entries will be spell checked as you enter them; leaving this set to Yes will reduce the number of typos and errors in your blog entries.
Open Hyperlinks in New Window	No	With "No" specified as the default, any hyperlinks that get clicked on from within the blog entry will open in the same window; if you want links to open in a separate window, you should change this to Yes.
Show Paragraph Formatting Toolbar	No	This turns off paragraph formatting in iBlog's toolbar.
Check for Updates at Launch	Yes	This automatically looks for updates every time iBlog is launched; by having this set to Yes, it ensures that you will be notified when there is a new release you should download.

Sounds

The Sound preferences panel, shown in Figure 8-6, allows you to have an alarm sound whenever you make a certain type of change to your blog.

If you don't want iBlog to make any sounds, you can simply uncheck all of the checkboxes next to the items listed in the Operations column.

Publish

Before you can publish a blog, you first need to specify a blog using the Publish preferences pane, shown in Figure 8-7.

At the bottom of this window is the Choose Location Type pop-up menu. By default, this menu is set to .Mac (which we'll want to use), but you can also opt to publish your blog to FTP, Local (your Mac's local domain), WebDAV, or AFP. Since we want to publish the blog to your .Mac HomePage, just leave this menu set to .Mac.

To add your blog to the list of Publish Locations, click on the New Location button at the bottom of the window. A sheet slides out of the window's titlebar, as shown in Figure 8-8.

Figure 8-6. iBlog's Sounds preferences pane.

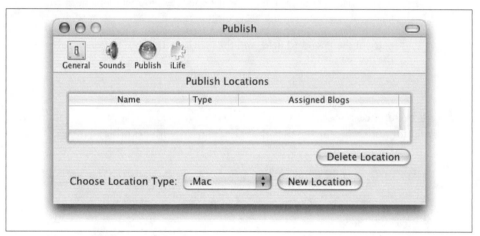

Figure 8-7. iBlog's Publish preferences pane.

Since the blogs you write will be posted to your iDisk, you will need to supply your .Mac username and password in the fields provided, as shown in Figure 8-8. For the Location Name, choose anything you'd like; for me, I've set this to Chuck's .Mac Blog, as shown.

By default, iBlog is set to save your blog entries in the */Sites/iblog* directory on your iDisk. iBlog creates the *iblog* folder and places that within the *Sites* folder on your iDisk the first time you create a blog entry.

Once you've filled in all of the blanks on this sheet, click on the Save button to save the new location for your blog.

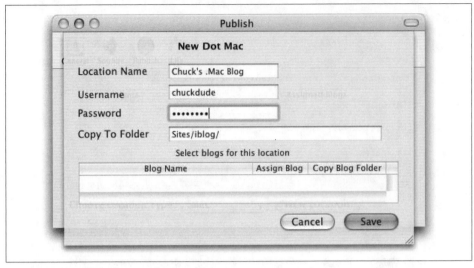

Figure 8-8. Specify the location for your blog.

 If you change your .Mac password frequently, you will also need to change its password in iBlog's Publish preference panel. To do so, just double-click on the blog location name to open the sheet, change the entry in the Password field, and then click on the Save button to save the new password.

iLife

The iLife preference panel, shown in Figure 8-9, is used for specifying the location and format for audio and image files that can be used with your blog entries.

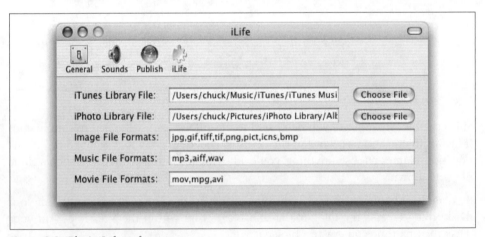

Figure 8-9. iBlog's iLife preferences pane.

Now that you've learned what iBlog is and how to configure its preferences, the next step is to actually create your blog.

Building Your Blog

Once you've configured iBlog's preferences and tested out the interface, you're ready to make your mark on the Internet with your blog. When you're first starting out, there are three things that you need to do:

- Create a blog
- Create a category (or multiple categories) for the blog
- Create entries for the category

Think of your blog in the same context as a book. Each book (a blog) has a table of contents (categories), and inside, the book has chapters (entries) that contain text and pictures. So, the first thing you'll need to do is create the blog, specify any categories (if needed), and then start making your blog entries.

How Often Should I Blog?

This is one question that many newcomers to blogging often ask, and the answer really depends on how much time you want to devote to blogging. Most people tend to post one blog entry a day, while others practically run a news service with all their posts.

Blog when the mood hits you, or when you have something worth sharing with your readers.

The big thing to keep in mind is that once you publish your blog, the entries are stored on your iDisk (in */Sites/iblog*), so you'll need to keep track of how much space your blogs are taking up and maintain them properly. (Prior to publication, your blog entries are stored locally in the *~/Sites/iblog* folder.) Fortunately, most blogs are just text and HTML coding, so those files shouldn't take up too much space.

Creating a Blog

The actual process of building a blog with iBlog is pretty simple. To create your first blog, select New Blog (Option-⌘-N) from the File menu; the sheet shown in Figure 8-10 appears.

As you can see from Figure 8-10, the sheet for creating a blog has two tabbed panes: Attributes and Display Settings. The Attributes pane is where you assign a name and description for your blog, specify whether your blog will have an RSS XML feed that other bloggers can pick up on and so you can add your name and email address to the blog.

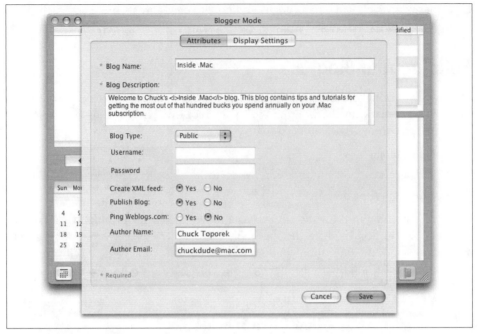

Figure 8-10. The Attributes pane.

There's also an option to select whether your blog will be Public (the default) or Private. If you opt to select Private from the Blog Type pop-up menu, you will need to assign a username and password. This is a good way to restrict access to certain blogs that you want to allow only a select few access.

 The only two required fields that you must fill out on the Attributes pane are the Blog Name and Blog Description fields; the others are optional.

The Display Settings sheet, shown in Figure 8-11, is what you use to set up the layout and specifics of your blog. From this sheet, you can specify:

- The width of the content and navigation areas of the web page
- The number of entries for each blog or category page
- The order in which blog entries and categories appear
- The number of entries on the feed page
- The template to use (left or right navigation)
- The CSS stylesheet to use

For most people, the default entries should be fine. However, if you want to change the stylesheet around so that you're not using the default, your options consist of

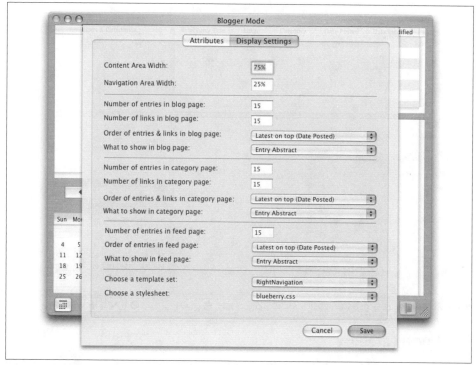

Figure 8-11. The Display Settings pane.

blueberry (the default), banana, blackberry, honeydew, mint, or plain. You can pre-view each of these stylesheets by selecting one, clicking on the Save button, and then clicking on the Preview icon in iBlog's main window. The page will build and then you can see how it will look.

When you've finished changing the settings for your blog on the Attributes and Display Settings sheet, click on the Save button. This creates a folder for the blog on your hard disk (in *~/Sites/iblog*); the blog also shows up in the Blogs & Categories section of iBlog's window, as shown in Figure 8-12.

As you can see, the blog shows up in the window as a folder with a black disclosure triangle to its left. To reveal the contents of the blog folder, click on the disclosure triangle so that it points downward. You can also use the right arrow key to reveal the folder's contents, just as you would in the Finder's List View. If a blog doesn't have any categories assigned to it, the folder will appear empty.

From here, you have one or two options. You can opt to create categories for your blog, or you can just start writing entries and publishing them up to your blog. Before showing you how to create a blog entry, though, I'll first cover blog categories.

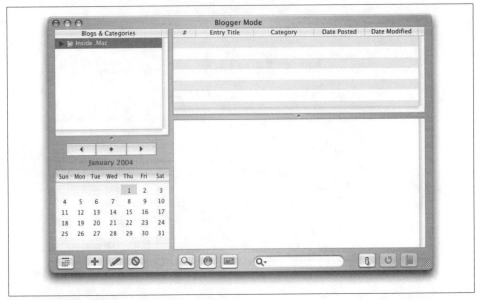

Figure 8-12. The Blogs & Categories section.

Creating a Category

To add a category to your blog, you can either select New Category from the File menu (Shift-⌘-N), or you can click on the plus-sign button at the bottom of iBlog's window, as shown in Figure 8-13. When you click on the plus-sign button, a context menu pops open, giving you the option to create a new blog, a new category, or a new entry.

Figure 8-13. Select New Category from the plus-sign button's context menu.

After selecting New Category, a sheet opens up with a text field so you can assign a name to the category, as shown in Figure 8-14. The only required field on this sheet is the Category Name field.

If you have an image you want to associate with the category, you can drag that from the Finder and drop it into the Category Image box. Images should be no more than 64 × 64 pixels square. Once assigned to a category, the image will appear along with any blog entry that fits into the category.

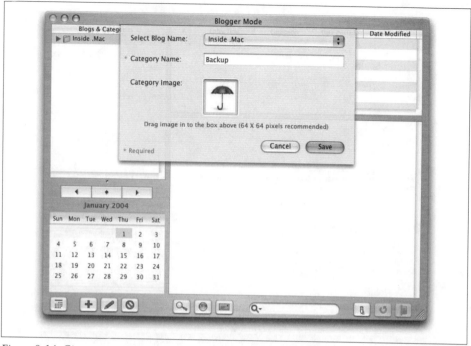

Figure 8-14. Give your category a name and add an image, if you desire.

When you have saved the name for your category (by clicking on the Save button in the sheet shown in Figure 8-14), the new category will appear as a folder within the blog's folder, as shown in Figure 8-15.

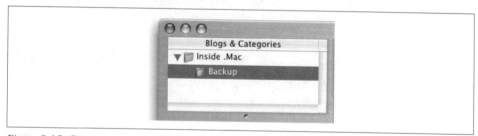

Figure 8-15. Categories appear as folders within the Blog folder.

Making an Entry

With two steps down, the only step remaining is actually creating your blog entry. As shown earlier in Figure 8-13, click on the plus sign button at the bottom of iBlog's window and select New Entry from the menu. Or, if you prefer, you can select New Entry from the File menu (⌘-N).

After selecting New Entry from the menu, the New Entry window shown in Figure 8-16 pops open. Just type in the information for your blog entry, and click on the Save button when you're finished.

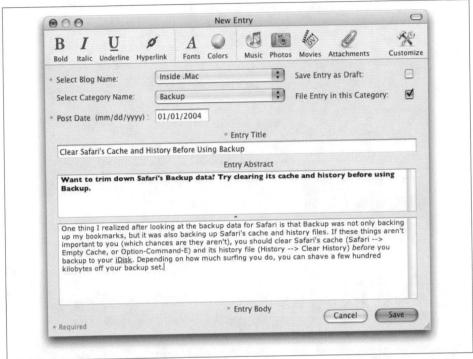

Figure 8-16. *The New Entry window gives you a place to create your blog entries; just fill in the blanks.*

 Make sure that you check your spelling before posting your blog to the Web; nothing will turn off readers more than a blog riddled with typos.

After you click on the Save button, the New Entry window closes and your blog entry appears in iBlog's window, as shown in Figure 8-17.

If you decide that you want to change something in your blog entry (maybe the title or some part of the body isn't quite right?), you can double-click on the entry in the list at the upper-right part of the window. This will open the blog entry in the editing window so you can make your changes; just click on the Save button when you're satisfied with the changes.

Previewing your blog entry

Now comes the moment of truth: the time when you get to see how your blog entry will look before it is published. At the bottom of iBlog's window, click on the button that looks like a magnifying glass; this is the Preview button. When you click on the Preview button, iBlog creates the web page for your blog entry, saves it into your *~/Sites/iblog* folder, and then opens the blog in your default web browser, as shown in Figure 8-18.

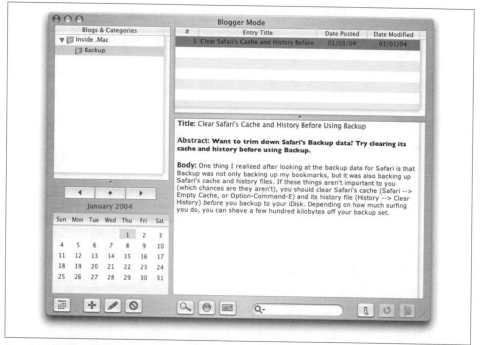

Figure 8-17. The saved blog entry, just waiting to be previewed and published.

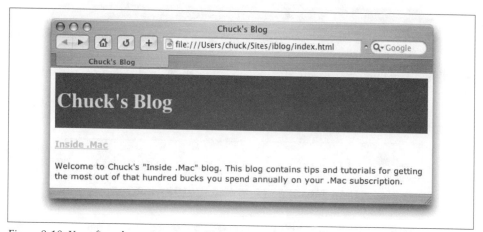

Figure 8-18. Your first chance to see your blog is in Preview mode.

As you can see from Figure 8-18, iBlog previews a page that lists the blogs you've created; in this case, it's my blog for *Inside .Mac*. If you click on the link for the blog title, you will be taken to another page (shown in Figure 8-19) that lists the blog entries and their categories.

Now let's take a closer look at what gets posted on the blog page. If you look at Figure 8-20, you'll see a close up of the blog entry itself. Here you can see that iBlog

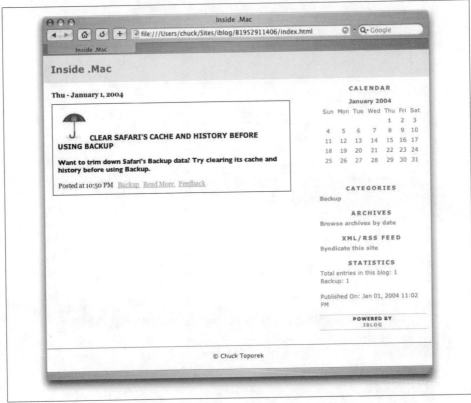

Figure 8-19. A preview of the blog entry created back in Figure 8-16.

places the entry in a box, assigns a date above the entry, and then uses the title and abstract you've given to the blog entry.

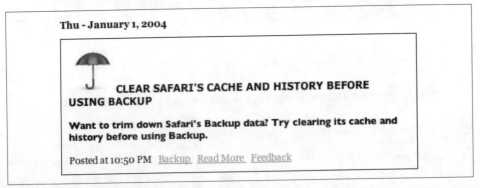

Figure 8-20. A closer look at the blog entry.

Beneath the entry's abstract, you'll see a timestamp that tells you when the blog entry was posted, followed by three links:

Backup

> The category link; this takes the reader to a page containing all of the blog entries for that particular category

Read More

> Takes the reader to the full-text of the blog entry

Feedback

> Takes the reader to a page where they can offer comments and feedback on that particular blog entry

Of the three, only the first link title should change for you (unless, of course, you're running a blog category named "Backup"). Figure 8-21 shows what the entire blog entry looks like, if someone were to click on the Read More link.

CLEAR SAFARI'S CACHE AND HISTORY BEFORE USING BACKUP

Want to trim down Safari's Backup data? Try clearing its cache and history before using Backup.

One thing I realized after looking at the backup data for Safari is that Backup was not only backing up my bookmarks, but it was also backing up Safari's cache and history files. If these things aren't important to you (which chances are they aren't), you should clear Safari's cache (Safari --> Empty Cache, or Option-Command-E) and its history file (History --> Clear History) *before* you backup to your iDisk. Depending on how much surfing you do, you can shave a few hundred kilobytes off your backup set.

Posted: Thu - January 1, 2004 at 10:50 PM   Inside .Mac   Backup   Feedback

Figure 8-21. View the full blog entry with the Read More link.

You can see that the blog entry carries three links of its own; these include:

Inside .Mac

> A link back to the blog's main page

Backup

> A link to the blog's category page

Feedback

> A link to the Feedback page

When a reader clicks on the Feedback link, a new email message window will open up in their default email client. The reader can then send their comments to you via email if you entered your email address in the Attributes sheet when you created the blog (see Figure 8-10, earlier in this chapter).

This is the one downside of iBlog over other blogging software. With other blogging software, readers of your blog can post comments back to your web site. However, since iBlog is publishing to your iDisk, readers can only send their feedback via email.

If you're satisfied with how the previews of your blog entry look and read, it's time to publish your blog.

Publishing your blog

To publish your blog, click on the Publish icon (the one with a little globe on it, just to the right of the Preview icon). When you do, you'll probably run into the error message shown in Figure 8-22.

Figure 8-22. What? No blogs found?!

Before you can publish your blog, you first need to specify which blogs are publishable in iBlog's preferences. Go to iBlog → Preferences (⌘-,),click on the Publish icon in the toolbar, and then double-click on the name of the item in the Publish Locations field. You'll see the name of the blog you created (in my case, *Inside .Mac*) with two empty checkboxes off to the right. Click on these checkboxes to enable publishing of the web log, as shown in Figure 8-23.

After clicking the Save button, close iBlog's preference window and try publishing your blog again. This time it should work and not give you any errors. The only time you should see an error now is if you're not connected to the Internet. The reason for that is because iBlog publishes to your iDisk, and it needs that Internet connection to create the files and folders in your iDisk's *Sites* folder (*/Sites/iblog*).

Sending an email notification

When iBlog connects to your iDisk, a message window appears and displays information about the files being transferred to your iDisk. After the files have transferred successfully, iBlog opens the entry in your default web browser. One thing that's

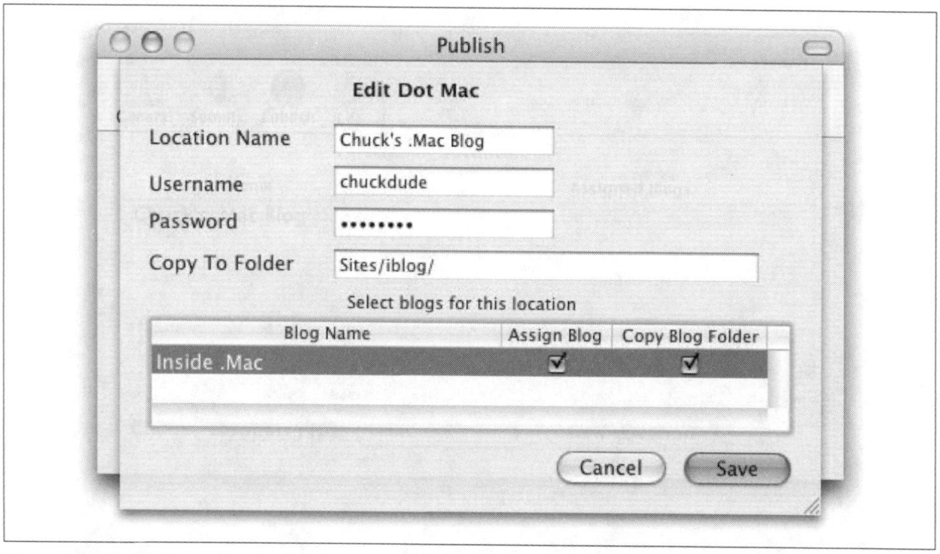

Figure 8-23. Click on the checkboxes to assign the blog as publishable.

particularly odd about the entry, though, is the naming scheme used isn't particularly user-friendly. For example, the link for the post created in this example is:

http://homepage.mac.com/chuckdude/iblog/B1952911406/index.html

Worse yet, if someone just goes to:

http://homepage.mac.com/chuckdude/iblog

the reader will see an error message, saying that the page doesn't exist.

To help you get around this, iBlog includes an email notification button at the bottom of its window. When you click on this button (which looks like an envelope), the sheet shown in Figure 8-24 appears. From here, you can select contacts in your Address Book and send them an email notification with the link to your blog entry, as shown in Figure 8-25.

Unfortunately, there's no way to automate this process; you'll have to point the readers to your blog each and every time.

Another solution to this problem is to take the *index.html* file that iBlog creates in *~/Sites/iblog* and just drag that to the */Sites/iblog* folder on your iDisk. This makes it so people can just go to the *iblog* directory with the link:

http://homepage.mac.com/membername/iblog

and they will see a page similar to the one shown earlier in Figure 8-18 that just lists blogs.

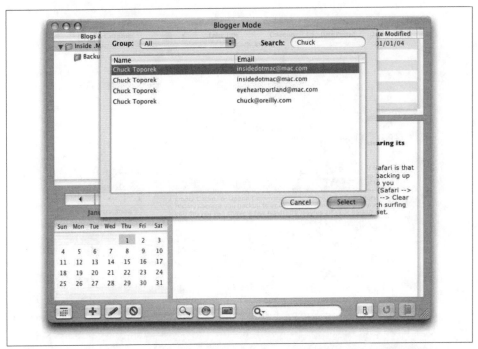

Figure 8-24. Use the sheet to select and/or search for the people whom you want to notify about your blog.

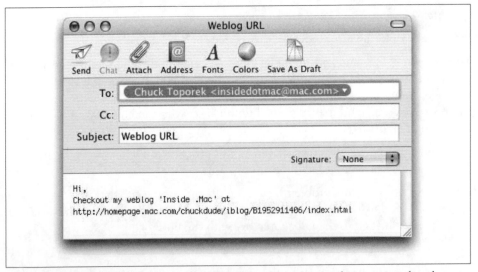

Figure 8-25. After clicking on the Email button, iBlog opens a new email message window that includes a link to the blog entry.

Further Exploration

As you can see, there's a lot more to iBlog than meets the eye, but for creating a basic blog that you can publish on your .Mac HomePage, it does the trick. Once you've mastered the basics of using iBlog, you might want to consider using iBlog to:

- Customize the stylesheets for your blog (Resources → Manage Stylesheets)
- Customize the templates for your blog (Resources → Manage Templates)
- Use iBlog in Reader Mode to read and subscribe to various newsfeeds and blogs (Window → Switch to Reader Mode, or Option-⌘-T)

For more details on using iBlog, visit Lifli Software's web site at *http://www.lifli.com*, or visit *http://www.ibloggers.net* to see what other people are doing with iBlog.

CHAPTER 9

Using iSync with .Mac

As part of its Digital Hub strategy, Apple not only paid close attention to how people were using their Macs, but also to the other devices that people use in their daily life. As Bluetooth technology spread from Europe and Asia to North America, more and more people—Mac users—found themselves with Bluetooth-enabled cell phones and PDAs, but didn't have a way to synchronize the devices with their Mac. Apple realized that something needed to be done to help Mac users share the information on their Mac with their devices, and the result was iSync (*http://www.apple.com/isync*). iSync is a small application that synchronizes contacts, calendars, and bookmarks from your Mac with your .Mac account and other devices that are part of your digital life.

Think of iSync as a conduit that shuttles information from your Mac to other devices and back again. iSync is used to synchronize the Address Book contacts, iCal calendars, and Safari's bookmarks to your .Mac account and to portable devices connected to or detected by your Mac. iSync provides a way for you to always have access to your contacts, calendar, and bookmarks from wherever you are, or on whatever device it is you're using.

This chapter starts out with a quick overview of what iSync is and goes on to show you how synchronize your contacts, calendars, and bookmarks with your .Mac account, other devices, and with another Mac.

Understanding iSync

One way to look at the whole synchronization process is to assign generic terms to the process. Since your Mac will most likely be the place from which all of the synced data will originate, it can be considered the *source*. On the other hand, the device that you want to sync data with can be called the *destination*. It's kind of like the old math equation where you want to get from Point A to Point C, but first you need to go through Point B. In this case, the source (your Mac) is Point A, the destination (the device) is Point C, and in the middle, you have iSync (Point B) acting as a conduit to shuttle the data from here to there. Figure 9-1 illustrates this relationship.

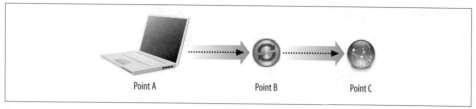

Point A   Point B   Point C

Figure 9-1. The synchronization process is as simple as getting from Point A to Point C, with iSync in the middle as Point B.

With iSync, you're not just limited to synchronizing your data with your .Mac account. You can synchronize your data with personal data assistants (PDAs), cellular phones, an iPod, and with other Macs, as shown in Figure 9-2.

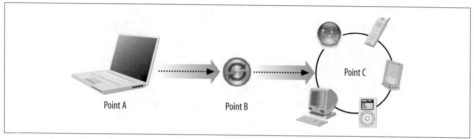

Point A   Point B   Point C

Figure 9-2. iSync also works as a conduit to shuttle data from your Mac to a variety of devices, including cell phones, iPods, and other Macs.

And the synchronization process is a two-way street, meaning that the data on your Mac is compared with any existing data on the device. If there is a slight change or something new, iSync will alert you to those changes and allow them to be made to the data on your Mac.

The important thing to remember is that iSync is mostly responsible for getting your data from Point A to Point C and back again. iSync enables you to use the contacts in your Address Book, iCal calendars and To Do lists, and Safari bookmarks on multiple devices. As such, iSync is an integral part of Apple's "Digital Hub" strategy, by fitting your Mac into your digital lifestyle.

Now that you know the basics of how iSync works, let's take a quick run-through of the application itself and show you how to put iSync to work.

Overview of iSync

Like most of the iApps, iSync is fairly small application with an intuitive interface. This section serves as a quick overview of iSync's interface so you can start pushing bits of data around. But first, let's take a look at the type of data you can sync, and to where you can sync that data.

What You Can Sync

There are only three types of data that you can synchronize from your Mac with other devices:

- Bookmarks from Apple's web browser, Safari
- The contact information stored in your Address Book
- Calendars and To Do items from iCal

To select which items you will synchronize, simply click on the checkboxes next to the desired item under the This Computer section, as shown in Figure 9-3.

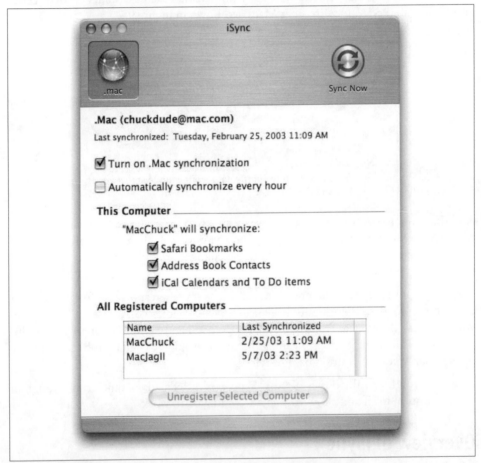

Figure 9-3. Select which items you can sync from your Mac by clicking on the checkboxes under the This Computer section.

Now let's discuss each of these items individually.

Syncing Safari's bookmarks

One of my most prized possessions (well, at least on my computer) is my bookmark list. If you're like me, you probably have hundreds of bookmarks that you've painstakingly categorized. However, the big problem with bookmarks is that they're typically available on one computer only. If you have more than one computer, the only way you can ensure that your bookmarks make it from one Mac to the other is to physically transfer the bookmark file. But that only solves one problem and creates another, because there really is no way to ensure that someone else didn't add bookmarks to the Mac while you were away.

 Safari bookmark syncing was introduced with iSync Version 1.1 (released June 2003). If you are running an earlier version of iSync, you should download a newer version from Apple's web site (*http://www.apple.com/isync*). To see which version of iSync is installed on your Mac, launch iSync and go to iSync → About iSync.

Unlike other web browsers (such as Internet Explorer and Netscape Navigator) that store their bookmarks as an HTML file, Safari's bookmarks are saved in the form of a property list (or *plist*) file. A *plist* file is nothing more than an XML file that contains data. Safari's bookmark file is located on your Mac in *~/Library/Safari/Bookmarks.plist*. If you know a little about XML and Schemas, it's fairly easy to interpret the *Bookmarks.plist* file, as well as any other *plist* file on your Mac. However, unlocking the secrets of a *plist* file is beyond the scope of this book.

 If you've installed Apple's Xcode Tools, you can use the Property List Editor (found in */Developer/Applications/Utilities*) to open, view, and edit *plist* files.

The Xcode Tools are available on CD, and can also be downloaded from the Apple Developer Connection (ADC) web site (*http://developer.apple.com*). The disk image containing the Xcode Tools weighs in at around 350 MB, so you'll need a high-speed Internet connection (cable, DSL, T-1, etc.) to download the package.

You can use iSync to place a copy of your *Bookmarks.plist* file on your iDisk, where it can be synced with another Mac, or to web-enabled PDAs and cell phones.

Syncing data from Address Book

When you add or change a person's contact information in the Address Book application, that person's information is stored in a set of files found in *~/Library/Application Support/AddressBook*. The files you'll find in that directory include:

ABPerson.index
>   This file is used to build the index of the contact information you've stored in your Address Book.

AddressBook.data
> This file contains all of the contact information for the entries you've made to your Address Book.

AddressBook.data.backup
> As the name implies, this is a backup file of the *AddressBook.data* file. The *AddressBook.data.backup* file is created automatically by the Address Book application whenever you make a change to the contacts.
>
> If your Address Book has gone haywire and you need to restore its data, this file will be used to rebuild the *AddressBook.data* file. As such, you should regularly make a backup of your Address Book's database, not just by using the Backup application (see Chapter 5), but also by using one of the methods described here.

AddressBook.data.beforesave
> This file is similar to the *AddressBook.data.backup* file in that it contains the information in your Address Book. The difference is that this file is created automatically when you quit Address Book; whereas, you need to actually do something to create the *AddressBook.data.backup* file. The *AddressBook.data. beforesave* file contains the information stored in your Address Book just prior to quitting time.

AddressBook.data.previous
> Like the *AddressBook.data.beforesave* file, this file contains the information found in your Address Book, both past and present. This means that the *.previous* file also contains contact information for people whom you've deleted from your Address Book. This file is regenerated whenever you finish adding, deleting, or making changes to records in the Address Book application. This is also regenerated just prior to when the *AddressBook.data.beforesave* file is created.

Images
> The Address Book application lets you add an image to individual records; this directory contains the data for rendering those images. The filenames for the images appear as a generic alphanumeric string, such as *8DF28640-B112-11D6-AB3C-00039398D26E*. Each of these files contains the raw TIFF image data for the image associated with an individual's Address Book record.
>
> Also within this directory is the *CachedMacDotComPhotos* directory. This directory contains TIFF image files for the people in your Address Book who have a photo associated with their record. The image filenames resemble that person's email address, but with a *.tiff* extension; for example, *chuckdude@mac.com.tiff* or *x180@mac.com.tiff*.

Syncing data from iCal

When it comes to synchronizing your iCal data, iSync looks in *~/Library/Calendars* for any *.ics* files. Files that end with a *.ics* file extension, which are the only type of files saved in the *~/Library/Calendars* directory, are the calendar files you've created or subscribed to using iCal.

Extracting Address Book's Images

You don't have to worry about resizing images when you drag a photo of a person into their record in your Address Book. Address Book takes the image—regardless of its original size—creates a smaller version of that file, and then assigns that image to that person's record in the Address Book.

When that image icon is created, Address Book saves one version in the */Cached-MacDotComPhotos* directory and assigns it a filename based on the person's email address, and another version in the *Images* directory with an alphanumeric filename, as mentioned earlier, but that isn't necessarily clear. The alphanumeric filename, as well as the data within that file, is very cryptic, but you can view the image by doing the following:

1. Open a new Finder window (File → New Finder Window, or ⌘-N) and navigate your way to *~/Library/Application Support/AddressBook/Images*.

2. Click on one of the alphanumeric filenames in that directory and select File → Duplicate (⌘-D) from the menu bar. A duplicate of the file is created in the same directory with "copy" added to the filename as a way of letting you (and the system) know that it's a copy of the original file.

3. Click on the "copy" file and hit the Return key; this selects the filename and allows you to give it a new name.

4. Type in a new filename, and give that file a *.tiff* extension (for example, *chuckdude.tiff*).

5. Press the Return key again to accept the new filename. You'll notice that the file's icon changes from a blank, generic icon to whatever application you've chosen as the default for viewing TIFF files. Most likely, the default application for viewing TIFF files will be Preview (*/Applications/Preview*).

To view the image file, simply double-click on its icon. If the application required to view the image isn't running, that application will launch and the image will be displayed in a window for your viewing pleasure.

Now you have a separate image file for that user, which you can then use for other purposes, including use in iChat.

When your iCal calendars have been synced with your iDisk, the synchronization and backup files are stored in *~/Library/Application Support/SyncService*. There will be two folders in the *SyncService* directory:

Backup Data

This directory contains three folders (*AddressBook*, *Calendars*, and *Safari*), which contain the backup data created by iSync the last time Devices → Backup My Data was selected. Also within this directory is a copy of the *com.apple.iCal.sources.plist* file; which is the property list file that contains the preferences information for iCal.

LastSync Data

This directory contains three folders (*AddressBook*, *Calendars*, and *Safari*), which contain the a copy of the Address Book, iCal calendars and To Do items, a copy of Safari's *Bookmarks.plist* file, and a copy of the *com.apple.iCal.sources. plist* file from the last time iSync was used to synchronize this information with any device.

The *com.apple.iCal.sources.plist* file found in *~/Library/Application Support/SyncService/Backup Data* and *~/Library/Application Support/ SyncService/LastSync Data* is sourced from the original file, which can be found in *~/Library/Preferences*.

Address Book's property list file, located in *~/Library/Preferences/com. apple.AddressBook.plist*, is not backed up or synchronized by iSync. Safari's main property list file is located in *~/Library/Preferences/com. apple.Safari.plist*.

While it might sound like the *Backup Data* and *LastSync Data* folders contain the same information, they can be completely different, depending on when you last performed a sync or backed up your data using iSync. If you don't use iSync's Backup My Data option from the Devices menu often, the information in that directory can get stale-dated. Meaning, if you haven't backed it up with iSync, the files are probably old and somewhat unreliable if you're hoping to recover recent changes from them.

If for some reason your Address Book, iCal information, or Safari's bookmarks gets lost or corrupt, and you haven't backed them up to your iDisk, you can recover your data from iSync using either Devices → Revert to Last Sync, or Devices → Revert to Backup.

What You Can Sync With

Before you set off to start using iSync, you'll need to think about what you're going to sync your Mac with. There are five different types of "devices" that you can sync your Mac with using iSync:

- Your .Mac account
- iPod
- Another Mac
- A personal data assistant (PDA), such as a Palm Tungsten or the Handspring Treo
- A cellular phone, such as the Ericsson T68i or Nokia 3650

iSync 1.3 supports a wider variety of cellular phones and services, and handheld devices. For a complete list of devices you can sync your data with, go to *http://www.apple.com/isync/devices.html*.

The most obvious place to synchronize your Mac with is with your .Mac account. By synchronizing your data with your .Mac account, the data is used to provide various web-based services offered through your .Mac membership, such as:

- The contacts in your Address Book can be used with .Mac's web-based Mail service (see Chapter 4), and can also be synchronized with other Macs
- Any calendars you create and publish with iCal, including To Do items, are stored on your iDisk, and can be synced to another Mac
- The bookmarks you save with the Safari web browser can be accessed online (see "Bookmark Syncing," later in this chapter) and shared with other Macs

If you were wondering if iSync could be used to duplicate the information on one Mac's hard drive and place that on the hard drive of another, in effect giving you one cloned system based on another Mac's digital DNA—think again. iSync cannot be used to synchronize entire hard disks between Macs on a local network. But don't worry, all hope is not lost.

To clone one Mac's hard disk to another, you'll have to resort to other tools, such as the *rsync* Unix command-line utility for remote synchronization, or Mike Bombich's Carbon Copy Cloner (*http://software.bombich.com*). Both of these utilities allow you to clone the data stored on one hard disk and place that on another. However, use of *rsync* and Carbon Copy Cloner are beyond the scope of this book. For more information on *rsync*, consult its manpage (via *man rsync* in the Terminal, or visit its web site at *http://rsync.samba.org*).

Where the Sync Goes

Now that you know what gets synced with iSync, you're probably guessing at where all that data goes. If you are using iSync to sync data with your .Mac account, the information is stored on your iDisk in the */Library/Application Support/Sync* directory. Depending on what you've synchronized, there can be three subdirectories within the *Sync* directory:

BKMK
    This directory contains the data for your Safari bookmarks.
CONT
    This directory contains the data for the contacts stored in your Address Book.
ICAL
    This directory contains the calendar and To Do items from iCal.

When syncing data with an iPod, Address Book data will be stored in the *Contacts* folder as *iSync.vcf*, and any iCal calendars and To Do items will be stored in the *Calendars* folder. The files placed in the *Calendars* folder by iSync will all begin with *iSync-* as part of their filename; for example, *iSync-Work.ics*, *iSync-Personal.ics*, etc. Since the current breed of iPods aren't Internet-enabled devices, Safari bookmarks will not be synced to your iPod.

When you use iSync to synchronize the data from your Mac with other devices such as a cellular phone or a PDAs, the data is stored on those devices in a format that can be interpreted and displayed by that device.

iSync's Preferences

Keeping true to its form, iSync's preferences are pretty simple. You can access iSync's preferences window, shown in Figure 9-4, in one of two ways: from iSync's application menu (iSync → Preferences), or by using its keyboard shortcut (⌘-,).

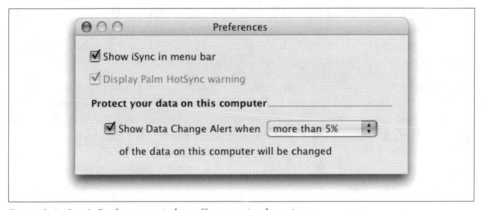

Figure 9-4. iSync's Preferences window offers two simple options.

As mentioned earlier, selecting the checkbox next to "Show iSync in menu bar" will place an icon for iSync in the menu bar. This "menulet," shown in Figure 9-5, gives you easy access to open or use iSync to synchronize your data. It also lets you know the date and time that you last performed a sync of any kind.

You can also view iSync's options from its Dock menu, as shown in Figure 9-6. To open iSync's Dock menu, simply click on its Dock icon and hold the mouse button down; after a few seconds, the menu will appear. The main difference between iSync's menulet and its Dock menu is that the Dock menu includes "Show In Finder" and Quit (or Force Quit, available by Option-clicking iSync's Dock icon) options.

The other option available in iSync's preferences is for displaying the Safeguard panel. As you can see from Figure 9-4, there is a pop-up menu that has four options for choosing whether the Safeguard panel will be displayed if "any," "more than

Figure 9-5. iSync's menulet gives you quick and easy access for using iSync or for seeing when you last synced your data.

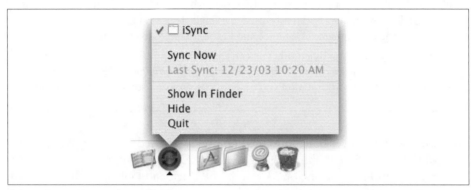

Figure 9-6. iSync's Dock menu.

1%," "more than 5%," or "more than 10%" of the data on your computer or any device will be changed. You can't miss the Safeguard panel when it appears because its titlebar will have a black and yellow construction zone–style pattern. For more information about the Safeguard panel, see the section "Performing Your First Sync" later in this chapter.

To close the Preferences window, either click on the red close window button or use the keyboard shortcut ⌘-W; any changes made in the Preferences window will be saved when the window closes.

Adding and Removing Devices

It's actually quite simple to add and remove devices to and from iSync's list of devices with which to synchronize data. There are four possible device types that you can add to iSync:

- .Mac account
- Bluetooth-enabled cellular phones
- Bluetooth-enabled PDAs
- iPods

The .Mac "device" is actually your iDisk, and is available by default and cannot be removed from the list of possible devices to sync with. Any other devices either need to be connected or within range of being detected via Bluetooth. For example, if you want to synchronize data from your Mac to your iPod, your iPod needs to be connected to your Mac with its FireWire cable (the data can't get there by itself, now, can it?).

What Is Bluetooth?

Bluetooth, which is not Bluebeard's ugly step-cousin, is a short-range (up to about 30 feet) wireless technology, primarily used by small devices such as cellular phones, PDAs, and the next generation of mice and keyboards for personal computers.

For more information on Bluetooth, you can either visit Apple's web site at *http://www. apple.com/bluetooth*, or the main Bluetooth web site, *http://www.bluetooth.org* (but keep in mind that the information you find on that site is mostly for propeller-heads).

For wireless syncing over Bluetooth, the first thing you need to do is make sure that your Mac supports Bluetooth. The easiest way to see this is to open the System Preferences application by clicking on its icon in the Dock and looking in the Hardware section. If your Mac supports Bluetooth, the first icon on the left of that section is for the Bluetooth preferences panel, as shown in Figure 9-7.

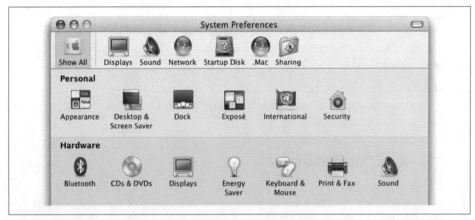

Figure 9-7. If your Mac supports Bluetooth, look in the Hardware section of the System Preferences window; if you see the Bluetooth panel listed on the left, you're good to go.

If you do not have a Mac with built-in Bluetooth (such as one of the new Aluminum PowerBooks), you can purchase a Bluetooth adapter that plugs into one of your Mac's USB ports.

Most any Bluetooth adapter can work with older Macs running Mac OS X 10.2 (Jaguar) and above; however, Apple recommends and stocks the adapters from D-Link (*http://www.dlink.com*) in their online Apple Store (*http://store.apple.com*) and in the Apple Stores (*http:// www.apple.com/retail*) scattered around the globe.

Likewise, if you have a Bluetooth-enabled device such as a cellular phone or PDA, and if you have one of the newer PowerBooks or a Bluetooth adapter, you can use iSync to synchronize data between your Mac and the device.

Quitting iSync

While this might seem trivial, there are few ways you can quit iSync:

- By selecting Quit iSync from iSync's application menu.
- By issuing the Quit command's keyboard shortcut, ⌘-Q.
- By closing iSync's window, either by clicking on the red close window button in iSync's titlebar, or by using the standard Close Window keyboard shortcut, ⌘-W.

Of course, you could always use the Force Quit option from the Apple menu, or open a Terminal window, issue the *top* command, and then find and kill iSync's process from the command line, but that would be overkill. You should reserve those options for when iSync is frozen and unresponsive.

Registering Your Mac with the Sync Server

There's a first time for everything, and this is true with iSync. There are a few things that you need to do the first time that you use iSync, the first of which is to register your computer with the .Mac synchronization server. To register your computer, follow these steps:

1. Make sure your Mac is connected to the Internet. To do this, open the Network System Preferences panel and look for an IP address in the TCP/IP tab. If you see an IP Address listed there, you're ready to go; if not, you should connect with your Internet Service Provider (ISP).

You cannot register your Mac with the .Mac synchronization server without a connection to the Internet (direct-connect, wireless, or dial-up).

2. Launch iSync by double-clicking on its icon in the Finder (*/Applications*), or by clicking on its Dock icon. When iSync launches, its window will be collapsed, as shown in Figure 9-8, with just a .Mac button on the left and iSync's button on the right, prompting you to "Sync Now".

Figure 9-8. At first sight, iSync's window is pretty simple.

3. To start the registration process, click on the .Mac icon on the left edge of the window. When you click on the .Mac icon, the status bar at the bottom edge of the window will slide downward (similar to how a sheet slides out of a window's toolbar) to reveal iSync's options.

To start the process of registering your Mac with the .Mac synchronization server, click on the Register button at the lower-right corner of iSync's window as shown in Figure 9-9.

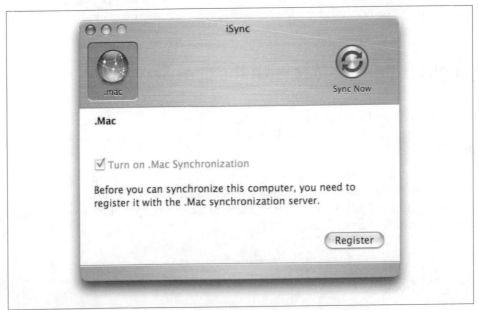

Figure 9-9. After clicking on the .Mac button, iSync's window opens up so you can register your Mac with the .Mac synchronization server.

4. The next thing you need to do is to give your Mac a name. This can be the same name you've set up in the Sharing preferences panel (System Preferences → Sharing), or something completely different.

To give your Mac a name, simply type in a name in the text field as shown in Figure 9-10. The Mac's name is used by the .Mac synchronization server to recognize your Mac whenever you perform a sync to your .Mac account. After entering a name for your computer, click on the Continue button.

Figure 9-10. Assign a name that the .Mac synchronization server will use to recognize your Mac whenever you attempt to sync its data.

5. After you click on the Continue button (noted in the previous step), there will be a short delay while iSync registers the name of your Mac with the .Mac synchronization server. To register your computer, iSync sends the name you have given to your Mac along with your .Mac Member Name and password, as specified in the .Mac preference pane (System Preferences → Internet → .Mac).

You can associate more than one Mac to your .Mac Member Name with the .Mac synchronization server by simply assigning a different name for each computer. For example, if you have two Macs, one at work and one at home, you could register them with the .Mac synchronization server as MacWork and MacHome, respectively, as long as your .Mac Member Name is the same on both Macs.

Once your Mac has been registered, iSync will notify you of this fact in the "This computer" section of its display (shown in Figure 9-11). If you've registered any other computers to your .Mac account, the names of those computers will be listed in the "Other computers" section.

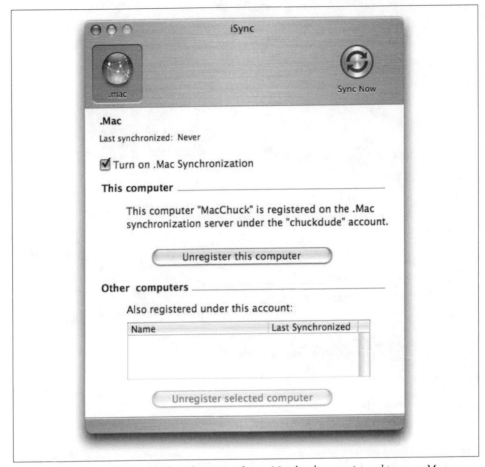

Figure 9-11. iSync informs you when the name of your Mac has been registered to your .Mac account.

Once your Mac has been registered with the .Mac synchronization server, you're ready to perform your first sync.

Performing Your First Sync

With the fine details out of the way, it's time to put iSync to work. With your Mac registered with the .Mac synchronization server, iSync can be used to transfer the data from your Mac to your iDisk; once there, your contacts, calendars, and bookmarks can be pulled over to other Macs or used by other .Mac services.

This section shows you how to add and remove devices to the sync list, and provides an overview of the windows and alerts you'll see along the way during the data transfer.

Add and Select Devices

By default, iSync is set up to synchronize data with your .Mac account, as denoted by the .Mac icon in top portion of iSync's window (see Figure 9-11). Try as you might, you cannot remove the .Mac icon from iSync's list of devices.

> Well, there is one way to remove .Mac from the list of devices, but that involves hacking iSync's *plist* file.

If you have other devices that you'd like to synchronize data with, you can add them to the list by selecting Devices → Add Device (⌘-N).

> To synchronize data with a PalmOS device, you need to use the HotSync Manager, which is installed on your Mac by the software that came with your Palm PDA. For more information about the HotSync Manager, visit Palm's web site (*http://www.palm.com*).
>
> Additionally, any time you upgrade to a new version of iSync, you should also upgrade the Palm Desktop software.

When you select Add Device from the Devices menu, iSync will search for any devices connected to or within Bluetooth range of your Mac. When iSync locates a device, an icon for that device is displayed in the Add Device window, shown in Figure 9-12. In this case, iSync has detected an iPod.

Figure 9-12. iSync's Add Devices window displays an icon for any devices it can sync data with.

To add a device to iSync's list of devices to sync with, simply double-click on the icon's device in the Add Device window. When you do, the device will transfer from the Add Device window to iSync's main window, as shown in Figure 9-13. The Add Device window stays open until you close the window, either by clicking on the red close window button or by using the close window keyboard shortcut (⌘-W).

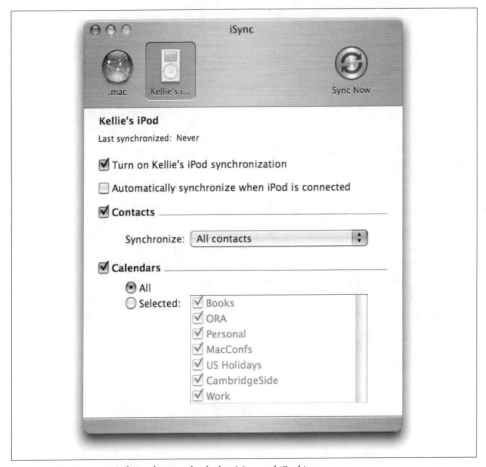

Figure 9-13. iSync's window, showing both the .Mac and iPod icons.

Once detected, iSync displays the name of the device and lets you know when the last time a sync was performed. The only data you can sync with an iPod are the Contacts from your Address Book or the Calendars from iCal. (Music syncing is handled by iTunes and is not discussed in this book.)

The Safeguard panel

One of the great things about iSync is that it not only synchronizes data from your Mac, but it also compares that data with the any existing data on devices with which it is synchronizing. When iSync encounters similar records that might have slightly different information, the Safeguard window, shown in Figure 9-14, appears.

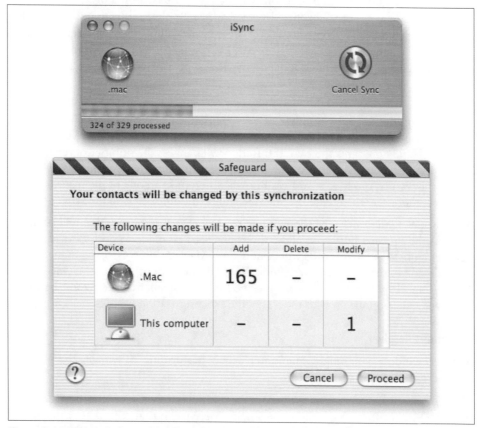

Figure 9-14. *iSync's Safeguard window alerts you when it finds differences in data on the destination device when compared with the source device.*

As shown in Figure 9-14, the Safeguard window is broken up into a table view with four columns:

Device
This column lists the devices with which you're synchronizing data.

Add
This column lists the number of new records that will be added to the device. Figure 9-14 shows that there are 165 records to be added to the .Mac account from the Address Book. We know that the additions are coming from the Address Book by the "Your contacts will be changed by this synchronization" message in bold text near the top of the window.

Delete

This column lists the number of records that will be deleted from the device. iSync determines whether a record will be deleted based on a previous sync. For example, if you've synchronized your Address Book's contacts once before but have deleted a few people between syncs, iSync will list that number of records in the Delete column. When you perform the sync, any records on that have been deleted from your Mac since the last sync will also be deleted from the device.

Modify

This column lists the number of records that will be modified on your Mac. When performing the sync, iSync looks at the records on your Mac and the device and compares the two. If it finds any changes, the number of records that will be modified is noted in the Modify column. In the case of Figure 9-14, one of the records on .Mac's Address Book is different from one of the records on the Mac; therefore, the record on the Mac will be modified during the sync.

After reviewing the Safeguard panel, if you're okay with the changes that will be made, click on the Proceed button to allow the changes to be made to both devices. In the case of Figure 9-14, 165 records will be added to .Mac's Address Book, and one change will be made to the Mac's Address Book. If you don't want to make the changes, click on the Cancel button. The changes specified in the Safeguard panel won't be made, and iSync will continue on with the rest of the synchronization process.

The Conflict Resolver

Another window you might encounter when performing a sync is the Conflict Resolver, as shown in Figure 9-15.

The Conflict Resolver appears when it finds similar records on the devices being synced with, but there might be some slight difference in that record. The portion of the record that iSync is trying to resolve is displayed as red text. In the case of Figure 9-15, the difference between my Address Book records is that there's a trailing slash on the URL for my work home page (*http://www.oreilly.com/* in .Mac's Address Book, versus *http://www.oreilly.com* in my Mac's Address Book).

The Conflict Resolver lets you choose which information to use. As you can see from Figure 9-15, the information for each device is placed within a box, one of which has a thicker, blue border; the box with the blue border contains the information that will be used to resolve the conflict. Meaning, the information in the box will be made the same on all devices being synced. If you want to choose the information in the other box, simply click on that box and it will be highlighted with the blue border.

Once you've selected the information that you want to be used, click on the Finish button. iSync resolves the conflict on the source and destination devices, and displays the sheet shown in Figure 9-16. To continue with the synchronization process, click on the Sync Now button; or to save the change and quit the synchronization process, click on the Sync Later button.

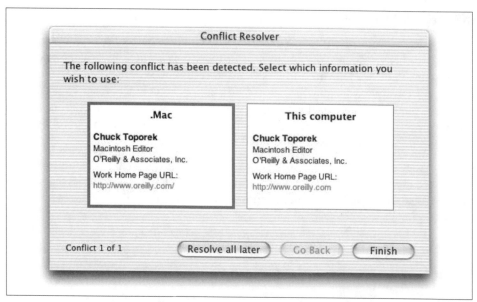

Figure 9-15. iSync's Conflict Resolver.

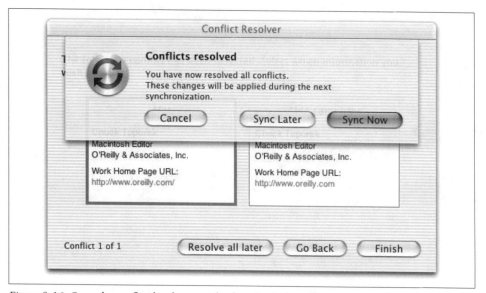

Figure 9-16. Once the conflict has been resolved on the devices, iSync gives you the option of continuing with the sync or saving those changes for a later sync.

The combination of iSync's Safeguard Panel and the Conflict Resolver helps to ensure that your data is the same on your Mac and any of the devices with which you're syncing.

Resetting a Device

Most syncs will go off without a hitch. You connect a device, sync the data with iSync, and then go about your business. But there may come a time when you want to erase the data you've synced to a device and restore it with the data on your computer. For example, you may have synced the all of the contacts from your Address Book to your cell phone, when all you wanted was your list of Friends, or maybe you didn't mean to sync the event calendar for the local Apple Store to your iPod. In times like these, iSync comes with a reset button of sorts.

To reset the synchronized data on a device, make sure the device you want to reset is connected to or detected by your Mac (Devices → Add Device). Next, select Devices → Reset All Devices, which opens the window shown in Figure 9-17.

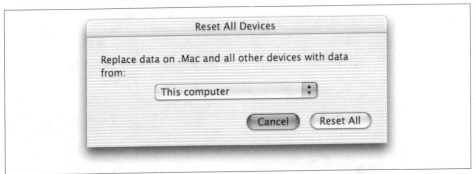

Figure 9-17. Clicking on the Reset All button resets the data on your devices, including .Mac.

 Before you click that Reset All button, you should keep in mind that any changes you've made to the data on your devices will be wiped out, including any changes you've made to the online version of your Address Book.

If you have something precious on any device, you should take the time to update the information on your computer first. For example, if you've entered a new phone number for a friend on your cell phone and you haven't made that change to your Mac's Address Book, you should go into the Address Book and make that change before you click on the Reset All button, which will wipe out and restore the data on the phone.

To start the process of clearing the old data off of the devices and replacing it with a fresh set of data from your Mac, click on the Reset All button. iSync's window will collapse, and you can track the progress of the data replacement by reading the messages shown in the window's status bar (the gray bar at the bottom of the window), as shown in Figure 9-18.

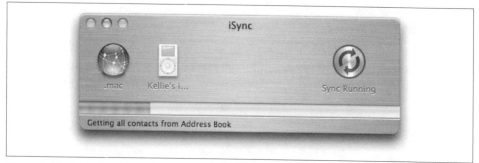

Figure 9-18. As the blue progress meter moves from left-to-right, the status bar at the bottom of the window displays messages about what iSync is doing.

If you are synchronizing data between two or more Macs, you should resynchronize the other Mac after you've reset the devices. When you synchronize the other Mac, you will see a message similar to the one shown in Figure 9-19.

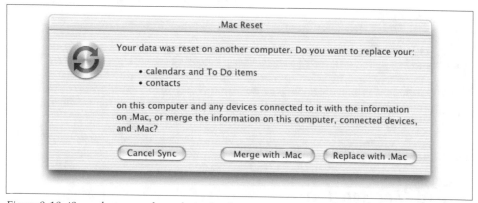

Figure 9-19. iSync alerts you after a device has been reset.

When you use iSync on the other Mac, the .Mac Reset window shown in Figure 9-19 appears. This window alerts you to the changes that were made and gives you one of three options to select from:

Cancel Sync
> Clicking on this button will cancel the synchronization process, leaving the data on the machine intact.

Merge with .Mac
> Clicking on this button will merge the data from your Mac with what exists on the .Mac (iDisk) server.

Replace with .Mac
> Clicking on this button replaces the data on the Mac with what exists on the .Mac (iDisk) server.

Since we want to keep the data the same across all of the devices and Macs, the option to choose here is Replace with .Mac.

Additionally, if you have used an earlier version of iSync and this is the first time that Safari's bookmarks had been synchronized, you will also see the alert message shown in Figure 9-20.

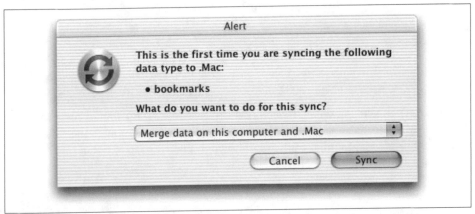

Figure 9-20. iSync alerts you if there's something new waiting on the server to synchronize.

The first time you synchronize Safari's bookmarks between two Macs, you will see a pop-up menu that gives you an option to merge the bookmark lists. Selecting this option (Merge data on this computer and .Mac) is probably the option you will want to choose. Why? Well, it lets iSync merge Safari's bookmarks on the different Macs so that they will be the same on both Macs.

Mac-to-Mac Syncing

As you've seen, iSync can be used to shuttle data from your Mac and store it on your iDisk. That makes it really convenient for accessing the information in your Mac's Address Book from anywhere, as well as using it with .Mac's web-based Mail services. But one of the really cool features of syncing with your .Mac account is that you can also sync that information back onto another Mac.

For example, say you have a PowerBook G4 that you tote around for work, and an iMac that you use at home. If both Macs are running Mac OS X, you can use iSync to synchronize data between the two Macs, with your .Mac account acting like a storage facility and iSync acting as a network router in the middle, as shown in Figure 9-21.

As you can see from Figure 9-21, synchronizing data between Macs is a multistep process:

1. Mac #1 (the PowerBook) uses iSync to store its data on the iDisk.

2. Mac #2 (the iMac) uses iSync to connect to the iDisk.

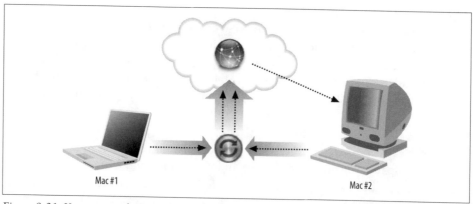

 is positioned in the note block below.

Mac #1

Mac #2

Figure 9-21. You can synchronize the data on two (or more) Macs using the .Mac synchronization server as a repository for the your data.

3. iSync then looks at the data stored on the iDisk and compares the data from Mac #1 with the information on Mac #2.

4. iSync compares Mac #2's information against Mac #1's information on the iDisk.

5. Mac #2 downloads the information from the iDisk and stores that on the hard disk where it is loaded into the Address Book, iCal, and Safari.

6. If Mac #2 has some different information that doesn't match up with the information on Mac #1, those differences are noted and synchronized with Mac #1's data on the iDisk.

7. The next time Mac #1 uses iSync, it will be notified of the changes from Mac #2, and those differences can be synchronized with Mac #1's data, if so desired.

The key here is that both Macs need to be registered with the .Mac synchronization server (described earlier) using your .Mac Member Name (you cannot sync your Mac with another .Mac member's Mac). Once registered, the sync server can be used as the conduit to transfer data back and forth between two or more Macs.

> So when you think about it, iSync is like a two-way street that meets up with a roundabout. Traffic can move in both directions toward and from the roundabout (iSync), and back out again, depending on what you decide to do. The only exception is that you'll probably never get stuck on the roundabout like the Griswold's in *European Vacation* ("Look honey, Big Ben!").

Now that you've seen the process in theory, let's see how Mac synchronization works in the real world.

Step 1: Sync Mac #1 to .Mac

The first step in this process is to use iSync and synchronize the information on your Mac with your .Mac account. If you haven't already used iSync and you've come here from some other place in the book (like maybe the table of contents or the index), you should go back and start reading this chapter from the beginning. You'll get a quick overview of iSync and see how to synchronize the information on your Mac with your .Mac account.

Step 2: Merge Mac #2's data with .Mac

Launch iSync on Mac #2 and select "Merge data on computer and .Mac" from the pop-up menu near the top of the window as shown in Figure 9-22.

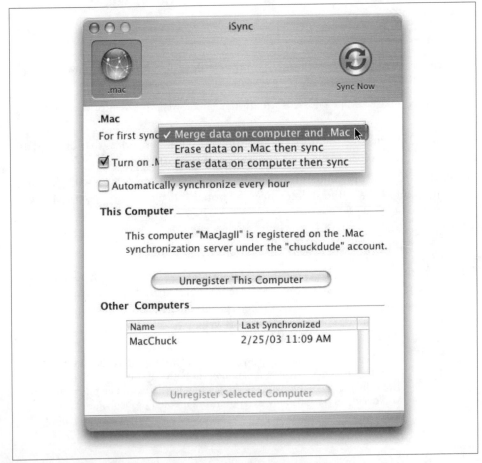

Figure 9-22. Select the "Merge data..." option from the pop-up menu.

It's worth noting here that there are two other options in the pop-up menu shown in Figure 9-22:

Erase data on .Mac then sync

Select this option only if you want to make the data on Mac #2 the primary source for information contained in Address Book, iCal, and Safari's bookmarks. Selecting this option will erase all of the data you've previously synced from Mac #1 to your .Mac account, and will then upload Mac #2's information to .Mac.

Erase data on computer then sync

Select this option to erase all of the information in Mac #2's Address Book, iCal, and Safari's bookmarks before syncing with the .Mac server. Select this option only if you're certain that the info stored on Mac #2 isn't important and can be replaced.

In the case of both Erase options, it's worth noting that once you've erased the data, either on the .Mac synchronization server or on the local machine, there's really no going back.

Your only recourse is to select either the Revert to Backup or Revert to Last Sync option from iSync's Devices menu.

Step 3: Click on the Sync Now button

To start syncing the data between the two Macs, click on the Sync Now button, located in the upper-right corner of iSync's window. iSync's window will collapse (as shown in Figure 9-23), and the synchronization process will begin.

Figure 9-23. After clicking on the Sync Now button, iSync starts downloading information from the .Mac synchronization server to Mac #2.

Step 4: Deal with any conflicts

Since you're merging data from one Mac to another through the .Mac synchronization server, you might encounter some conflicts with the data. The Safeguard panel and the Conflict Resolver (discussed earlier) will appear, alerting you to the changes that will be made on Mac #2. You will need to resolve all of the conflicts, as described earlier in the section, "The Conflict Resolver."

Step 5: Process complete (almost)

After Mac #2 has finished the sync with the .Mac synchronization server, iSync's window will slide open again, as shown in Figure 9-24. A message next to "Last synchronized" displays the day, date, and time of the last synchronization, which in this case is the sync that's just been performed.

Figure 9-24. With the sync complete for Mac #2, iSync's window slides back open and displays information about the sync.

Step 6: Sync Mac #1 to close the loop

Again, since you're merging data between the two Macs, you should go back to Mac #1 and run iSync again to sync it with the .Mac synchronization server. This ensures that the data on both Macs are now the same. The circle is now complete, Obi Wan.

To view the changes made on either Mac, you can access iSync's log, discussed in the next section.

Bookmark Syncing

Before iSync came along, the biggest problem with bookmarks is that they were a one-computer-only thing. Meaning, the bookmarks you made on one computer weren't easy to get at from another computer, and there was no way of synchronizing them with another, or using them while you were visiting a friend or on vacation.

One of the nice things about using the Safari web browser (*http://www.apple.com/safari*) and iSync, is that you can make your bookmarks available to other Macs and use them online from wherever you are. Just imagine the following scenario: you're on vacation at your friend Marsha's place, and you're telling her about some article you read online and bookmarked with Safari a few weeks ago. Of course, Marsha now wants to read it, but finding the article could take a lot of time.

If you've synced your bookmarks with your .Mac account, all of your bookmarks can be accessed quickly, and with very little trouble. Best of all, you can access your bookmarks from any machine: Mac, Windows, whatever. All you need is a web browser.

Once you've used iSync to synchronize your Safari bookmarks, the bookmark data is stored on your iDisk in two places:

/Library/Application Support/Sync/BKMK

> This directory contains a series of binary files (raw data) used by iSync. These files store the bookmarks in a format that can be transferred to another Mac using iSync, making them available in the Safari browser on the other side.
>
> The files in this directory have odd filenames, too, such as *3D7E19DE-926B-11D7-BA79-00039398D26E.D000*. The first part of the filename (*3D7E19DE-926B-11D7-BA79-00039398D26E*) is a unique identifier for your .Mac account. The extension (*.D000*, *.D001*, *.D002*, etc.) denotes a synchronization. Each time you use iSync to synchronize your bookmarks, a new file will be created, but with a differently numbered extension; the one with the higher number (e.g., *.D002* is higher than *.D001* and *.D000*), contains the data from the most-recent sync.

/Library/Application Support/Bookmarks

> This directory contains but one lone file, *Bookmarks.xml*, which contains all of your bookmarks. When you view your bookmarks over the Web, the *Bookmarks.xml* file is used to supply the bookmarks displayed in the Bookmarks Window.

Synchronizing Safari's bookmarks with your iDisk makes them available to other Macs, and they can also be used over the Web from any computer with a graphical web browser such as Netscape Navigator (*http://www.netscape.com*), Camino (which dupes the .Mac servers into thinking it is Netscape; *http://www.mozilla.org/projects/camino*), and even Internet Explorer, which still ships with Mac OS X (*/Applications*). If you try to use a nonstandard browser, such as Opera (*http://www.opera.com*), you will be redirected to the page shown in Figure 9-25, telling you that the Bookmarks Window can only be viewed with Safari, Internet Explorer, or Netscape.

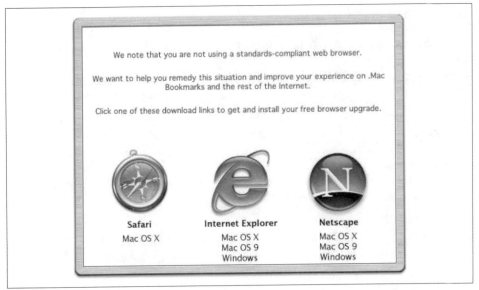

We note that you are not using a standards-compliant web browser.

We want to help you remedy this situation and improve your experience on .Mac Bookmarks and the rest of the Internet.

Click one of these download links to get and install your free browser upgrade.

Safari
Mac OS X

Internet Explorer
Mac OS X
Mac OS 9
Windows

Netscape
Mac OS X
Mac OS 9
Windows

Figure 9-25. This page appears when you try to use a nonstandard browser for accessing your bookmarks over the Web.

Using Your Bookmarks on the Web

To use your bookmarks over the Web, follow these steps:

1. Click on the Bookmarks icon on the .Mac homepage, as shown in Figure 9-26.

- Mail
- Address Book
- Bookmarks
- HomePage
- iDisk
- iCards
- Backup
- iSync
- Virex
- iCal
- Support

Figure 9-26. Click on the Bookmarks icon to gain access to your Safari bookmarks.

2. Now you'll need to get past the password page. If you've enabled Keychains to work with Safari (Safari → Preferences → AutoFill, and have checked "User names and passwords"), all you will need to do is click on the Enter button or hit the Return key.

3. Once your .Mac Member Name and Password have been authenticated by Apple's servers, you will be greeted with the Bookmarks Welcome page, shown in Figure 9-27.

Figure 9-27. The Bookmarks Welcome page.

4. To start using your Safari bookmarks, click on the Open Bookmarks button. After clicking this button, another browser window will open, giving you access to all of your synchronized bookmarks, and the main browser window will return you to the .Mac homepage. The Bookmarks Window is shown in Figure 9-28.

The Bookmarks Window pops up as a separate browser window that you can move around on your screen as needed.

Using the Bookmarks Window

The Bookmarks Window (shown in Figure 9-28) gives you quick and easy access to your bookmarks from wherever you are, and from whatever system you're using. You can use this window to open existing bookmarks, and add or delete bookmarks as well.

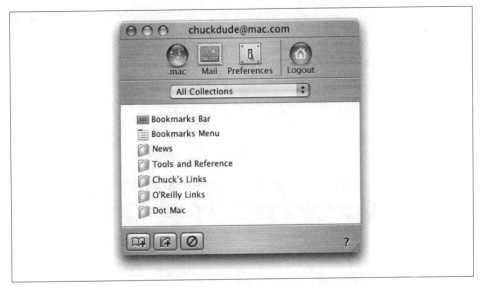

Figure 9-28. The Bookmarks window.

Along the top of the window is a row of four buttons, which perform the following functions:

.Mac
Opens the .Mac homepage (*http://www.mac.com*) in a new browser window.

Mail
Opens the .Mac Mail page in a new window (of course, you'll have to authenticate yourself again to get at your Mail).

Preferences
Opens a Bookmarks Preferences window (shown in Figure 9-29).

The Bookmarks Preferences window gives you the following options:

Always open pages in a new browser window
This ensures that any bookmarks you click on will open in a new browser window. This option is enabled as the default.

Always open pages in the same browser window
This option will open any bookmark you click on in the same window as the Bookmarks window.

Since the purpose of having the Bookmarks Window open as a separate window is to make your bookmarks easily accessible, enabling this option is not recommended. The reason is because you will need to resize the narrow Bookmarks window to view the bookmarked page you selected, and you'll have to use the Back buttons to get back to the Bookmarks Window (which you can either leave large or resize to be smaller).

Figure 9-29. The Bookmarks Preferences window.

Save my password (Bookmarks log in not requried on this computer)
> This option, which is unchecked by default, makes it so you won't have to authenticate yourself on the computer you're using in order to gain access to your bookmarks.
>
> If you plan to use the Bookmarks Window often, it is recommended that you enable this option by clicking on the checkbox.

Language
> There are only two language options available in the drop-down menu: English or Japanese.

Turn on .Mac Bookmarks Synchronization
> This option, which is checked by default, enables (or disables, if unchecked) Safari bookmark synchronization. Beneath this option, you will also see the date and time that your bookmarks were last synchronized with the .Mac server.

If you have made any changes to the Bookmarks Preferences, click on the Save button to save your settings. If not, you can click on the Cancel button to go back to viewing your bookmarks.

Logout

Clicking this button simply closes the Bookmarks Window, which can also be accomplished by clicking on the red close window button or by using the keyboard shortcut, ⌘-W.

Using the Bookmark Category menu

Located just below the row of buttons is a pull-down menu that you can use to quickly gain access to different folders of bookmarks. When the Bookmarks window first opens, the pull-down menu is set to All Collections, which shows you the basic set of your bookmarks. To view specific folders, simply click on the set of arrows on the right side of the pull-down menu and select another category, as shown in Figure 9-30.

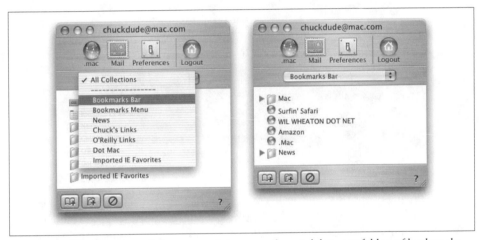

Figure 9-30. The Category pull-down menu let's you easily switch between folders of bookmarks.

After letting go of the mouse button on one of the bookmark categories, the bookmarks for that category are displayed in the center (white) portion of the window as seen on the right of Figure 9-30. As you can see in the Bookmarks window on the right, there are two folders (Mac and News) that have disclosure triangles next to them. This means that there are other folders within, each containing their own set of categorized bookmarks. If a folder doesn't have a disclosure triangle next to it, it means that the folder contains only bookmarks; there are no other folders within.

Here, the disclosure triangles act just as they do from within the List View of the Finder. To see the contents within, simply click on the disclosure triangle (which makes it point downward), as shown in Figure 9-31.

To collapse an open folder, simply click on the downward-pointing disclosure triangle.

Figure 9-31. Clicking on a disclosure triangle next to a folder reveals its contents within the view.

Managing your bookmarks

Running along the bottom of the Bookmarks window are three buttons that let you manage your bookmarks. These buttons, shown in Figure 9-32, let you add bookmarks, categories (or folders), as well as delete bookmarks from your collection.

Figure 9-32. The Bookmark window's controls for managing your bookmark collection.

With the Bookmark window open and another browser window open off to the side, you can click on the Add Bookmark button to create a bookmark for the site you're visiting. If you decide that you need to add a new folder to store some bookmarks in, click on the Add Category button. And finally, to delete a bookmark, click on the Delete Bookmark button. The next time you use iSync, the changes you've made to the bookmarks online will be applied to Safari's *Bookmark.plist* file on your Mac.

At the bottom-right edge of the Bookmarks window, near the window-resizing grabber, is a simple little question mark. When you click on this icon, the .Mac Help window, shown in Figure 2-5 (see Chapter 2) pops open, giving you access to all of Apple's .Mac help files.

iSync's Logs

iSync keeps track of every sync you perform and stores that information in a log. To display iSync's log, select Window → Show Logs (⌘-L) from the menu bar. Selecting this option opens the iSync Log window, shown in Figure 9-33.

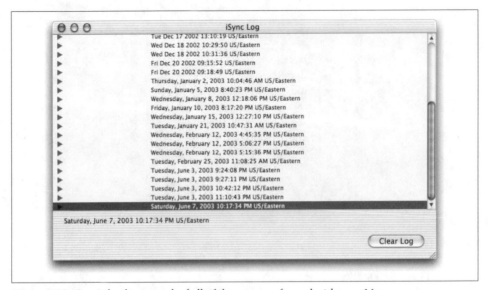

Figure 9-33. iSync's log keeps track of all of the syncs performed with your Mac.

Each line of iSync's log displays the day, date, and time of the syncs. The information contained in iSync's log can be used to help you diagnose problems you might encounter when trying to perform a sync, or just so you can see what happened during the sync process.

To view the specific details for a particular sync, click on the black disclosure triangle at the far-left edge of the window. The triangle will point downward, and the information for that date's sync is displayed in the iSync Log window, as shown in Figure 9-34.

The log gives you a second-by-second account of what transpired during the synchronization process.

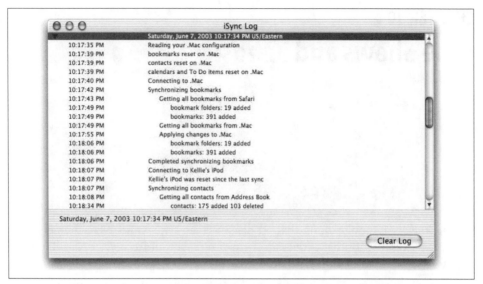

Figure 9-34. iSync's log keeps track of everything that transpired during a sync, including the time when each task was performed.

You can also view iSync's log using a text-editing application, such as TextEdit or BBEdit, by opening the *output.synclog* file, located at */Library/Application Support/ SyncService/501* on your Mac's hard drive.

To reset iSync's log, click on the Clear Log button at the lower-right corner of the iSync Log window. This will erase any data stored in the *output.synclog* file and clear the display of the iSync Log window.

CHAPTER 10

Slide Shows and iCards

Beyond the basic applications that Apple provides with your .Mac membership, there are a number of other services to help you reach out from your Mac and connect with your friends, family, and other Mac users.

This chapter covers the use of the Mac Slides Publisher and iPhoto to create a screensaver (or Public Slide Show) from images and photos, and it shows you how to send custom iCards.

Creating a Public Slide Show

One of the free pieces of software that Apple provides to .Mac subscribers is the Mac Slides Publisher. This small application allows you to create a Public Slide Show (a screensaver) that you can not only use on your computer, but also share with other .Mac members.

While Mac Slides Publisher is a standalone application, it was integrated into iPhoto 2 to make it easier for users to create slide shows using the images in their iPhoto libraries. This section covers the use of Mac Slides Publisher in both forms. Each has its advantages, but iPhoto makes it a heck of a lot easier to create a Public Slide Show, since all you need to do is select the images and click a button. This is just one of the many great things Apple has done to integrate .Mac services into the iApps. Just a few clicks and you're done; that's the way it should be.

The Mac Slides Publisher is found on your iDisk in the */Software/Apple Software/Mac Slides Publisher* directory. iPhoto 2 is installed by default with Mac OS X Panther, and iPhoto 4 (*http://www.apple.com/iphoto*) is included as part of iLife '04 (*http://www.apple.com/ilife*).

Image Formats

The most important thing to note before you set off to create your Public Slide Show is that you can only use JPEG images. You cannot use GIF, TIFF, BMP, PNG, etc.

From GIF to JPEG in a Jiffy

Have an image in GIF (or any other) format that you'd like to include as part of your Public Slide Show? Well, don't fret; there is a quick solution for converting your images to JPEG. The answer: Preview.

While mostly thought of as the default viewer for PDF files, Mac OS X's Preview application (*/Applications*) is actually quite powerful. For example, to convert a GIF image to a JPEG image, follow these steps:

1. Launch Preview by double-clicking on its icon in the Finder.
2. Open the image you would like to convert.
3. Select File → Export (Shift-⌘-E) from the menu bar.
4. Near the bottom of the sheet that slides down, you will see a drop-down menu next to the word "Format"; click on that menu and select JPEG. Notice how the file extension changes to *.jpg* in the "Save as" field at the top of the sheet.
5. Click on the Save button to save the image in JPEG format.
6. Quit Preview (⌘-Q).

It's worth noting that the image will probably change some when you convert it to JPEG format. You should open the image in Preview before you finally decide whether to use it as part of your slide show.

If you purchased a Power Mac or PowerBook that came with GraphicConverter, you should use that application instead since it will do a better job at handling the file conversion. If GraphicConverter didn't come with your new Mac, you can download it from Lemke Software's web site (*http://www.lemkesoft.com*). GraphicConverter is a powerful tool, and it's highly scriptable with AppleScript. A quick Google search will most likely turn up many results for an AppleScript droplet that uses GraphicConverter to batch-convert files.

Using Mac Slides Publisher

The trick to using Mac Slides Publisher is not to launch it. Instead, Mac Slides Publisher acts like a droplet. This means that instead of launching the application by double-clicking on it and loading the images in that way, you simply drag and drop images onto Mac Slides Publisher's application icon.

Since Mac Slides Publisher is a droplet application, it's easier to use if you place it in your Dock. That way, you can just drag and drop image files onto its Dock icon to create your public slide show. To place Mac Slides Publisher on your Dock, go to the *Applications* folder in the Finder, locate Mac Slides Publisher, and drag its icon to the Dock.

 To quickly go to Mac Slides Publisher in the second Finder window, type "Ma" and the icon for Mac Slides Publisher will highlight.

The following example assumes that the JPEG images you want to use for your slide show are saved in your *Pictures* folder (*~/Pictures*), and that you've placed Mac Slides Publisher in your Dock. To create a Public Slide Show, follow these steps:

1. Open a new Finder window (⌘-N) and go to your *Pictures* folder.
2. ⌘-click on the JPEG images you want to include in your Public Slide Show.

Drag the images from the Finder window and drop them onto Mac Slides Publisher's icon in the Dock. When you do, Mac Slides Publisher launches and starts to optimize and copy the images up to your iDisk, as shown in Figures 10-1 and 10-2.

Figure 10-1. Mac Slides Publisher first optimizes the files for your slide show...

 The other caveat to using Mac Slides Publisher is that you must be connected to the Internet in order to create your Public Slide Show. The reason is because the application probes your iDisk and creates a place to save the slide show. If you are not connected to the Internet, Mac Slides Publisher will crash.

After the images for your Public Slide Show are copied to your iDisk, Mac Slides Publisher displays the message shown in Figure 10-3. If you want to send an email message to fellow Mac OS X users, telling them about your Public Slide Show, click on the Announce Slideshow button; if not, click on the Quit button to close Mac Slides Publisher. The email message, shown in Figure 10-4, includes instructions on how to configure Mac OS X's preferences to use the Public Slide Show.

When you create a Public Slide Show, the image files are saved on your iDisk in */Pictures/Slide Shows/Public*. When another Mac OS X user opts (via System Preferences → Desktop & Screen Saver → Screen Saver) to use your .Mac Public Slide Show

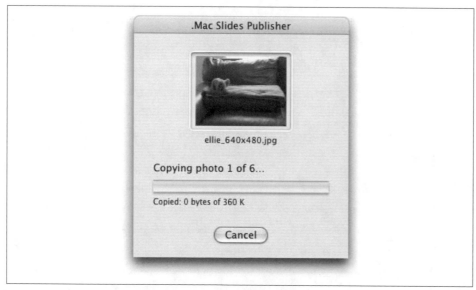

Figure 10-2. ...and then it copies the image files to your iDisk.

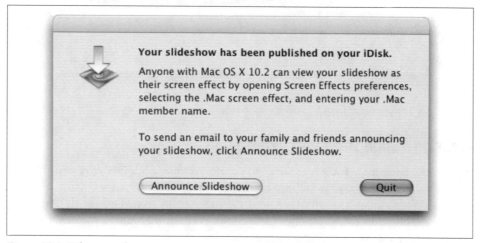

Figure 10-3. When complete, you can announce your Public Slide Show, or quit Mac Slides Publisher.

as their system's screensaver, their Mac connects to your iDisk and downloads the images for your Public Slide Show, placing the files on their system in *~/Library/ Caches/com.apple.iToolsSlideSubscriptions/membername/Public Slide Show*. Each image of the slide show has a similar name, ranging from *Image-001.jpg* to *Image-999.jpg*, depending on how many images you opt to use for your Public Slide Show. There is also a *config.plist* file, which the Desktop & Screen Saver preference panel uses to run the screensaver.

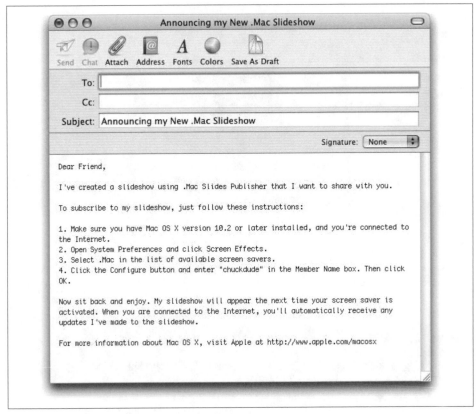

Figure 10-4. Let your Mac friends know about your slide show.

Creating a Slide Show with iPhoto

As mentioned earlier, the easiest way to create a Public Slide Show is with iPhoto. Part of the reason is because iPhoto is installed with Mac OS X by default, and you have to download and install Mac Slides Publisher from your iDisk. With iPhoto, all you'll need to do to create a Public Slide Show is select the images you want to use, and then click on the .Mac Slides button.

 The example provided here works with iPhoto 2 or higher.

To create your public slide show from iPhoto, follow these steps:

1. Launch iPhoto by clicking on its icon in the Dock, or by double-clicking on its icon in the Finder (*/Applications*).

2. Select the images you want to use as part of your screensaver from one of your image libraries by either selecting all of the images (⌘-A) or by ⌘-clicking on the images you want. The images you select will have a blue border around them in iPhoto, as shown in Figure 10-5.

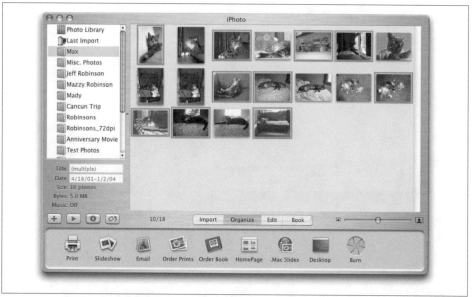

Figure 10-5. Select the images you want to use in your public slide show.

3. Locate and click on the .Mac Slides icon at the bottom of iPhoto's window; when you do, a message window is displayed (shown in Figure 10-6), asking you whether you want to publish the public slide show. If you're certain that you've selected the images you want to use, click on the Publish button.

Figure 10-6. Click on the Publish button to create the public slide show.

After clicking on the Publish button, iPhoto optimizes and copies the images to your iDisk, placing them in the */Pictures/Slide Shows/Public* folder.

4. When the public slide show has been created, you will see another message (shown in Figure 10-7), giving you the option to announce your slide show or to quit the process.

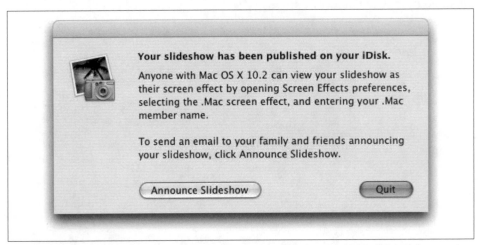

Figure 10-7. Click on the Announce Slideshow button or Quit, depending on what you want to do.

If you click on the Announce Slideshow button, iPhoto launches your email client and creates the email message shown earlier in Figure 10-4. The email message includes instructions that tell other Mac OS X users how to configure the Desktop & Screen Saver preference panel to use your public slide show.

Using Your Screensaver

Once you've created your screensaver, you will need to configure your Mac to use it. To do this, launch the System Preferences and follow these steps:

1. Click on the Desktop & Screen Saver preference panel.

2. Click on the Screen Saver tab.

3. In the Screen Savers area on the left, select .Mac.

4. In the Preview section on the right, you will see a quick message that says "Looking For Slides...", after which, the default Apple-produced .Mac slides will appear in the Preview window.

5. Click on the Options button.

6. To add the slide show you just created, enter your .Mac Membership Name in the appropriately named text field.

7. Click on the OK button. The sheet slides back up into the window's titlebar, and you're ready to go.

While it may appear that your job is over, it isn't quite yet; you still have some tweaking to do:

1. Click on the Options button.
2. At the top of the sheet, you will see a listing of slide show Subscriptions, as shown in Figure 10-8.

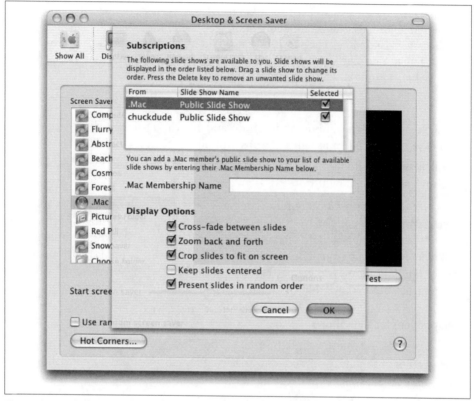

Figure 10-8. The Screen Saver preference panel's Subscriptions sheet.

As you can see, your slide show is listed beneath the .Mac Public Slide Show, which means that Apple's .Mac screensaver will take precedence over yours. However, since both checkboxes to the right of the slide shows have been selected, the images from each slide show will be combined for your screensaver. The images from the first slide show will be used first, followed by the others in the list.

But what if you want your slide show to be used instead? To do this, you have a few options:

- Uncheck the checkbox in the Selected column by clicking on the checkbox for the .Mac Public Slide Show. This turns off that slide show, making yours the main source for your screensaver.

Finding Other .Mac Slide Shows

Great. You've created your own screensaver, put it up on your iDisk so others with Mac OS X can use it, and you know how to configure your Mac to use someone else's screensaver. The problem is, unless you know a ton of other people who have .Mac memberships, how are you going to find other screensavers?

Well, look no further than DotMac.info (*http://www.dotmac.info*), a web site where other .Mac members can share information and search for other .Mac HomePages, screensavers, and more. The site also lets you do keyword searches to help you find other Public Slide Shows, as well as connect with other .Mac members. There's no charge for using the site; all you need to do is create an account and log in.

- Click on the .Mac Public Slide Show and hit the Delete key to permanently remove that item from the list of Subscriptions.
- Click on your Public Slide Show and drag it to above the .Mac Public Slide Show, as shown in Figure 10-9.

When you drag your (or any) Public Slide Show around, a solid black bar appears to indicate where the item you're dragging will be relocated. In looking at Figure 10-9, you can see that the black bar appears above the .Mac Public Slide Show. If that's the place where you want your slide show to appear, let go of the mouse button and the order of the slide shows will change appropriately. Now when your screensaver kicks in, the images from your Public Slide Show will be used first.

Display options for Slide Shows

When you click on the Options button on the Screen Saver preference pane, the lower portion of the sheet contains the following Display Options for slide shows:

Cross-fade between slides
> When selected, this option is responsible for the fade effect when one image in your slide show transitions to another.

Zoom back and forth
> When selected, this option is responsible for zooming in or out of an image in the slide show, making it appear as though the image is moving closer or farther away. This option is only available if the "Cross-fade between slides" option is selected; otherwise, it is grayed out.

Crop slides to fit on screen
> This item will resize the images so they fill your entire display area; otherwise, the image will appear in its original size.

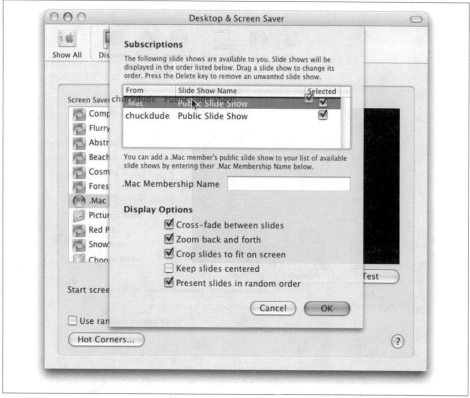

Figure 10-9. Giving your Public Slide Show precedence by dragging it above the .Mac Public Slide Show.

Keep slides centered

> This option is only available when "Crop slides to fit on screen" is selected. This option will do as its name implies: it centers the images of your slide show on screen. If "Crop slides to fit on screen" isn't selected, this option is grayed out and selected by default.

Present slides in random order

> This item will jumble the images in your selected slide shows so they appear out of order. If you have subscribed to multiple slide shows (see Figure 10-9), the images from all selected slide shows will intermix as well.

These options give you greater control over how the images of your slide show will appear and act when your Mac goes into screensaver mode.

iCards

In addition to your .Mac email account and HomePage, Apple gives you yet another way to keep in contact with your friends: iCards. iCards are electronic postcards you can send out for any occasion. To access the main iCards page, go to *http://www.mac.com/icards* (or *http://www.apple.com/icards*), as shown in Figure 10-10.

Figure 10-10. iCards let you send electronic postcards.

As you can see from looking at Figure 10-10, the main iCards page has an iCards Categories sidebar to the right, to help you quickly find the iCard you want. You'll also find quick links for special Holiday iCards and the Top Cards Sent. The iCards have been categorized for every occasion, including:

- Browse All
- Create Your Own
- Apple
- Holidays
- Celebrations
- Thinking of You

- Something Special
- Art & Photography

You'll also find subcategories listed beneath these categories to make it even easier for you to find the right iCard. For example, if you're on the road and want to send a quick iCard to your lovely wife, you can click on Missing You, found within the Love and Friendship category. Additionally, the subcategories in the Holidays section will rotate around so you'll have access iCards for Valentines Day in February, and Halloween in October.

To create an iCard, follow these steps:

1. Click on one of the categories, and you'll be taken to another page from which you can select an image to use with your iCard, as shown in Figure 10-11.

2. When you select an image to use with your iCard, you will be taken to the page shown in Figure 10-12. This page provides a space for you to type in your message as well as select the font style.

3. After you've typed in your message and selected the type style to use, click on the Continue button (either at the top or bottom right of the page). You'll then be taken to the page shown in Figure 10-13, which you use to enter the email address (or addresses, if you're sending the iCard to more than one person) for the person to whom you're sending the iCard.

   Adding a person's email address couldn't be any easier. From this page, you have three different options to choose from; you can:

   a. Select the name of someone in the Quick Address pop-up menu (see Chapter 4 for more information on how to add someone to the Quick Address menu).

   b. Type the email address in the "Enter emails" field.

 If you are sending an iCard to more than one person, you can separate the email addresses with a comma. For example:

> chuckdude@mac.com, insidedotmac@mac.com, chuckthewriter@mac.com

   c. Click on the Address Book button and you'll be taken to a page that lets you select the people in your online Address Book by placing a checkmark next to each name. Once you've selected the person (or persons) in your Address Book, click on the Choose button and their email address appears in the "Enter emails" text field.

   If you have more than one recipient on the email message and you don't want everyone to see who else received the iCard, click on the checkbox next to "Hide distribution list".

Figure 10-11. Select the image to use with your iCard.

4. When you've finished adding the recipients to the iCard, click on the Send Card button (either at the top or bottom right of the page). After your iCard has been sent, you will see the message shown in Figure 10-14.

If you want to sent the same iCard to someone else, click on the Send Same iCard button. To send a different iCard, you can return to the main iCards page or click on the Return to Category button.

Personalize iCards with Your Photos

In addition to the hundreds of stock iCards provided by Apple, you can also use your own photos to create an iCard with a personal touch. To use your personal images,

Figure 10-12. Type in your message and select the type style to use.

simply save them in the *Pictures* folder on your iDisk. The only real stipulation is that the images need to be saved as either JPEG or GIF; you cannot use TIFF or PNG images for your iCards.

> If you've created a Public Slide Show or a Photo Album page for your .Mac HomePage, the images used for these are saved in your iDisk's *Pictures* folder, making them readily available for use as iCards.

Although it isn't necessary, your images will look best if they are sized 416 × 312 pixels for landscape (horizontal) images, or 312 × 416 for portrait (vertical) images. If your images are of another size, they will be stretched or squished to fit. As mentioned earlier, you can use either GraphicConverter or iPhoto to resize and export images files.

Figure 10-13. Enter the email address for the iCard's recipient(s).

 You must be a .Mac member to create custom iCards, and you must use a supported web browser. These browsers include (at a minimum) Safari 1.0 or later, Microsoft Internet Explorer 5.0 or later, or Netscape 4.7. Versions of Netscape higher than 4.7.*x* will not work with this feature.

To use one of your own images for an iCard, follow these steps:

1. Go to the iCard site (*http://www.mac.com/icards*) and click on the Create Your Own icon.

2. The page that appears shows you the contents of your iDisk's *Pictures* folder, as shown in Figure 10-15.

Figure 10-14. When you see this message, your iCard has been sent.

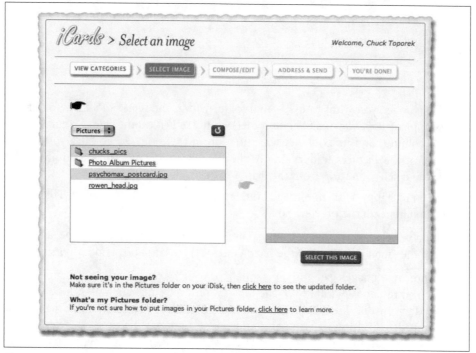

Figure 10-15. Create your own iCard from the images in your iDisk's Pictures folder.

3. To use one of your pictures, select the image file in the listing to the left, and the image will instantly appear in the preview box to the right, as shown in Figure 10-16.

Figure 10-16. Preview your image before creating the iCard.

If the image you want to use is in a folder within the iDisk's *Pictures* folder (for example, the *Public Slide Shows* folder), double-click on the folder's name in the left column, and its contents will show up in this box. To go back to the root level of the *Pictures* folder, simply click on the folder pop-up menu above the box and select Pictures from the list.

4. If you're happy with the image you've selected, click on the Select This Image button beneath the preview box.

Once you've selected the image to use, enter the message, choose the type style, and then add the email addresses of the recipients for the iCard and send it on its way.

Using your own images can add a personalized touch to the iCards you send, particularly if you're handy with any of the illustration programs, such as Adobe Illustrator or Macromedia Freehand, or with image editing programs such as Adobe Photoshop. If you think that some of your images are worthy of use by other .Mac members, you can save them to your iDisk's *Public* folder. That way, if people have access to your iDisk's *Public* folder (say, through your .Mac HomePage), they could download and use the images for their own iCards.

Creating a Members' Portfolio

If you think your images are good enough and you'd like to share them with other .Mac members, you could always consider creating a Members' Portfolio. If you click on the Member's Portfolio link in the iCards Categories list (shown in Figure 10-10), you will be taken to a page that instructs you how to submit your images for consideration.

The requirements are that the images must be sized correctly (416 × 312 pixels for horizontal images, or 312 × 416 for vertical images), and you must be the person who created the images. To submit your images to Apple for consideration, first place the images in the *Pictures* folder on your iDisk, and then go to the Members' Portfolio page and click on the Submit Image icon in the upper-right corner, as shown in Figure 10-17.

Figure 10-17. Click on the Submit Image icon to submit your images for possible inclusion in the Members' Portfolio section.

If Apple likes the image you submitted, they will contact you and ask you to sign an agreement to include it on the Members' Portfolio page.

Becoming a Featured Artist

Think you're a pro? Why not submit some of your images to Apple for inclusion in the Featured Artist section (access from the iCards page at *http://www.mac.com/icards*). Click on the Featured Artist link in the iCards Categories list (see Figure 10-10). When you get to the Featured Artist page, click on the Artist's Site icon in the upper-right corner of the page. This takes you to another page that runs through the submission requirements.

You can submit from 8 to 12 images for consideration through the iCards web page. If Apple likes the images you've submitted, you will be contacted and asked to sign an agreement that grants Apple rights to include your images for use as iCards.

PART IV

Appendixes

This part of the book includes information that every .Mac member will find useful. Here you'll find a listing of the keyboard shortcuts for all of the applications used as part of the .Mac services, even those for iBlog and tips for using Safari. You'll also find some troubleshooting tips for any iDisk errors you might see, as well as instructions for how to use the iDisk Utility for Windows XP.

This book finishes up with the following appendixes:

- Appendix A, *.Mac's Keyboard Shortcuts*
- Appendix B, *Common iDisk Error Codes*
- Appendix C, *Installing and Using the iDisk Utility for Windows XP*

.Mac's Keyboard Shortcuts

This appendix lists the keyboard shortcuts associated with each .Mac application. Application shortcuts listed here include those for:

- Backup (Chapter 6)
- iBlog (Chapter 8)
- iDisk Utility (Chapter 3)
- iSync (Chapter 9)
- Safari (Chapters 2, 8, and 9)
- Virex (Chapter 5)

Backup

Table A-1 lists the keyboard shortcuts used with the Backup application.

Table A-1. Backup's keyboard shortcuts

Menu	Item	Keyboard shortcut	Description
Backup (the application menu)	About Backup	None	Opens a window that tells you what version (and build number) of Backup you're using.
	Go to .Mac	None	Opens the .Mac web site (*http://www.mac.com*) in your default web browser.
	Buy Storage	None	Takes you to the .Mac Upgrade page (*http://www.mac.com/1/addstorage.html*), which gives you options for purchasing more iDisk or Email storage space.
	Buy Media	None	Opens the online Apple Store in your default web browser so you can purchase additional storage media (CD-R/RW and DVD-R/RW).

Table A-1. Backup's keyboard shortcuts (continued)

Menu	Item	Keyboard shortcut	Description
	Provide Backup Feedback	None	Takes you to a page on Apple's web site where you can send feedback to Backup's developers. You can use this form to submit things such as bug reports and feature requests.
	Services	None	None of the items in the Services menu work with Backup, even if you select an item in the QuickPick list.
	Hide Backup	⌘-H	Hides the Backup window.
	Hide Others	Option-H	Hides open windows for other applications.
	Show All	None	Brings the Backup window to the front.
	Quit Backup	⌘-Q	Quits Backup. If you quit while performing a backup, you will need to start the backup over again. Additionally, the backup will become corrupt.
File	Add	None	Adds a file or folder to the backup Items list.
	Find	None (not even the standard ⌘-F works)	Opens a Find dialog that lets you search for files and folders that meet a certain criteria. Unfortunately, you cannot add these items to the backup Items list directly from the search results window. See the section "Finding and adding items to the backup list" in Chapter 6 for more information on using the Find feature.
	Show/Hide Info	⌘-I	Opens the QuickPick list when you have an item selected.
	Show Log	⌘-L	Opens the log that keeps track of the backups you've performed.
	Eject	⌘-E	Ejects a CD or DVD, if one is in the disc tray.
	Backup Now	None	Starts a backup; this is the same as clicking on the Backup Now button on Backup's window.
Edit	Cut	⌘-X	This option is grayed out and cannot be used.
	Copy	⌘-C	This option is grayed out and cannot be used.
	Paste	⌘-V	This option is grayed out and cannot be used.
	Remove From List	None	Removes a selected item from the backup Items list.
	Restore All Quick-Picks	None	Select this menu item if you've removed one of the QuickPick packages from the Backup List and want to get it back.
	Clear iDisk Backup Folder	None	Deletes all of the items in your iDisk's *Backup* folder. Even though you'll be warned before your backup data is deleted, you should think twice before you select this option; once you agree to remove your backup data, there's no going back.
	Select All	⌘-A	Selects all of the items in the backup list. Using this option with the QuickPicks list open will close the QuickPicks list and select all of the items in Backup's main window.
	Check All	Shift-⌘-A	Selects all of the items in the backup list.
	Uncheck All	Shift-⌘-D	Deselects all of the items in the backup list.

Menu	Item	Keyboard shortcut	Description
	Special Characters	None	This menu item is irrelevant to using Backup.
View	Back up to iDisk	None	Starts backing up the selected items to your iDisk.
	Back up to CD	None	Starts backing up the selected items to CD.
	Back up to Drive	None	Starts backing up the selected items to a specified external or networked drive.
	Restore from iDisk	None	Starts the process of restoring data to your Mac from a previous backup to your iDisk.
	Restore from CD/DVD	None	Starts the process of restoring data to your Mac from a previous backup to CD or DVD.
	Restore from Drive	None	Starts the process of restoring data to your Mac from a previous backup to an external or networked drive.
Window	Minimize	⌘-M	Minimizes the Backup window to the Dock.
	Close Window	⌘-W	Simultaneously closes and quits Backup.
	Bring All to Front	None	Since Backup only has one window, this menu item is pretty useless; if you can select this menu item, it already means that Backup is at the top of the window stack.
Help	Backup Help	⌘-?	Opens Backup's help file.

iBlog

Table A-2 is an overview of iBlog's menu hierarchy. Included in this table is a listing of iBlog's keyboard shortcuts, which will help you work faster with the application in producing your blog entries.

Table A-2. iBlog's menu hierarchy and keyboard shortcuts

Menu	Item	Keyboard shortcut	Description
iBlog (Application menu)	About iBlog	N/A[a]	Displays details about iBlog, including its version name.
	Preferences	⌘-;	Opens iBlog's preference window.
	Register	N/A	Opens a window that lets you register your copy of iBlog.
	Check for Updates	N/A	Compares the version of iBlog you're using with the most recent version available on Lifli Software's server. If a new version is available, you will be prompted to download a new version.
	Services	N/A	
	Hide iBlog	⌘-H	Hides iBlog's window.

Table A-2. iBlog's menu hierarchy and keyboard shortcuts (continued)

Menu	Item	Keyboard shortcut	Description
	Hide Others	Option-⌘-H	Hides the windows of any other applications that may be open.
	Show All	N/A	Brings all of iBlog's windows to the front of the window stack.
	Quit	⌘-Q	Quits iBlog.
File	New Blog	Option-⌘-N	Creates a new Blog.
	New Category	Shift-⌘-N	Creates a new blog category.
	New Entry	⌘-N	Creates a new entry for the presently selected blog category.
	New Group	Option-⌘-G	Creates a new blog group.
	New Newsfeed	Option-⌘-F	Allows you to add a new RSS newsfeed to your blog site.
	New Stylesheet	Option-⌘-S	Lets you create a new CSS stylesheet for your blog's site.
	Save Entry	⌘-S	Saves the blog entry.
	Close	⌘-W	Closes the blog entry window.
Edit	Undo	⌘-Z	Reverts back to the previous state.
	Redo	Shift-⌘-Z	Redoes something that was undone using the Undo command.
	Cut	⌘-X	Cuts the selected text and places it in the clipboard.
	Copy	⌘-C	Copies the selected text, placing it in the clipboard.
	Paste	⌘-V	Pastes whatever is in the clipboard to where the text insertion marker is.
	Select All	⌘-A	Selects all of the text in the window.
	Edit Selectioon	N/A	Allows you to edit the currently selected text.
	Delete Selection	N/A	Deletes the currently selected text.
	Spelling	⌘-:	Allows you to spellcheck your entries, either as you type or for a selected word or words.
Fonts	Show Fonts	⌘-T	Opens the Fonts window, from which you can specify the font, style, and size for your blog entries.
	Bold	⌘-B	Makes the selected text bold.
	Italic	⌘-I	Makes the selected text italic.
	Underline	⌘-U	Underlines the selected text.
	Kern	N/A	Applies kerning (the space between characters) to the selected text.
	Ligature	N/A	Applies ligatures to selected text.
	Baseline	N/A	Allows you to change the baseline for a given character or word in a blog entry.
	Show Colors	N/A	Opens the colors palette.

Menu	Item	Keyboard shortcut	Description
	Copy Style	Option-⌘-C	Copies the style of the selected text so it can be applied to something else.
	Paste Style	Option-⌘-V	Pastes the copied style (see the previous menu entry) to the selected text.
Blogs	Preview	Option-⌘-P	Allows you to preview the blog entry.
	Publish	Shift-⌘-P	Publishes the entry.
	Reset Preview State for All Blogs	N/A	Changes the state of all blog entries to Preview (i.e., unpublished).
	Reset Publish State for All Blogs	N/A	Changes the state of all blog entries to Published.
	Reset Publish State	N/A	Resets the Publish state for all blog entries.
	Show Navigation Editor	N/A	Opens the Navigation Editor window.
	Export Blogs by Category	N/A	Exports all of the blog entries in the specified category.
	Export Blogs by Date	N/A	Exports all of the blog entries published on a particular date.
Feeds	Reload	Shift-⌘-R	Reloads any RSS feeds currently being fed into your blog.
	Subscribe	Shift-⌘-S	Opens a dialog that allows you to specify the URL for an RSS feed.
Window	Minimize	⌘-M	Minimizes iBlog's window to the Dock.
	Customize Toolbar	N/A	Used to customize iBlog's toolbar.
	Switch to Reader Mode	Option-⌘-T	Switches from edit to reader mode.
	Show/Hide Feeds Drawer	Option-⌘-D	Toggles the RSS feed drawer on/off.
	Bring All to Front	N/A	Brings all of iBlog's windows to the front of the window stack.
	Blogger Mode or Reader Mode	N/A	Depending on whether you've flipped the light switch on iBlog's interface, iBlog will either be in Blogger Mode (for creating blog entries) or Reader Mode (for subscribing to RSS feeds or other blogs).
Help	iBlog Help	⌘-?	Opens iBlog's help file in Apple Help.
	E-Mail Feedback	N/A	Opens a new email message in your default email client so you can send comments, feedback, or questions to iBlog's developers.

^a "N/A" indicates that there is presently no keyboard shortcut available for that menu item.

iDisk Utility

The keyboard shortcuts listed in Table A-3 can be used with the Mac OS X version of the iDisk Utility (*/Applications/Utilities*).

Table A-3. The iDisk Utility's keyboard shortcuts

Menu	Item	Keyboard shortcut	Description
iDiskUtility	About iDisk Utility	None	Provides basic information about the version and build number of the iDisk Utility installed on your Mac.
	Services	None	Provides access to the Services submenu.
	Hide iDisk Utility	⌘-H	Hides the iDisk Utility window.
	Hide Others	None	Hides the open windows for other applications that are running.
	Show All	None	Brings any hidden windows back into view.
	Quit iDisk Utility	⌘-Q	Quits the iDisk Utility.
View	Open Public Folder	⌘-1	Changes the window's view so you can open another .Mac member's iDisk *Public* folder.
	Open iDisk	⌘-2	Changes the window's view so you can open an iDisk.
	Public Folder Access	⌘-3	Changes the window's view so you can check or change the settings for your iDisk's *Public* folder.
	iDisk Storage	⌘-4	Changes the window's view so you can see how much space is used on your iDisk; can also be used for purchasing additional storage space for your iDisk.
Window	Minimize	⌘-M	Minimizes the window to the Dock.
	Bring All to Front	None	This is a useless menu option, since you can only have one iDisk Utility window open at a time.
	Hide Toolbar	None	Hides the toolbar at the top of the window.
	Customize Toolbar	None	Opens a sheet, from which you can customize the toolbar.
Help	iDisk Utility Help	⌘-?a	Launches the Help Viewer, which gives you information on how to use the iDisk Utility.

a The keyboard shortcut for opening the iDisk Utility's Help file (⌘-?) does not work. Instead, if you need Help, you will need to use the menu bar.

iSync

As with most Mac applications, iSync has its own set of keyboard shortcuts that you can use to help speed things up. Instead of using the menus and selecting items from there, you can use the keyboard shortcuts listed in Table A-4 to help make you a master iSync'er.

Table A-4. iSync's keyboard shortcuts

Menu	Item	Keyboard shortcut	Description
iSync (the Application menu)	About iSync	None	Provides basic information about iSync, including its version number and Apple's copyright statement.
	Preferences	⌘-,	Opens iSync's Preferences window.
	Provide iSync Feedback	None	Takes you to Apple's web site in your default web browser, from which you can send comments and bug reports to iSync's developers.
	Register iSync	None	Before you can use iSync, you will need to register it with Apple; select this option if you haven't already registered iSync.
	Services	None	None of Mac OS X's regular services are available to iSync.
	Hide iSync	⌘-H	Hides iSync's window from sight.
	Hide Others	Option-⌘-H	Hides the windows of any other applications.
	Show All	None	Reveals any hidden windows, but keeps iSync's window at the top of the window stack.
	Quit iSync	⌘-Q	Quits iSync.
Devices	Add Device	⌘-N	Adds other devices, such as Bluetooth-enabled cellular phones and PDAs, and iPods to iSync's list of devices with which to synchronize data.
	Remove Device	None	Removes a device from the list of gear to which iSync will synchronize data.
	Sync Now	⌘-T	Synchronizes data from your Mac to any connected or detected devices.
	Reset All Devices	None	Transfers the data that's currently on your computer and overwrites the information on all devices.
	Backup My Data	None	Creates a backup file of your Address Book and iCal information.
	Revert to Backup	None	Restores your Address Book and iCal information from the previous backup performed from iSync (don't confuse this with the Backup application).
	Revert to Last Sync	None	Restores your Address Book and iCal information from the last time you used iSync; this is helpful for instances when the data on your Mac has been inadvertently deleted, or worse, if your Mac has to be replaced after it has been stolen.
Edit	Undo	⌘-Z	Not available to iSync.
	Redo	Shift-⌘-Z	Not available to iSync.
	Cut	⌘-X	Not available to iSync.
	Copy	⌘-C	Not available to iSync.
	Paste	⌘-V	Not available to iSync
	Delete	None	Not available to iSync
	Select All	⌘-A	Not available to iSync

Menu	Item	Keyboard shortcut	Description
Window	Minimize	⌘-M	Minimizes iSync's window to the Dock
	Close	⌘-W	Closes and quits iSync simultaneously
	Show Logs	⌘-L	Opens a window that displays information about recent uses of iSync
	Bring All to Front	None	Brings all of iSync's windows to the front of the window stack
Help	iSync Help	⌘-?	Opens iSync's help file in the Help Viewer
	Keyboard Short-cuts	None	Displays the keyboard shortcuts that you can use with iSync (basically, the same information you find here in this table, just on your computer)

Safari's Keyboard Shortcuts

Table A-5 lists some keyboard shortcuts you can use in Safari; however, they should work in almost any web browser—including Internet Explorer, Camino (formerly known as Chimera), and Mozilla.

Table A-5. Browser keyboard shortcuts

Keyboard shortcut	Description
Down Arrow	Scroll down (similar to clicking on the down arrow in the scrollbar)
Up Arrow	Scroll up (similar to clicking on the up arrow in the scrollbar)
Option-Down Arrow	Scroll down one screen
Option-Up Arrow	Scroll up one screen
Option-Right Arrow	Scroll the web page to the right
Option-Left Arrow	Scroll the web page to the left
⌘-Down Arrow	Quickly scroll to the bottom of the page
⌘-Up Arrow	Quickly scroll to the top of the page
⌘-Left Arrow	Go back one page (similar to clicking on the Back button)
⌘-Right Arrow	Go forward one page (similar to clicking on the Forward button)
⌘-[	Go back one page (similar to clicking on the Back button)
⌘-]	Go forward one page (similar to clicking on the Forward button)
⌘-R	Refresh, or reload, the current page in the browser
⌘-N	Open a new browser window
⌘-W	Close the current browser window
⌘-M	Minimize the current browser window
⌘-P	Print the current page
⌘-F	Opens a Find dialog so you can search for something on the current web page
⌘-Q	Quit the browser

Virex

Table A-6 lists the keyboard shortcuts available for use with Virex 7.2.

Table A-6. Virex's keyboard shortcuts

Menu	Item	Keyboard shortcut	Description
Virex 7.2 (the Application menu)	About Virex	None	Provides basic information about Virex, including its version number.
	Preferences	None	Opens Virex's Preferences window.
	Services	None	None of Mac OS X's regular services are available to Virex.
	Hide Virex	⌘-H	Hides Virex's window from sight.
	Hide Others	None	Hides the windows of any other applications.
	Show All	Option-⌘-A	Reveals any hidden windows, but keeps Virex's window at the top of the window stack.
	Quit Virex	⌘-Q	Quits Virex.
File	Save Results	⌘-S	Saves the output displayed in the Results window to a file.
	Page Setup	Shift-⌘-P	Opens the Page Setup window for configuring how the Results will be printed.
	Print	⌘-P	Prints the output displayed in the Results window to the default printer.
Edit	Copy	⌘-C	Copies the output displayed in the Results window.
	Select All	⌘-A	Select all of the information shown in the Results window.
	Clear Results	⌘-L	Clears the output in the Results window.
	Special Characters	None	Opens the Character Palette.
View	Hide Toolbar	⌘-B	Hides/shows Virex's toolbar.
	Customize Toolbar	None	Opens a sheet for customizing Virex's toolbar.
Window	Minimize	⌘-M	Minimize Virex's window to the Dock.
	Bring All to Front	None	Unminimizes Virex's window from the Dock, bringing it to the front of the window stack.
Help	Virex Help	⌘-?	Displays Virex's help file in the Help Viewer.
	Virus Information Center	None	Takes you to Network Associate's web site, listing all of the currently known viruses.

APPENDIX B
Common iDisk Error Codes

Every now and then, you're going to encounter some problems when working with your iDisk. Whether you're trying to connect, disconnect, or upload files to your iDisk, if you're doing something wrong, Mac OS X spits back some unfriendly error codes that give you no guidance whatsoever as to what you've done wrong.

Table B-1 contains a listing of some of the more common error codes that may pop up when working with your iDisk, and offers some solutions to correcting the problem.

Table B-1. iDisk error codes

Error code	Displayed when...	Solution
-34	Uploading files to your iDisk	This error will appear when your iDisk is full. You should go to System Preferences → iDisk and verify whether your iDisk *is* full. If it is, consider removing or compressing some items on your iDisk.
-36	Trying to mount your iDisk	This is an input/output (I/O) error, which is typically the result of a proxy when trying to connect to your iDisk from an ISP. There are three possible solutions to this problem: • Double-check your Network preferences (System Preferences → Network, or via Internet Connect) to make sure that you are connected to the Internet. Without a proper Net connection, you cannot mount your iDisk. • Contact your ISP and ask them to update their proxy for WebDAV support. • Finally, try going to System Preferences → Network → Proxies. In the "Bypass proxy settings for these Hosts & Domains" field, enter *idisk.mac.com*, or its IP address, *204.179.120.77*.
-37	Uploading files to your iDisk	The filename is more than 31 characters in length. While Mac OS X allows filenames to be up to 256 characters, files stored on an iDisk can only be up to 31 characters; rename the file and try uploading it again.
-38	Files uploaded to the iDisk appear to be empty when viewed in the Finder	This error message appears when you try to upload files to, or modify files within, directories that cannot be directly modified from via the Finder.

Table B-1. iDisk error codes (continued)

Error code	Displayed when...	Solution
-43	Trying to mount your iDisk from the Finder, or when attempting to upload files	This could be the result of a corrupt */tmp* directory. Open the Terminal (*/Applications/Utilities*) and issue the following command: `ln -s /private/tmp /tmp` This will link the */private/tmp* directory to */tmp*, which should correct the problem.
-47	Trying to mount your iDisk	Your iDisk may already be mounted. Look in the Finder to see whether it shows up in the Computer section (Shift-⌘-C). If the iDisk doesn't appear in the Finder, restart your system (⌘ → Restart), launch the Terminal (*/Applications/Utilities*), and follow these steps: 1. `cd /Volumes`. 2. `ls -l`. If you see your iDisk's name in the *Volumes* directory, go to Step 3. 3. `sudo rm -rf USERNAME`. This will remove the hung mount point for your iDisk. Save the work you're doing in other applications, then restart your system (⌘ → Restart) and try mounting your iDisk again.
-50	Uploading files to a specific directory of your iDisk	This is an error in the user parameter list, which means that one or more files or directories in the path might be corrupt. For example, if you receive this error code when attempting to upload files to */Public/mysite*, follow these steps: 1. Create a new path: */Public/mysite2* 2. Move the files from */Public/mysite* to */Public/mysite2* 3. Delete */Public/mysite* 4. Rename */Public/mysite2* to */Public/mysite* 5. Continue uploading files.

APPENDIX C

Installing and Using the iDisk Utility for Windows XP

Realizing that many .Mac members were using Windows by day and a Mac at night, Apple released a Windows XP version of the iDisk Utility.* The Windows XP version of the iDisk Utility is similar to the Mac OS X version; however, there are a couple caveats:

- It can only be used to mount iDisks and *Public* folders.
- It does not have the capability to change the access privileges or password-protect your *Public* folder.
- It does not directly provide you with details about your iDisk, similar to the iDisk Storage option in the Mac OS X version.

The iDisk Utility for Windows XP can be downloaded from the Mac.com web site (*http://www.mac.com/1/idiskutility_download.html*).

The following sections will walk you through the process of downloading, installing, and using the iDisk Utility for Windows XP.

Installing the Windows XP iDisk Utility

After downloading the iDisk Utility for Windows XP, your first step before using it, obviously, is to install it. The following steps will walk you through the installation process:

1. Locate the file *iDisk Utility for Windows v1.0.2.zip*, and double-click on the icon to unpack the Zip file.
2. Double-click on the installer to launch the iDisk Utility for Windows Setup Wizard, shown in Figure C-1. After reading the Warning note, click on the Next button to proceed with the installation process.

---

* At present, Apple does not have plans to port the iDisk Utility to other versions of Windows, including Windows 95/98/NT/ME/2000.

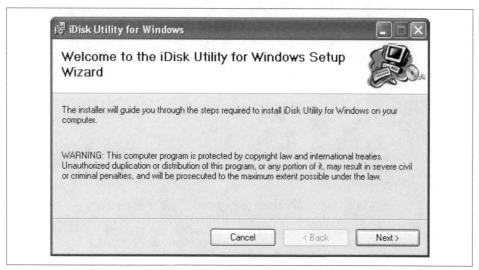

Figure C-1. The iDisk Utility for Windows Setup Wizard.

3. Next comes Apple's License Agreement for the iDisk Utility, shown in Figure C-2. As with all software license agreements, you should read through this carefully. Once you've done so, click on the radio button next to "I Agree", and then click on the Next button to proceed. If you click on the radio button next to "I Do Not Agree," the iDisk Utility will not be installed.

4. Next, you need to select the folder where the iDisk Utility will be installed on your system. By default, the Utility will be stored in *C:\Program Files\Mac Utilities\iDisk Utility for Windows*, as noted in Figure C-3. If you would like to choose another location, click on the Browse button. The lower portion of this window also lets you decide whether the iDisk Utility for Windows will be available to all users on the system, or to just you. After selecting the appropriate options, click on the Next button to proceed.

5. Before the iDisk Utility for Windows is installed, you'll have to pass through the Confirm Installation window, shown in Figure C-4. This is your last chance to make sure you're installing the application on your system. If you are unsure of anything you've set or selected in the previous four steps, you can click on the Back button to go backwards in the installer. Otherwise, if everything's copacetic, click on the Next button to start installing the iDisk Utility, as shown in Figure C-5.

6. After the iDisk Utility has been installed, you will see the Installation Complete window, shown in Figure C-6. To quit the installer and start using the iDisk Utility, click on the Close button.

Once the iDisk Utility has been installed, you can delete the Zip file and start using the program, as detailed in the following section.

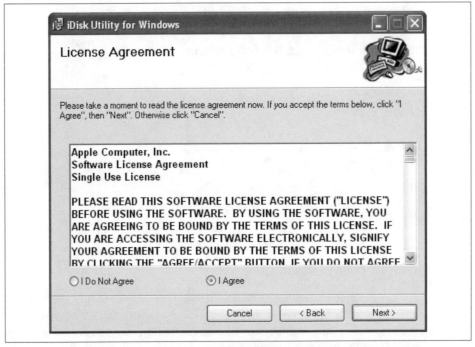

Figure C-2. More legal mumbo-jumbo, but you should still read the License Agreement.

Connecting to Your iDisk on Windows XP

After installing the iDisk Utility for Windows XP, the next thing you'll want to do is try using it to make sure that it's running fine. To launch the iDisk Utility, go to Start → All Programs → .Mac Utilities → iDisk Utility for Windows → iDisk Utility for Windows. After launching, you'll see the iDisk Utility's connect window, as shown in Figure C-7.

Unlike the Mac OS X version of the iDisk Utility (see Chapter 3), the Windows XP version offers two options only for working with an iDisk: either connect to an iDisk or connect to an iDisk's *Public* folder. It does not allow you to manage an iDisk's access privileges, purchase additional iDisk space, or readily view how much space is available on your iDisk.

To connect to an iDisk, simply type in your .Mac Member name and Password in the provided spaces and then click on the Connect button. A progress meter (shown in Figure C-8) will appear as your Windows machine attempts to connect to your iDisk.

After the connection has been made, you can use the Windows Explorer to view and interact with your iDisk, just as you would with the Finder. From the My Computer window (Figure C-9), you can see that the iDisk is mounted as a Network Drive. To

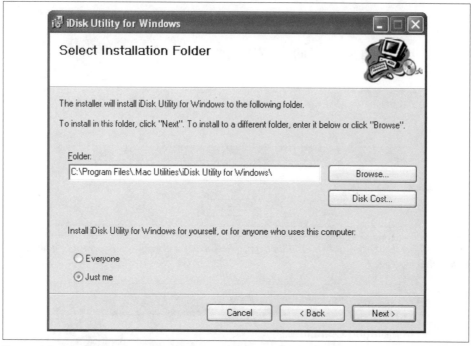

Figure C-3. Select where the iDisk Utility for Windows will be installed, and whether other users on the system will be able to use it.

Figure C-4. If you're sure you want to install the iDisk Utility, click on the Next button to start the installation process.

view the contents of your iDisk, simply double-click on the icon for your iDisk. A sample view from my iDisk, *chuckdude*, is shown in Figure C-10.

To open a folder, double-click on its icon in the view. To move around on your iDisk, you can use the Explorer's Back or Forward buttons, or enter a directory path in the Address field. For example, if you want to view the contents of the *graphics*

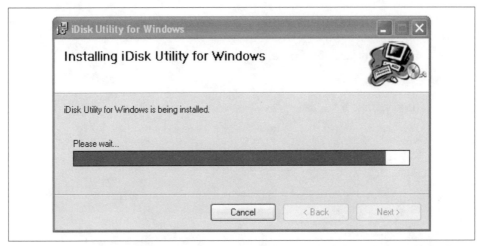

Figure C-5. As the iDisk Utility is installing, a progress meter will keep you informed of how the installation is going.

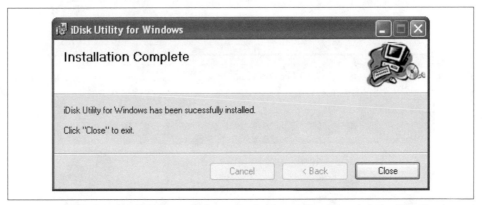

Figure C-6. With the iDisk Utility installed on your Windows XP system, click the Close button to quit the installer.

directory that you have added to the *Sites* directory, you could enter the following in the Address field:

```
E:\Sites\graphics
```

Pressing the Go button at the right edge of the Address field, or hitting Return will take you to the specified directory. Figure C-11 shows different views of the iDisk.

One thing you'll notice in Figure C-11 is that the dot files files whose name begin with a period, such as *.Update*, which are hidden by default in Mac OS X's Finder appear in the Windows Explorer. Both files and folders can begin with a period in their filename. Dot files are common on Unix-based systems. Dot files are used to hide important configuration files or applications from users who might otherwise damage their system with them. Some dot files you'll encounter on your iDisk are

Figure C-7. The iDisk Utility for Windows XP offers a means for you to connect to an iDisk or another .Mac member's Public folder.

Figure C-8. This progress meter lets you know that the iDisk Utility for Windows is attempting to make the connection to your iDisk. When the connection is complete, the message on the right will appear.

harmless, such as the *.Updates* directory, which contains software updates for Virex, while others contain information used Apple's servers for managing information about your account. Unless you know what you're doing, you shouldn't mess with the dot files you encounter, as doing so could break something critical.

To unmount your iDisk, click on the Back button, or type "My Computer" in the Address field and hit Return. Right-click on the name of your iDisk, and then select Disconnect from the menu that appears, as shown in Figure C-12.

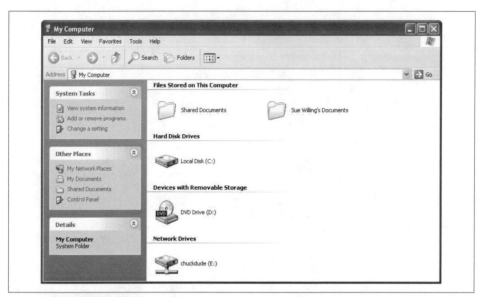

Figure C-9. Windows Explorer's My Computer view shows that the iDisk is connected under the Network Drives section.

Figure C-10. The view of chuckdude's iDisk.

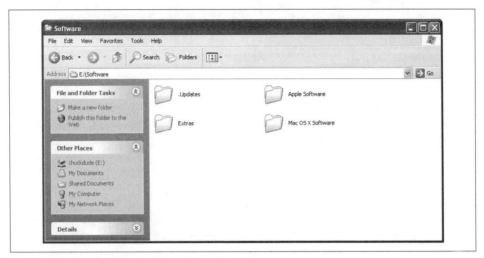

Figure C-11. A view of the iDisk's Software directory.

Figure C-12. When it comes time to disconnect from your iDisk, switch back to the My Computer view in Windows Explorer.

Wishful Thinking on Windows XP

One thing you'll notice after looking at Figure C-12 is that the Windows Explorer does reveal some information about your iDisk. If you click once on your iDisk to select it, a Details section will be added to the left pane of the window. The information provided here, however, doesn't give you the specific information about your iDisk.

For example, the Free Space and Total Size of your iDisk are somewhat skewed. Rather than showing you the information for your specific iDisk, the information you see in the Details section pertains to the entire networked drive of which your iDisk is a part. Figure C-12 shows that my iDisk (*chuckdude*) lives on a disk partition that's 5.59 GB in size.

While it's easy to think that you've suddenly inherited lots of iDisk space, don't be fooled. Instead, if you want to find out specifics about your iDisk, right-click on its name in the Explorer and select Properties from the menu.

Connecting to a Public Folder on Windows XP

Mounting a *Public* folder using the iDisk Utility for Windows XP is very similar to mounting an iDisk. To mount another .Mac member's *Public* folder, follow these steps:

1. Launch the iDisk Utility for Windows XP from the Start menu (Start → All Programs → .Mac Utilities → iDisk Utility for Windows → iDisk Utility for Windows).

2. In the Connect window (shown in Figure C-13), click on the radio button next to Public Folder.

Figure C-13. Connecting to another .Mac member's Public folder is as simple as selecting Public Folder in the Connect To section, entering the Member name, and clicking on the Connect button.

3. In the "Member name" field, enter the .Mac member's name. Notice that the Password field is unavailable.

4. Click on the Connect button to mount the specified member's *Public* folder.

If the .Mac member's *Public* folder isn't password-protected, it will promptly mount on your system. However, if it is password-protected, you will be asked to enter a password to gain access, as shown in Figure C-14.

Figure C-14. If the Public folder you want to connect to is password-protected, you will see this alert window.

If you know the password, enter that in the Password field and click OK. If the password you entered is correct, the *Public* folder will mount as a Network Drive; however, if you enter an incorrect password, the window shown in Figure C-15 alerts you to that fact.

Figure C-15. Enter a bad password, get another try. There's no limit to the number of times you can try connecting to a password-protected Public folder.

There is no limit to the number of times you can be challenged for a *Public* folder's password. You can keep trying until you either get it right or turn blue in the face. When you're finally connected to the *Public* folder, the iDisk Utility for Windows XP informs you of that, as shown in Figure C-16.

Figure C-16. The iDisk Utility for Windows XP will let you know when you've finally connected to the Public folder to which you've requested access.

Once you've connected to the *Public* folder, use the Windows Explorer to view its contents. The My Computer view, shown in Figure C-17, shows the *Public* folder mounted as a Network Drive. Unlike *Public* folders mounted on a Mac OS X system, *Public* folders mounted on a Windows XP system also tell you to which .Mac member the folder belongs.

To view the contents of the *Public* folder, double-click on its icon, or enter *E:\ membername-Public* in the Address field and then click on the Go button or hit Return. To download a file or folder from a *Public* folder, simply drag the appropriate item to your Windows XP desktop and the item will be copied to your machine. Likewise, to upload a file or folder from your Windows XP system to a .Mac *Public* folder, drag the item to the *Public* folder's view. However, this assumes that the *Public* folder has read-write access turned on. If the *Public* folder is read-only, you will not be able to copy items to the *Public* folder.

When you've finished your business with the *Public* folder, you can unmount it by going back to the My Computer view in the Windows Explorer. Once there, right-click on the icon for the *Public* folder in the Network Drives section and then select Disconnect from the menu, as shown in Figure C-18.

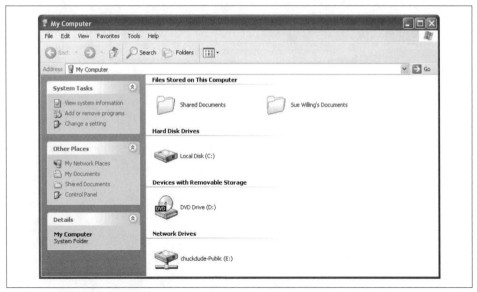

Figure C-17. The My Computer displays the Public folder's .Mac member name as part of the directory path, shown here as chuckdude-Public.

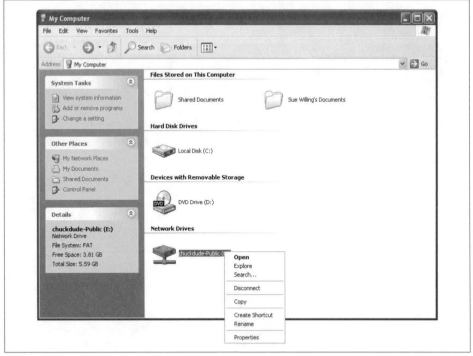

Figure C-18. Unmounting a Public folder is as simple as right-clicking on its icon in the My Computer view and selecting Disconnect from the menu.

Index

A

B

We'd like to hear your suggestions for improving our indexes. Send email to *index@oreilly.com*.

Support icon (.Mac Services Sidebar), 36
Switch to Reader Mode (iBlog) keyboard
        shortcut, 331
Sync Now keyboard shortcut, 333
synchronization process, 271
synchronizing
    Address Book, iCal, and Safari, xiii
        (see also iSync)
    iDisk, 69–76
        automatic or manual, 70
        turning off, 75
System Preferences application
    iDisk pane, 6
    .Mac pane, 6

T

Themes icon (HomePage), 211
Time Zone option (Viewing pane (Mail)), 90
/tmp directory, corrupted, 337
Total Size of iDisk on Windows XP, 346
Trash folder versus Deleted Messages
        folder, 104
trial .Mac membership, 49
Turn Off Font Styling in Preview option
        (iBlog), 254
Turn on .Mac Bookmarks Synchronization
        option (Bookmarks), 301
Type codes, 158–160

U

Uncheck All keyboard shortcut, 328
Underline keyboard shortcut, 330
Undo keyboard shortcut, 330
unmounting iDisk, 60
.Updates subfolder (Software folder), 48
USB drives, backing up to, 176–180
USB flash memory key, backing up
        to, 176–180

V

Viewing pane (Mail)
    Messages Per Page option, 90
    Show "All Headers" option, 90
    Time Zone option, 90
Virex, xiii, xv, 115–137
    Advanced Scan options, 120
    Automatically delete infected files
        option, 120
    Automatically scan at login option, 119

Check for new virus definitions at launch
        option, 120
Clean options, 120
configuring preferences, 118–122
Customize my eUpdate server settings
        option, 120
.dat files, 126
Download page, 115
downloading, 26
infected files, 127
installing, 115–117
keyboard shortcuts, 335
language support, 115
Perform an advanced scan of applications
        and macros for previously unknown
        viruses option, 120
proxy problems, 129
Remove macros from potentially infected
        files option, 120
running, 117–130
Scan inside compressed (.gz) and archived
        (.tar) files option, 119
Scan options, 118
scanning email attachments, 130–132
scanning for viruses from Terminal
        application, 132–137
Show detailed results information
        option, 119
testing, 124–127
tips, 127
toolbar, 122–124
    additional items, 124
    default items, 123
versions, 116
Virus Update options, 120
Virex Help keyboard shortcut, 335
Virex icon (.Mac Services Sidebar), 36
.VirexLogin process, 117
virus protection, xv
volumes, scanning for viruses, 122
vscanx utility, 132–137
    adding to command path, 132
    running as cron job, 136

W

web design, learning more about, 245
web sites, building
    creating your own, 244
    (see also HomePage)
WebDAV, 42
Windows XP, connecting to iDisk, 64

About the Author

Chuck Toporek is an avid Mac user and has been since the dawn of time (which was when he first laid hands on a Mac II system). Chuck is a Senior Editor with O'Reilly Media, Inc., and is the editor in charge of O'Reilly's Macintosh publishing efforts. In addition to editing books for Macintosh users, developers, and system administrators, he's found some spare time to write or contribute to Mac books as well, including the *Mac OS X Panther Pocket Guide* and *Mac OS X Panther in a Nutshell* (coauthor). He is also the coauthor of *Hydrocephalus: A Guide for Patients, Families, and Friends* (also published by O'Reilly).

Originally from a (very) small town in southeastern Michigan, Chuck has lived in various places on the west coast of the United States and Canada, and at sea in the Pacific and Indian Oceans, when he served in the U.S. Navy aboard the USS Hewitt (DD-966). After leaving the Navy to be a landlubber, Chuck pursued a career in publishing, and has worked in magazines, books, and online media.

When he's not writing or editing or tinkering with his Mac, Chuck can be found exploring the backwoods and coastal regions of the Pacific Northwest, watching cartoons, pursuing the next-best roller coaster, or working on one of the many side projects that keep him from riding his bike into a tree. He lives in Portland, Oregon with his wife, Kellie Robinson, and their cat, Sophie. To learn more about Chuck, visit his .Mac HomePage at *http://homepage.mac.com/chuckdude*.

Colophon

Our look is the result of reader comments, our own experimentation, and feedback from distribution channels. Distinctive covers complement our distinctive approach to technical topics, breathing personality and life into potentially dry subjects.

The animals on the cover of *Inside .Mac* are Eskimo dogs, also known as huskies. This dog stands between 20 and 27 inches high and can weigh anywhere from 60 to 100 pounds when fully grown. Its coat can be of any color and its eyes are brown, blue, or gold, or a combination of all or some of these colors. An Eskimo dog has a thick coat of fur, which helps it tolerate temperatures as low as 90 degrees below zero.

Eskimo dogs are workers, having a long history as sled dogs, both pulling and racing sleds. They have great physical endurance and an instinctual desire to run. Because of this, owners should make sure to allow these dogs plenty of outside time for exercise, but should also ensure that their dogs are not left to roam free, as they may run off too quickly. These dogs are very intelligent and loving. They have a considerable amount of energy and thrive when allowed to be around other dogs.

Mary Brady was the production editor and the copyeditor for *Inside .Mac*. Emily Quill and Claire Cloutier provided quality control. Julie Hawks wrote the index.

Edie Freedman designed the cover of this book. The cover image is an original engraving from *Royal Natural History*. Emma Colby produced the cover layout with QuarkXPress 4.1 using Adobe's ITC Garamond font.

David Futato designed the interior layout. This book was converted by Julie Hawks to FrameMaker 5.5.6 with a format conversion tool created by Erik Ray, Jason McIntosh, Neil Walls, and Mike Sierra that uses Perl and XML technologies. The text font is Linotype Birka; the heading font is Adobe Myriad Condensed; and the code font is LucasFont's TheSans Mono Condensed. The illustrations that appear in the book were produced by Robert Romano and Jessamyn Read using Macromedia FreeHand 9 and Adobe Photoshop 6. The tip and warning icons were drawn by Christopher Bing. This colophon was written by Mary Brady.